P9-DNQ-646

black ants and buddhists

**Thinking Critically
and Teaching Differently
in the Primary Grades**

Mary Cowhey
Foreword by Sonia Nieto

Stenhouse Publishers
Portland, Maine

Stenhouse Publishers
www.stenhouse.com

Copyright © 2006 by Mary Cowhey

All rights reserved. No part of this publication may be reproduced or transmitted in any form or by any means, electronic or mechanical, including photocopy, or any information storage and retrieval system, without permission from the publisher.

Every effort has been made to contact copyright holders and students for permission to reproduce borrowed material. We regret any oversights that may have occurred and will be pleased to rectify them in subsequent reprints of the work.

Credit
Page 146: Excerpt from *Lies My Teacher Told Me.* Copyright © 1995 by James Loewen. Reprinted by permission of The New Press.
Pages 180–181: This first aired as a public radio commentary on WFCR in Amherst, MA.

Library of Congress Cataloging-in-Publication Data
Cowhey, Mary, 1960–
    Black ants and buddhists : thinking critically and teaching differently in the primary grades / Mary Cowhey ; foreword by Sonia Nieto.
        p. cm.
        Includes bibliographical references.
        ISBN 1-57110-418-6 (alk. paper)
        1. Multicultural education—United States. 2. Elementary school teaching—United States. 3. Cultural awareness—Study and teaching (Primary)—United States. 4. Minorities—Education (Primary)—United States. I. Title.
LC1099.3.C699 2006
370.117—dc22   2005058138

Back cover photo courtesy of Susan Fink
Cover and interior design by Martha Drury

Manufactured in the United States of America on acid-free paper
11 10 09 08 07 06 9 8 7 6 5 4 3 2

For my mother, Mary Rose Cowhey, the first and best teacher I ever had.

CONTENTS

Foreword by Sonia Nieto   *vii*

Acknowledgments   *ix*

prologue Black Ants and Buddhism   1

1 Introduction   14

2 Compassion, Action, and Change   22

3 Routines: A Day in the Life of the Peace Class   36

4 It Takes a Village to Teach First Grade   57

5 Talking About Peace   81

6 Learning Through Activism   101

7 Teaching History So Children Will Care   122

8 Nurturing History Detectives   140

9 Seeing Ourselves and Our Families Through Students' Eyes   164

10 Responding When Tragedy Enters the Classroom   179

11 Building Trust with Families and Weathering Controversy   193

12 Going Against the Grain   208

afterword "Take This Hammer"   224

Appendix   *229*

  Sample Progression for "Exploration and Contact" Unit   *229*

  Sample Peace Class News   *240*

References   *241*

FOREWORD

When I was a junior in high school, my English teacher Dr. Carlin asked the class if we had read a particular book. Most of us said that we hadn't, and she responded, "Oh, how I envy you! What a treat you have in store." Although I no longer recall the name of the book after all these years, I remember what Dr. Carlin said because it seemed to me an unusual but wonderful way of introducing others to a great book. That's how I feel about the experience you are about to have as you read *Black Ants and Buddhists*. It is a book you will find hard to put down. In fact, in preparing to write this foreword, I thought I would just leaf through the manuscript since I was more than a little familiar with its contents. After all, I had seen the book in its several iterations, and heard about it even when the book was just an idea in Mary Cowhey's mind. But once again, I was drawn into it, as mesmerized with the many moving stories as I had been the first time I read them. So, once again, I spent hours reading, crying, and laughing out loud. Mary Cowhey's writing has that effect, as you will see.

I met Mary Cowhey several years ago when she was in the masters program in which I was teaching at the University of Massachusetts. I was privileged to be her advisor, and in the years since then I have treasured our continuing relationship. Perhaps what struck me most about Mary when I first met her was the quiet strength and dignity that she possesses. She speaks quietly and at times seems so young and innocent that she looks to be no older than a high school student. But underneath that reserved exterior is a woman of great love and integrity, with a steely determination the likes of which I have rarely encountered. Lucky, I always think, that she's on our side, that is, on the side of equity and justice, and on the side of children.

Mary Cowhey is also a masterful storyteller. I would be surprised if you got through this book without shedding a tear. Who would not be moved by these stories? In these pages, you will read about kids who organize a successful voter registration drive, who insist on opening up their school on a snow day to bring food to a local shelter, and who learn the meaning of—rather than simply recite—the Pledge of Allegiance. But *Black Ants and Buddhists* is more than a series of lump-in-your-throat vignettes, although of course it is that too. It is a book about what it means to create a caring community in a classroom of students of enormously diverse cultures and experiences, and about the high expectations that their teacher holds for all of them regardless of what others might expect from children of some of these backgrounds. In this book, you will read about an extraordinary teacher and the vision she has for her students and for the world. While she teaches them to achieve high levels of science and math and reading, and she teaches them to love art and nature and animals, she also teaches them how to work for peace, a difficult challenge in a world filled with war, devastation, and hate. As Mary writes, "Making peace is hard, hard, hard, but that's the price we must learn to pay for living on this planet."

Black Ants and Buddhists describes a teacher's dedication to forging a nurturing and caring environment where children learn to become socially responsible and critical. While it is a book about creating community and hope in a first- and second-grade classroom, this powerful book is mostly about real children coming to consciousness about the world around them and taking steps, to paraphrase Paulo Freire, to learn to read both the word and their world. How I envy you the experience of reading it for the first time!

Sonia Nieto

black ants and buddhists

ACKNOWLEDGMENTS

While in graduate school at the University of Massachusetts, juggling my teaching, a new baby, and a second-grade son, I always looked forward to reading for my multicultural education course and writing my weekly reflection journals for Sonia Nieto. It was a way for me to make sense of my work, which sometimes felt isolated, in a larger framework. It was my chance to connect, to tell someone the stories of my classroom and my students. It was Sonia who said, "You should really do something with all these stories." She kept saying that, even after I started giving her some of my stories for her books. Sonia nudged me to write a book of my own, but I didn't know how to begin. When I asked her, she pointed me in the right direction. I would like to thank Sonia for her wisdom, knowledge, advice, and encouragement as a teacher, mentor, and friend.

If I didn't work at Jackson Street School, I probably wouldn't be writing this book. Thanks to my principal, Gwen Agna, for her educational leadership and friendship, and for her exquisite ability to cultivate a community within a school, as well as a school within a community. Gwen understands and supports teacher innovation, reflection, and research, in practice as well as in theory.

I so appreciate my colleagues at Jackson Street School, including Susan Fink, Kathy Malynoski, Maria Garcia, Mary Bates, Linda Barca, Maria de la Vega, Holly Ghazey, Janet Benoit, Molly Burnham, and all the other teachers and aides who nurture each other, as well as the remarkable river of children we teach. Heartfelt thanks to Susan Fink for her technological support and sense of humor. Thanks especially to Kim Gerould, who read, critiqued, and encouraged so much of the manuscript along the way. Kim, Kathy, and I team-taught for a couple of the earlier years described in this book. They demonstrated remarkable stamina, patience, courage, flexibility, and willingness to collaborate in the face of my wildly developing curriculum. After a couple of years, I could hardly discern them flinching when I'd say, "I've got this idea . . ."

Thanks to the education program at Smith College, to Cathy Huntley, Lucy Mule, Susan Etheredge, and the many wonderful student teachers with whom I've worked over the years, especially Jackie Bushey and Sara Johnson, whose brave willingness to fill my shoes here and there helped this book get written.

I'd like to thank my fellow teachers and writers of the Western Massachusetts Writing Project, especially the Teachers as Writers program and the writing and response group, for their critiques and their encouragement to "do something" with my writing.

Thanks to Brenda Power, my editor, for graciously and enthusiastically guiding me through this process as a first-time author.

As I began to write more seriously, and share my writing process with my students and their families, I was encouraged by their support. I want to thank all of those families, without whom my teaching would not have taken shape this way. I would like to especially thank Karen and Beth Bellavance-Grace, Jo Glading-DiLorenzo, Rachel Wysocker, Denise Lello, Kay Saakvitne, Denise Elliott, Heidi and Gina Nortonsmith, Laurie Herzog, and Elizabeth Porto for their help with reading drafts and valuing the idea of a book like this.

Thanks to the many friends of the Peace Class who so generously share their time and wisdom, including Norma Sandowski, Taietsu and Alice Unno, Sister Kalilah Karim-Rushdan, Aneesa Uqdah, Tom Wartenberg, Mayor Clare Higgins, Mary McKitrick, and so many others.

Thanks to my students, who daily challenge, inspire, motivate, amaze, frustrate, engage, and amuse me. I am happy to have this opportunity to share their brilliance. One great pleasure in writing this book has been keeping the memories of these children alive by retelling their stories.

Thanks to David Sedaris for having a sense of humor about work and family and reminding me not to take myself too seriously.

Thanks to Rita and Terry Rowan, my seventh- and ninth-grade English teachers, who took me seriously as a writer when I was still a kid. It worked.

Thanks to my family, including my children, Robeson and Mairead, who patiently missed me many a weekend while I holed up to write and revise. I look forward to more adventures together. Thanks to my mom, who believes all things are possible. She makes me pause to appreciate the beauty of nature every day.

Most of all, thanks to my husband, Bill Blatner. I know this wasn't exactly what we had in mind when I said, "I'll just write" instead of taking classes while you finished graduate school. Thanks for your honest criticism of draft after draft, your flexibility in freeing me up to write, and the depth of your love.

black ants and buddhism

It was snacktime, with the normal jostling commotion of hand washing just accomplished. Most of my second graders were settling down to eat their snacks. I was eating an apple while pulling together my math lesson. Suddenly Gloria shrieked, "Black ants! Ugh! There are black ants over here!" I looked up, not surprised that black ants would invade in Gloria's vicinity. She might sooner slide her chair over spilled juice to hide it than wipe it up.

Sadie screamed from across the room, "Agh! They're biting me!" and slapped her back and thigh for dramatic effect. She rushed to Gloria's side and began crushing the ants under the staccato rhythm of her glittery red shoes. Ben, not one to miss the action, quickly joined Sadie in stomping the ants.

Som Jet stood up at his table and said, "They are black ants. Do not kill them!"

Ben, still stomping, looked up and said, "Yeah, we know they're black ants. That's why we're killing them."

Som Jet, normally a soft-spoken boy, opened his hands in a pleading gesture and raised his voice. "No! Do not kill them! They are living things! Black ants do not bite people!"

"Well, they bit *me*!" Sadie said impatiently. She stopped stomping for a moment to pull up her shirt, searching for some spot on her skin that could pass for an ant bite to bolster her argument.

Perhaps sixty seconds had passed since Gloria's first hysterical mention of the ants. "Everyone freeze," I said. Som Jet had a desperate look in his eyes. "Sadie and Ben, sit in your seats. Som Jet is trying to tell us something very important, and I think we all need to listen carefully to his words. Som Jet, would you tell us again?"

Som Jet breathed in. "They are black ants. They are living things. Black ants clean up mess. They do not bite people."

Calvin, an avid reader of nonfiction books and therefore a respected scientific authority in our class, said quietly, "That's true." Sadie narrowed her eyes at him and twisted her face defiantly.

Som Jet continued, "It is not right for us to kill living things." He sat down.

"But we always kill ants," Ben said. "We can kill ants if we want to." Many classmates nodded in eager agreement.

"Well, let's think about this together," I said. "What are our class rules?"

"Be kind. Work hard," Sovan volunteered, adding, "We don't have a rule about ants."

"Maybe our rules cover it. If there is even one person in our class who would feel very sad or upset about us killing even one ant, would it be kind for us to go ahead and kill that ant anyway?" I asked.

"Not really," Ben shrugged.

"Could a person work hard if he felt very sad or upset?"

"Definitely not!" said Sadie, emphatically slicing an X in the air. Sadie usually stomped to the classroom library quiet area at least once a day when too angry or upset to work. "We shouldn't do things on purpose to upset people."

"So what should we do about our ants?"

"Well," Michelle began, "we definitely shouldn't kill them."

"We should not kill them," Krish said. "They are living things."

Michelle paused thoughtfully, then added, "But I don't really like the idea of ants crawling around the floor when we're sitting on the rug and stuff."

"Why not?" Jack challenged. "We have crickets and milkweed bugs over there, and remember, we had butterflies, and you brought in so many caterpillars. Same thing."

Michelle pursed her lips. "They are all insects. You're right about that, but those were all in the habitats we made for them and these ants are *loose*."

"Maybe we could get an ant farm to put them in," Samuel suggested.

"Then they wouldn't be free and these are *wild* ants," Ann said quietly.

"Why did the ants come here?" Stan asked.

"Black ants clean up mess," Som Jet said.

"Maybe because we're not very tidy," Sadie suggested brightly. "Look at all our crumbs," she said, surveying her table with a sweeping gesture.

"When juice spill, it's sticky if you don't clean it," Ramadan said, looking under Gloria's chair.

"How could each of us take personal responsibility to make our room a less attractive habitat for black ants?" I asked.

"The leader could sweep after snack," Angela suggested.

"That's a good idea," I said, walking to the closet. "Here's where I keep the broom and dustpan. Let me show you all how to use it." First I gently swept up the ants and let Som Jet take them outside. Then I demonstrated sweeping and asked a few volunteers to model it.

Jasmine suggested that they all wash their tables. Angela said there weren't enough sponges. They decided that one person from each table

each day should do it, taking turns. Angela said the sponge should not be too wet, so I did a quick demonstration of sponge wringing and crumb catching. Sadie said that she and Gloria often forgot to take home their lunch boxes, and left them in the room, full of food, so they should be more responsible about taking them home every day. We talked about how taking more personal responsibility at school and at home is part of growing up. After an enthusiastic cleanup, we started our math lesson, a little late.

I continued thinking about Som Jet and Ben throughout the day. Ben was right. It was completely acceptable in our American culture to crush ants. Should I have told Som Jet, "Buck up and get used to it. You're in America now"? I thought of a similar argument in our school around the holidays a few years back. Some more traditional teachers argued that it was fine to continue to sing Christmas carols at a concert and have Christmas parties in classrooms and color pictures of Santa Claus, because everyone in America knows what Christmas is, and if they don't, they should learn. I thought more about what Ben had said. Not only is it culturally acceptable for Americans to crush ants, but we Americans also slap mosquitoes, bomb fleas, and swat flies. Heck, we land-mine and carpet-bomb countries. We defoliated much of Vietnam. We carry out "shock and awe" bombing campaigns in the cradle of ancient civilizations. Won't Som Jet have a tough time in America if he can't get used to a few crushed ants? Surely Som Jet will learn all this without my help, living in America and watching television, but what will *we* learn? I figured Som Jet felt the way he did because he is a Buddhist.

what would mohammed do?

A couple of days later, I attended a community *iftar* at Smith College. (*Iftar* is an evening feast to break the fast during the Muslim holy season of Ramadan.) While speaking to Sister Kalilah Karim-Rushdan, Muslim chaplain for the college who had visited my class earlier in the year, I told her the story about the black ants. She said, "In Islam, we should not kill the ants because all life is created by Allah." "Hmmm," I thought. "So much for stereotypes."

Less than a week later, it was Thanksgiving. During a snacktime discussion about Thanksgiving, Krish told a friend that he didn't know what his family was doing for Thanksgiving. Krish's family had come from India in July. I invited Krish's family to my home for Thanksgiving dinner. His father politely responded, "We do not know this Thanksgiving tradition. What is it appropriate for us to do?"

"Just come and eat with us," I said. Remembering only as they were arriving that they were vegetarians, I felt a bit awkward about our chicken and gravy, but we had lots of squash, beans, rice, and corn bread. At dinner, I told the story of the black ants. Ranjit, Krish's father, said that Hindus should not kill black ants because they are living things. I asked if that was why his family was vegetarian. He said it was because of that, and for health reasons. Ranjit then explained that his father was a poultry farmer and sold live chickens, but did not eat them.

"Hmmm," I thought. "You could live your whole life, hanging with White Christian Americans, crushing ants and swatting mosquitoes, thinking you were acting like everyone else on the planet, and you'd be wrong." I talked with my students about it when we returned to school. I explained that so far we had learned that Buddhists, Muslims, and Hindus had rules against killing living things and would not crush the ants. Ben leaned forward and whispered loudly across the rug to Michelle, "Do we have that rule in Judaism?"

We decided we should ask our friend Norma Sandowski what her friends in South Africa thought about this. Norma was a friend of Angela's mothers, and had heard of our class through them. She introduced herself to me the summer before at the community garden, where we both have plots. Norma is a retired chemical engineer and industrial safety consultant who decided, at the age of seventy, to pack up and go to a rural school in South Africa as a volunteer teacher. Norma visited our class before she left. We had been in fairly regular e-mail contact with her and her students. We e-mailed her at Itsoseng Center, her school near the South African border with Lesotho. Because of health reasons, Norma was not at the school when she got our e-mail, but she wrote back that on the Indian reservation in Oklahoma where she grew up, she learned it was not right to kill ants. She also learned that sprinkling black pepper would discourage them from coming in, without hurting or killing them. I shared this news with our class, and brought in a can of black pepper.

By this time, our personal responsibility campaign was working wonders. With minimal squabbling, the tables were being wiped and the floor was being swept. Som Jet regularly carried any found ants outside. Gloria still had a hard time remembering to take home her lunch boxes (she always had several in circulation), but we put a sign in her mailbox to remind her. Sadie often spotted ant activity that eluded others (including me) and would not rest until she had thoroughly sprinkled black pepper on the area. Gabriella's mother asked me what I had said to the children about personal responsibility, because Gabriella came home, cleaned her bedroom, and sorted all the laundry. When her shocked mother asked what had inspired her, Gabriella said, "I'm just taking personal responsibility."

The children had grown fond of the black ant story, and when a visitor came to the room, they would often say, "Let's tell her about the black ants." It was a loose survey, not seeking numerical data in the form of a vote, but rather a quest for different perspectives on this question.

Honestly, I know little about Buddhism. I know less about Hinduism and only a little more about Islam. I remembered that the previous year Jack, a blond-haired, blue-eyed child with college-educated theater carpenter parents, had said he was a Buddhist. Jack also has a good imagination and tells a lot of stories. Jack's parents hadn't mentioned being Buddhist when I visited the family, and I hadn't noticed any Buddhist artifacts when I visited their home, but I gave Jack the benefit of the doubt. Jack also has a slight lisp, and I have auditory processing disorder. Sometimes when other children talked about going to temple or church, he would say, "I go to *sangha*." When I asked what that was, he said, "You know, *sangha*, where you learn Buddhism." I didn't know. Anyway, I assumed that if Jack was a Buddhist, his parents must be Buddhists too.

I called and reached Jack's mom, Ann, to see if she'd be willing to come in and explain to the class a little more about Buddhism. Jack had already told her the story about the black ants. She said neither she nor Jack's father were Buddhist and that Jack knew more about Buddhism than she did. I was a little surprised and asked where he had learned about it. She said that the previous year he had started going to a Dharma school, taught by Dr. Taietsu Unno, a retired professor from Smith College and the husband of a retired teacher from our school. Ann offered to contact the Unnos to ask them to come visit our class.

It took us a couple of weeks to reach the Unnos, because they had gone to Japan, Thailand, and Bhutan. After some phone tag and e-mail messages, we arranged for them to visit. The children took turns telling parts of the black ant story to the Unnos, who listened carefully. Mrs. Unno then explained why Buddhists would not harm a living thing. Dr. Unno explained the Wheel of Dharma and the Noble Eightfold Path, which consisted of right thoughts, speech, conduct, livelihood, effort, mindfulness, meditation, and views. He also told the story of Buddha and led a meditation exercise with the class. Together we all said the following:

Breathing in, I relax
Breathing out, I smile

Breathing in, I feel calm
Breathing out, I feel good

Breathing in, no more anger
Breathing out, peace and quiet
—Adapted from Thich Nhat Hanh

It struck me how this quiet breathing and sitting in their chairs with good posture was different from the children's previous imitations of "meditating," when they would contort themselves into some version of the lotus position, pinch their thumbs and index fingers together (pinkies extended), gaining as much attention as possible in the process. I wondered where they had learned that caricature of meditation, the superficial "look" of it without the substance.

The next day, we wrote a thank-you note to the Unnos and asked a few more questions that we hadn't thought to ask when they visited.

"can you believe the government did that?"

Ben picked up a book from the display in our classroom library, called *Baseball Saved Us,* about children playing baseball in a Japanese American internment camp during World War II. Ben likes baseball and football. I saw him studying the illustrations. Although Ben was the most impulsive and physically aggressive student in my class, he was also intensely spiritual and poetic. Ben looked up and said, "The people in this book look like Mr. and Mrs. Unno, don't they?" I studied the illustration he was pointing to.

"You're right. Mr. and Mrs. Unno are Japanese American, and this story is about Japanese Americans during a sad time in our country's history. In fact, Dr. and Mrs. Unno lived that history. When they were your age, they were sent to live in an internment camp like that." Later, I noticed Ben reading *Baseball Saved Us*. Ben is an average reader and tends to pick books that are on the easy side. I knew this book was above his reading level, so I said it would be all right if he borrowed it to read at home with a parent's help. He was intent on reading it right then and said, "It's okay. I think I can read it. I'll just ask my friends if I get stuck on a word." A few times, during quiet reading time, I looked up from

my reading group and saw Ben out of his seat. Just before speaking to him, I'd realize that he had gone over to Michelle or Seamus to ask them to read a tricky word, and then returned to his seat.

Later I asked him to read some of it to me. Although he was not fluent, he was working very hard at reading it, very hungry for the story. He shook his head and looked at me, asking, "Can you believe the government did that?"

When I asked how he would feel if the government did that to his family, he said he'd feel angry. I said that was how I thought I would feel, but I remembered some years ago, when Mrs. Unno had visited my class and told my students what it was like to be in those camps. I was surprised when she said she forgave the people who did that to her. She was not bitter. Ben's eyes grew wide. I asked Ben how he thought she was able to let go of all that anger. He thought a moment and said, "Probably 'cause she meditates."

I remembered I had another book, *The Bracelet,* about a Japanese American girl sent to an internment camp. She was forced to leave her home and best friend, who gave her a bracelet to remember their friendship. Ben asked if he could read it. I brought it in the next day. Again, the text was difficult for him, but he tackled it vigorously. He noticed in the dedication of the book that the author thanked the Uno family of Northampton (spelled with one *n* and not two), and we wondered if those were "our Unnos." He decided he would have to write them to find out.

I photocopied the meditation that Dr. Unno had given us and told the children I was putting one in each of their mailboxes to take home. Ben raised his hand and said, "I need two copies, one for my family's refrigerator and another one in my bedroom, where I go for time-out. If we feel angry or upset, we could use that to meditate."

"Hang one in our library, Ms. Cowhey," Sadie said. "I'll use it a lot when I go there."

making connections

Every day, I read aloud to my class: lots of picture books, lots of fiction, some nonfiction, as well as letters, news articles, and items from the Internet. We always discuss these readings, both to ensure the understanding of the English language learners and to deepen the comprehension of all the students. In these discussions I model and teach comprehension strategies described by Ellin Keene and Susan Zimmerman in *Mosaic of Thought*. For example, one approach is to teach children to use schema by making connections between the text and their own lives (text-to-self), other books and stories (text-to-text), and to the world (text-to-world). After some experience, this comprehension habit becomes second nature. In addition to these read-alouds, which focus on enjoyment and comprehension, I do another read-aloud each week for the purpose of philosophical discussion, where the emphasis is on listening skills and oral language development.

For our philosophical discussion, I decided to read *Hey Little Ant!* by Phillip and Hannah Hoose. It is a humorously illustrated story, written in verse, depicting a debate between a boy who is poised to squish an ant on the sidewalk, and the ant, who thinks he shouldn't do it. The story ends by asking what you would do. We began our discussion there. Krish said, "Leave the ant. Imagine how the ant would feel."

Jack added, "In Buddhism, no one would kill another living thing, big or small."

"Under some STOP signs," Stan said slowly, "there's a sticker that says, Eating Animals."

"That's vegetarians," said Jasmine.

I asked who was more powerful in the story, the boy or the ant. At first, children said the boy was more powerful, because he could kill the ant, could run faster than the ant if the ant tried to run away, and so forth. Gabriella said, "The kid, because he's big. He can squish the ant, but I don't think he should. Everything is made by God."

Then Samuel said no, the ant was more powerful. "His voice is powerful, and what he says is true."

"The ant is more powerful because ants can lift ten times their weight," Gloria said. "Humans can't do that."

I asked the children, "What is power?" Krish said it is strength. Jasmine said it could be magical powers.

Ivan said it is "things that you are good at, like reading, not just strength." Gloria mentioned "strength in words, like writing." Ben talked about the power of running machines.

Calvin talked about the power of courage and the power of building. He added, "You might have powers you don't even know, like Hanuman the Monkey King. He didn't know he could fly." Calvin was making a text-to-text connection with the *Ramayana,* the sacred Hindu text. In preparation for Divali, the Hindu festival of lights, Krish's mother, Sonu, had visited our class and told the story of Lord Rama, his wife, Sita, and the critical role played by Hanuman the Monkey King. Ben had recognized the story, and brought in a picture book called *Hanuman* from

home that I read to the class. Hanuman quickly became a class favorite. Here he was back again.

Sovan added "the power of illustrating" (of art). Angela added the power of science. Michelle added the power of love, and Jasmine added the power of friendship. Gloria suggested the power of imagination. I told her I thought Einstein would agree with her because he thought imagination was more important than knowledge. Seamus, an avid football player and fan, added "the power of football" with a giggle, then said more seriously, "Athletes are strong, so athletic power."

Krish pointed to the picture of Gandhi on the bulletin board and said, "Gandhi had the power of peace and bravery."

Sadie had been agitated at the start of the discussion because of an incident at recess and had gone to the classroom library to meditate and listen. Now she joined us in the circle and returned to the question of who was more powerful. "I think the ant was more powerful because he was able to get the boy to *stop*." I said that stopping a situation could in fact be very powerful, that when workers go on strike, they stop making things in the factories to make the factory owners listen to what they say they need.

"It's easier to be small, you know," Jack said with a sly smile, being one of the shorter members of class himself. "The ant could lie down in the crack so the boy's foot couldn't squish him." He rolled to lie down on the rug, demonstrating, then continued, "Plus, he could communicate very well." I commented that that was an interesting observation that illustrated a principle of guerrilla warfare: a relatively poor, small, ill-equipped group fighting the oppression of some powerful invading force might operate like a flea on a horse, biting here and then moving somewhere else, like an ant in a crack, usually too small to see or to catch. I told them the American colonists used that style of warfare early in the American Revolution, fighting against the powerful British Army, and the North Vietnamese used it against the Americans. Those using that style were successful in both cases. I said the current attacks on American troops in "post-war" Iraq reminded me of that kind of fighting.

Stan agreed with Jack. "When you are small, you can hide from your enemy."

Som Jet walked over to a table and patted it, saying, "A table is big and strong, but it's not powerful, because it's not alive and can't do anything."

Ramadan agreed. "A chair holds you up, but it can't do nothing."

Soon it was International Day for Human Rights, December 10. I read aloud *For Every Child* by Caroline Castle. We brainstormed a list of human rights. Ramadan, a Muslim Albanian refugee from Kosovo, named rights such as "To not get killed, to not get your house blown up." They added others to the list: the right to get an education; the right to have clean water, food, shelter, and medical care; and the right to be called your own name. Ben added, "To believe your own religion." The children made captioned drawings of the human rights they chose.

"his painting . . . it's kind of like protesting."

The next day, we had a philosophical discussion of *Matthew's Dream* by Leo Lionni, in which a mouse dreams that art can change his world. We returned to Sovan's idea about the power of art.

We looked at Pablo Picasso's *Guernica*. Ramadan noticed, "The people look sad and scared."

Stan said, "Not all the stuff is in the right place." They noticed parts of a cow up in the air.

"I think it needs a body," Ramadan said.

"That's part of art," Ben answered.

"It shows people getting hurt," Jasmine said.

Ramadan touched one of the faces and said, "He looks scared."

"He's getting tortured," Ben said seriously.

Ramadan asked, "Was he [Picasso] in *my* country? Was he in *my* war?"

I told them the story of the painting, how the fascists had bombed the Spanish city of Guernica during the Spanish Civil War. Picasso painted *Guernica* to show the world the horror of that war. Calvin said, "Maybe if someone was for war and saw that, it could make them be against war." The children were quiet for a minute. Calvin kept looking at *Guernica,* then continued thoughtfully, "His painting . . . it's kind of like protesting."

• • •

On Christmas, the restaurant where Som Jet's family works was closed. They all came to dinner at my home. The conversation eventually got around to the black ants. His mother explained the five precepts of Buddhism, which include avoiding harming living things, not stealing, and not committing adultery. My mother said that sounded like some of the Ten Commandments.

I kept thinking back to Ben's loudly whispered question, "Do we have that rule in Judaism?" It's a good question. The basic rules of

Judaism and Christianity are the Ten Commandments. The sixth one is "Thou shalt not kill." That's pretty broad, pretty clear. It doesn't specifically say, "Thou shalt not kill people, but bugs are okay," or vice versa, or "Thou shalt not kill good people, only evil ones," or "Thou shalt not kill except during a war," or "Thou shalt not kill unless the other guy kills first." It just says, "Thou shalt not kill." I thought about politicians who so loudly profess their Christianity, and wondered how they reconcile this contradiction. I wondered if Emperor Hirohito was a Buddhist.

My students and I didn't know the answers to all these questions. Sister Khalilah was leaving for Mecca in a few days to make her *hajj* (holy pilgrimage). There would be more than a million pilgrims from all over the world gathered there. She said she would tell some people she met there the story of the black ants. When she came back, she would tell us what she learned. We planned to keep searching and asking. On the way to finding answers, we knew we would find more questions.

reflections on black ants and critical teaching

I chose to begin with this story because it illustrates what critical teaching and learning look like in my classroom. In the fast-paced days of teaching young children, I often need to step back and ask myself, "What is really going on here?" The story of "Black Ants and Buddhism" starts with a conflict. Human nature draws us to conflict. We become curious about the overheard argument at the next table in a restaurant, or a conflict between parent and child in the supermarket. Too often textbooks and other teacher-proof curriculum for young children provide a pat and happy presentation, devoid of conflict. Not surprisingly, these materials and this approach to teaching often bore many children, who are then labeled "inattentive." The small-scale invasion of black ants into our classroom, met by vigorous stomping and a cry of protest, engaged every member of the class, within seconds. Everyone had an opinion. Everyone cared.

In these days of fast food, instant messaging, music videos, call waiting, and fast cash, our society in general and our media in specific actively and aggressively shorten our attention span. As a teacher of critical thinkers, part of my job is to deliberately nurture sustained interest in questions over time. I want these children to grow into critically thinking citizens, not passive consumers of mass media fed by spin doctors. This kind of sustained attention is a process, not a hit-the-buzzer or click-the-mouse reflex. The black ant questions have been under investigation for two months now, and the interest continues.

The story of the black ants illustrates students' sense of ownership of the story itself and its central questions: *Doesn't everyone think it is fine to crush ants? If not, why not? Who disagrees? Do they see the world differently from people who think it is fine?* The story belongs to the children. They tell it often and well, to whomever will listen. Their questions are unique. In the tradition of critical pedagogy, it is a problem they have posed for themselves. Much of the learning takes place through dialog: conversations during a snack or meal, questions, comments, visits, philosophical discussions, and book talks.

Critically teaching this conflict and the subsequent investigation changed student behavior at school and at home, to make the world a little better. Gandhi says it is not so important how large the thing you do, but simply that you do it.

Teaching critically listens to and affirms a minority voice that challenges the status quo. Instead of forcing assimilation and acceptance of dominant culture, it reexamines cultural assumptions and values and considers their larger ramifications. Every student's voice was heard in this process, through philosophical discussions, meetings with guests, reflecting on books, listening and talking with visitors, and writing to friends and elders to ask their opinions.

The black ants helped us explore a variety of perspectives and helped us to learn, then compare and contrast, the rules of a variety of spiritual traditions. The ants helped us look at ants and the world and ourselves as Americans through others' eyes. Not bad, for some black ants at snacktime.

CHAPTER 1

introduction

Homework: Write your own story problem.

Write and solve an addition story problem. Write about an adding situation you might find in your home. Use words, number or pictures to show how you solved the problem.

At my house. There were 58 ants. 22 more come to my house. How many ants are at my house?

$$
\begin{array}{r}
58 \\
22 + \\
\hline
80
\end{array}
$$

Knowledge emerges only through invention and re-invention, through the restless, impatient, continuing, hopeful inquiry human beings pursue in the world, with the world, and with each other.

—Paulo Freire

My first encounter with Paulo Freire was accidental. I was a thirty-four-year-old student, taking my first undergraduate education course at Smith College. I felt awkward in my new Ivy League surroundings, having recently moved from the ghetto in South Philadelphia. My professor gave us an article to read and asked us to write a "response paper." I had dropped out of college sixteen years earlier to become a community labor organizer, and I couldn't remember having ever been asked to write a "response paper." Something in the article reminded me of when I was an organizer in Trenton, New Jersey. That's what I wrote about in my "response."

A couple of Guatemalan car washers came to the weekly workers meeting and complained that they had just been fired from the car wash because they had told the other workers that the boss was skimming most of the tip money out of the tip box. The workers had been strip-searched and beaten with brushes before being fired. The meeting also drew nearly a dozen Puerto Rican welders, whose case we'd been fighting with the National Labor Relations Board. The welders urged the car washers to fight their case. The car washers said no, they did not trust our government to help them, and they could not risk being sent back to Guatemala, where they might be killed. Frustrated, the welders asked them what they wanted then.

"We want to learn English," one young car washer said, "so we can defend ourselves." The other members considered this and argued about it. Eventually a middle-aged man named Bonifacio and a young single mother of four named Ivette volunteered to teach them. They were both somewhat fluent in English, although neither had any formal teaching experience or a high school diploma. Several of the welders agreed to help out, if the car washers would help them with a renovation project at our office.

The next Tuesday evening, I met with Bonifacio, Ivette, and Ramón, the leader of the welders, before the class was to begin. Teaching English was not part of my organizing repertoire; I asked the others how they thought we should start. Ramón was definite. "First class: words for work." He began to dictate sentences, in Spanish, English, or Spanglish. "My name is ___. I am Puerto Rican. My Social Security number is ___. How much is the pay?" Ivette and Bonifacio helped with the translations. Ivette typed the lesson on a mimeograph stencil. When the Guatemalan car washers arrived with nearly a dozen of their coworkers, Ramon taught two of them how to run the mimeograph machine and recruited them to come early each week to run it before the class started.

At the next meeting, there was a report about the Survival English class and a lively discussion in Spanish about what else the class members should learn. When one of the car washers reported how his brother's hand had gotten mangled in the rollers that week, and how the boss had threatened to fire him if he didn't repair the rollers by morning, they decided that the next lesson should be "words for getting hurt," which included an orientation to workers' compensation rights and occupational safety issues.

Another week, some of the Guatemalan workers, who rented cot space in overcrowded apartments divided by sheets, complained that they had no heat. That inspired "words for where you live" about tenant rights and finding apartments. There were "words for police" and "words for doctors." The lessons arose directly from the immediate struggles the workers faced in their daily lives. There were no lessons about conjugating verbs or making plurals.

The Central American workers learned their rights and the inequities of American society as they learned English. Each week more of them came and brought their friends—gravediggers, nursery workers, and roofers—to the Survival English classes, the meetings, and the renovation sessions. In the meantime, the American workers, mostly Puerto Rican and African American, realized that many of the rights they were learning about and using in their organizing did not extend to undocumented workers, just as many of the labor laws did not recognize domestic, agricultural, or temporary workers. They began to consider labor issues more globally. Together they developed strategies and organized for mutual benefit and protection.

I was nervous when the professor returned the papers. I didn't know if telling the story of the Survival English classes was an appropriate "response." On the paper the professor had written a comment asking when I had read Paulo Freire's *Pedagogy of the Oppressed*. I went to her after class and asked her what that was. She said she thought I'd read it already. She said that it was dense to read but that she thought I would like it.

getting to know paulo

The following summer, I had a work-study job at the Smith College library. Most of our patrons were students in the summer session of the School for Social Work. I worked at the reserve window and soon discovered that *Pedagogy of the Oppressed* was on reserve. That entire summer, between checking materials in and out for people, I struggled through *Pedagogy of the Oppressed.* I read a paragraph, reread it, read the next, and then reread the previous two. The theoretical language made my head swim. Because I had been an organizer for many years, the political aspect of the book was more familiar than the pedagogical aspect.

The following summer, I worked on the reserve desk and read it again. It was hard for me to picture Paulo Freire as an organizer. I couldn't imagine this guy sitting down with a bunch of illiterate Brazilian peasants, let alone Puerto Rican welders and Guatemalan car washers, gravediggers, and roofers.

After two labored readings, I grasped a few big ideas. Freire said that teaching was a political act; I agreed. Freire criticized the "banking concept" of education, in which the students are viewed as ignorant, empty receptacles, to be filled with deposits of knowledge, provided by the teacher. He said that the traditional "banking concept" approach stifled creativity and critical thinking and served to enforce oppression. He contrasted this with what he called "problem-posing" education, in which students and teachers are coinvestigators of problems that arise organically from their daily experiences.

In problem-posing education, the teacher isn't the sole source of knowledge. Dialog between students and a teacher is part of an inquiry process that encourages critical thinking. I could see the connection between Freire's concept of problem-posing education and the Survival English class story, but beyond that, I felt pretty stupid and thought I really didn't get it.

Then I started teaching. I became a teacher because I knew I wanted to make a positive change in the world. I had a head packed full of theory and a one-year teaching contract. I knew already that every new teacher in my district would get a layoff notice before the year was over. I had nothing to lose. I taught like I had a year to live and everything to learn. I had no furniture and no supplies in my classroom to set up, so I spent the week before school started going door to door in the community, visiting the families of my students. That felt familiar. I could teach like an organizer. I didn't worry about not understanding everything Paulo Freire wrote. I was ready to teach.

A couple of years later, in graduate school at the University of Massachusetts, Dr. Sonia Nieto reintroduced me to Paulo Freire, with his *Teachers as Cultural Workers: Letters to Those Who Dare Teach.* By then, I felt Freire was more like a wise old friend. I could make out, relate to, understand, and use some of what he said. Needless to say, I am not an

academic authority on Freire's theory, but I can humbly and honestly say that his theory informs my work.

teaching critically

I choose to teach critically because I believe young children are capable of amazing things, far more than is usually expected of them. I am not talking about raising a score on a standardized math test (although that often happens). I am talking about thinking critically and learning to learn, learning to use basic skills like reading, writing, solving mathematical problems, analyzing data, public speaking, scientific observation, and inquiry as an active citizen in your community. I believe young children can think about fairness and are deeply moved and highly motivated by the recognition of injustice. I choose to teach critically because it lets me keep learning alongside my students. It keeps my work fascinating, funny, and fast-paced. I teach this way so that I can hear every child's voice and see each jewel sparkle.

I decided to write this book because people often ask me questions about the way I teach. The central question seems to be, How can teachers of young children use language and literacy to teach about the world (history, geography, social studies, science) with rigor, depth, and challenge in a way that engages and empowers young students? I believe theory emerges from the practice, and that the very best teaching merges theory, practice, and reflection.

. . .

In the introduction to *Rethinking Our Classrooms* edited by Bigelow, Christensen, Karp, Miner, and Peterson, the editors describe several interlocking components of what they call a social justice classroom. They argue that the curriculum and classroom practice must be:

- Grounded in the lives of our students
- Critical
- Multicultural, antiracist, pro-justice
- Participatory, experiential
- Hopeful, joyful, kind, visionary
- Activist
- Academically rigorous
- Culturally sensitive

I strive to teach critically in a social justice classroom. My teaching is always evolving toward that goal.

Here is Sonia Nieto's definition of multicultural education in a sociopolitical context (2003, p. 305):

> Multicultural education is a process of comprehensive school reform. And basic education for all students. It challenges and rejects racism and other forms of discrimination in schools and society and accepts and affirms pluralism (ethnic, racial, linguistic, religious, economic and gender, among others) that students, their communities, and teachers reflect. Multicultural education permeates the schools' curriculum and instructional strategies, as well as the interactions among teachers, students and families, and the very way that schools conceptualize the nature of teaching and learning. Because it uses critical pedagogy as its underlying philosophy and focuses on knowledge, reflection, and action (praxis) as the basis for social change, multicultural education promotes democratic principles of social justice.

The seven basic characteristics of multicultural education in this definition are:

Multicultural education *is antiracist education.*
Multicultural education *is basic education.*
Multicultural education *is important for* all *students.*
Multicultural education *is pervasive.*
Multicultural education *is education for social justice.*
Multicultural education *is a process.*
Multicultural education *is critical pedagogy.*

background notes

In many ways, I look like a typical American elementary schoolteacher: a forty-five-year-old White native English-speaking female from a large Irish-American Catholic family, married, with two children. Perhaps less typically, I was a farmworker and temporary worker before becoming a volunteer community organizer of farm, seasonal, service, and temporary workers in Oregon, Philadelphia, and Trenton for fourteen years. Later, as a low-income single mother of a biracial child, I attended Smith College on a scholarship, worked part time, and received welfare and a child care subsidy. I graduated when I was thirty-six years old. I had pic-

tured myself working in an inner-city school in Holyoke or Springfield, but those districts never even called me for an interview. I began teaching first grade in a bilingual class at the school across the street from the subsidized apartment complex where I lived, and I teach there still.

I teach at Jackson Street School, a public elementary school of 400 children in the small city of Northampton in Western Massachusetts. I have taught first grade and second grade, which I currently teach. I team-taught a combined first- and second-grade classroom for several years, and have often looped up with first graders to second grade. In my first year of teaching, I had fourteen students. Nine years later, I have twenty-four, and know that my class will likely grow.

About a third of my students live in homes where languages other than English, including Albanian, Thai, Hindi, Khmer, Russian, and Spanish, are spoken. Three of my students arrived in the United States in the last six months. Bilingual education was outlawed in Massachusetts in 2002. Because I am certified in teaching English as a Second Language, English language learners in second grade are clustered in my class. Some of my students have identified special needs, such as autism or developmental delays. Some have significant attention issues and/or emotional needs, such as depression or explosive behavior. Quite a number of my students have witnessed domestic violence or have been abused. Ten of my students are children of color (Asian, Latino, and African American), and many of them are biracial, i.e., Pakistani Panamanian or Jewish African American. My students are Jewish, Muslim, Buddhist, Protestant, Hindu, Unitarian, Catholic, and atheist.

Economically, my students come from a wide range of families. Thirty-seven percent of the students at our school receive free or reduced-price lunch. Most of my students' parents work outside the home. About half are service workers, in fast food or other restaurants, hotels, colleges, universities, supermarkets, and nursing homes. One is in the military. Others work in various professions, including law, psychology, nursing, veterinary medicine, higher education, and social work. Each year about 10–15 percent of my students are in transition, living with friends or relatives, in foster homes, or in shelters because of financial hardship; long-distance moves; separation; domestic violence, abuse, or neglect; or the mental illness, incarceration, or addiction of a parent. I have had second graders for whom Jackson Street School is their fourth, fifth, or even seventh elementary school.

We have great family diversity at our school as well. We have students being raised by biological, foster, or adoptive parents, grandparents, aunts, friends, or other guardians. I have always had one or more adopted children in my class. They are adopted from other countries or from within the United States, through agencies or through the Department of Social Services, sometimes as infants or toddlers and sometimes as five-to-seven-year olds. Some years as many as one-third of my students have lesbian parents.

Jackson Street School is one of four elementary schools in the district. It has a reputation for multiculturalism and respect for diversity. It is led by Gwen Agna, a well-respected principal deeply committed to equity, whose own children attended the school. The Parent Teacher Organization has a very active Cultural Arts Committee that writes grants to bring artistic residency programs on Latino dance, Indian culture and movement, world rhythms, and more each year. It has a Language Sharing Program, in which a strand of classes (including mine) from kindergarten to fifth grade receives approximately an hour of Spanish instruction in the content areas each week.

Northampton is a liberal city of about 29,000. It is home to Smith College, a women's liberal arts college. I have a student teacher from Smith College each semester, and we have access to its plant house, art museum, machine shop, and other facilities for field trips. Northampton is in the Five College Area, which includes Smith, Mount Holyoke College in South Hadley, and Hampshire and Amherst Colleges and the University of Massachusetts in Amherst. There are numerous opportunities to collaborate with professors and graduate students on research projects.

Each chapter in this book tells a story about teaching and learning and attempts to answer by illustration some of the questions teachers ask about teaching critically: How do you keep the teaching age-appropriate? How do you keep it authentic and relevant, so that children will care about the topic? How can I do all this myself? Do families ever react negatively? How can you tell if the kids are "getting it"? What about when it doesn't work the way you planned? What if you don't know all this stuff?

I don't have answers to all these questions. As I tell you these few specifics about my city, my school, and my class, it is with the understanding that no class is "typical." With each new group of students, the nature of my class changes. Even when I loop up from first to second grade with a dozen of my students from the previous year, my class is not the same. All this is to say that the stories in this book are not meant to be blueprints, but rather possibilities, as you listen to the children you know, pursue their burning questions, tell and retell their stories.

compassion, action, and change

It is not enough to be compassionate. You must act.

—Dalai Lama

Welcome to the s

survival center

We went to the surviva center and delivered food.

*I*n the course of studying the life cycle of plants, my first graders learned about the importance of plants as a human food source. This brought us to the idea of hunger, and why some people go hungry, which led to other questions of fairness, such as why some people don't have a place to live. I had a student teacher from Smith College and was looking for ways to support her in tackling a community service-learning project. I noticed in the newspaper that a local organization was organizing its annual Thanksgiving dinner for homeless and low-income people at a church downtown and needed volunteers and donations. I introduced the concept of compassion and action with a quote from the Dalai Lama: "It is not enough to be compassionate. You must act." I worked with my student teacher to braid these strands together.

The Tuesday before Thanksgiving, a crew of family volunteers helped my students bake and mash the pumpkins I had brought in from my garden to make a dozen pumpkin pies and several batches of cookies. Then we munched on roasted pumpkin seeds for snack. Our plan was to put the pies and cookies in boxes donated by a local bakery and carry them downtown on the public bus the next day. We would go first to city hall to meet with Mayor Clare Higgins and Rebecca Mueller, an advocate for the homeless, then walk down the block to the church, deliver the pies and cookies, and volunteer to set up the church hall before catching the bus back to school in time for early dimissal. I had never done this before, but it seemed like a reasonable plan.

That Tuesday afternoon someone mentioned that it might snow the next day, the first snow of the season. My students asked if we would still go. I said, "Of course we'll still go! First graders are tough! We're not scared off by a little snow! Besides, people don't stop being hungry when it snows. We promised to deliver these pies and help set up for that dinner. A promise is a promise!"

When I woke up the next morning, there was nearly a foot of snow on the ground. I turned on the radio. School was canceled. As I sat eating breakfast, thinking about our pies locked up in the school, the phone rang. It was Jack's mother, Ann. "I told Jack it's a snow day. I told him school is canceled, but he's insisting he has to go to school anyway, to deliver those pies. He said you said first graders were tough and wouldn't be scared off by a little snow. I told him it's a lot of snow, but he said you promised to deliver the pies. He keeps saying, 'A promise is a promise.'" Sometimes the ability of first graders to quote their teachers almost verbatim is scary.

I took a deep breath. "It's all true," I admitted. "We just need to make a plan." Ann said that her workplace also was closed for the day. I said I'd call her back in a few minutes. I called my principal and asked if she would open the school for us to liberate the pies and cookies. She agreed to meet us in two

hours, after the roads had been plowed a bit; I called Ann back and asked if she and Jack would meet me at school at 9:45 A.M. to get the pies. Ann and I split the class list and called everyone about meeting at the school for a "family field trip." I called our contacts downtown and told them we'd be coming.

As families continued to arrive in the school lobby, the children used colored markers to write Thanksgiving messages on the pie boxes. At 10 A.M., we took off in a long, slow caravan of cars. More families met us at city hall. As we settled into a large conference room with Mayor Clare Higgins and Rebecca Mueller, I took a quick count. Many families had brought along extra children they were taking care of that day while other parents went to work. We had more than twenty-five children and twenty parents.

Mayor Higgins thanked the children for their hard work and determination. She introduced Rebecca, who began by asking the children if they thought anything was unfair in the world. Sadie raised her hand and said, "I think it's unfair that some people have homes and other people don't." Rebecca then told the story of efforts to organize homeless people in Northampton over the last twenty years. She described some of their protests, like sleep-outs in the downtown park by homeless people and their allies. She explained some of the reasons people become homeless, how working a minimum-wage job without health care benefits or reliable transportation creates a fragile existence that can easily unravel. She described some of the services that exist for homeless people in Northampton, both families and single adults.

My students asked her what life was like for homeless people and what they could do to help. She told them very specific items they could collect, such as lip balm and hand lotion, adult-size socks and laundry detergent. Rebecca described how homeless people could trade in a pair of dirty, wet socks for a pair of clean, dry socks each night at the shelter. She also explained how people could use washers and dryers for free but needed laundry detergent.

After hot cocoa served by the mayor's staff, we bundled up and carried our pies down the steps of city hall, across Main Street and down to the church basement. I looked over my shoulder and saw this long trail of brightly booted children, proudly and seriously carrying boxes of pies and tins of cookies, stretching down the slippery steps of city hall, across the slushy crosswalk and up the block.

When we reached the site of the dinner, we rolled up our sleeves as the bemused volunteer coordinator explained the task at hand to this large crew of small helpers. They nodded with looks of complete understanding and took off like a swarm of ants. People often look at young children and say, "Don't you wish you could bottle that energy?" It was thrilling to see all of that youthful energy, which as a teacher I often struggle to contain, channeled so powerfully

and effectively. The volunteer coordinator was stunned by the efficiency of their setup work and asked how they did it so quickly. Sadie rolled up her sleeve to show her skinny arm and said fiercely, "Because we're powerful!"

Next, tables were set up in the freshly swept day-care rooms for preparing meals for delivery to homebound people. Then we moved on to the main hall, where dozens of long tables and folding chairs were to be set up for the dinner. As Jack and I worked together to set up chairs, I said, "Good idea, Jack." He smiled broadly and said, "You know what the Dalai Lama says, Ms. Cowhey: 'It is not enough to be compassionate. You must act'!"

• • •

In many ways, our pie project would seem to reflect the spirit of caring for others and remembering those in need at the holidays, which seems central to the American values promoted in our schools. Teachers are often looking for community service–learning projects that will demonstrate that spirit of care and engage their students, but I feel the need to look critically at each and every project I undertake.

Consider the typical model of the school food drive, usually held during the holiday season. Sometimes these drives involve a competition between classrooms to collect the largest number of cans, which really reflects how much disposable income, more than how much concern, the families of that class have. A parent told me of a food drive at another school in which the students of the class that brought the most cans were rewarded with a pizza party. There are mixed messages there. Although school food drives are well meaning, they may inadvertently be

- reinforcing stereotypes about poor people,
- oversimplifying the problem and the solution,
- failing to teach an understanding of the causes of poverty or local efforts to improve conditions, and
- further stigmatizing low-income children in the school.

I don't want children to think that a turkey dinner or a pumpkin pie will solve the problems of a homeless person or an unemployed family. Without a doubt, the holidays are hard and stressful for low-income people, but the reality is that things get a whole lot more miserable in January, February, and March when the seasonal jobs disappear and heating costs increase, along with medical costs and days of work lost to sickness.

When kids collect canned goods for "poor people," it makes "poor people" seem like a predestined, anonymous group. It makes poverty seem like a permanent, almost genetic condition. The children have no idea where the food goes after they drop the cans their mothers bought into the box. If we leave it at that, it is a child's imitation of an adult's token gesture of charity: tossing a coin in a beggar's cup. Does the tossed coin absolve the adult of responsibility for addressing the societal contradictions that create such poverty even here, in the richest country in the world?

A "give the helpless a handout" approach does nothing to increase children's understanding of the complex reasons why people go hungry or cannot afford housing. By oversimplifying the problem—i.e., they are hungry because they are poor—it oversimplifies the solution: a bag of food. It stereotypes low-income people as passively "in need." Although young children are less aware of (and should not be taught) them, society is burdened with a slew of stereotypes about poor people being lazy, unintelligent, dirty, and so forth. It fails to acknowledge the creative problem solving, resourcefulness, resilience, persistence, and enduring spirit of people who take nothing for granted. Perhaps most painfully, the traditional school food drive can further stigmatize low-income children in the class by reinforcing these stereotypes.

who are "poor people" anyway?

When I was a child growing up in suburban Long Island, there were school food drives each holiday season, "to help poor people." I always wondered who these poor people were and where they lived.

I remember one Christmas when we were having bologna for dinner. We always had peanut butter and jelly for lunch, so I thought of bologna as an exotic treat. I was six or seven years old, a curious little girl, and innocently asked, "Why are we having bologna for dinner?" My father jumped up from his chair and yelled, "We are not poor! We are not poor!" I hadn't particularly associated having bologna for Christmas dinner with being poor, but my father's reaction impressed upon me the idea that poor was something we did not want to be.

In my family, we were not allowed to use the term *poor people*. My mother taught us early on to use the phrase *those less fortunate than ourselves at this time*. It didn't exactly roll off the tongue, but we used it with relish as we sorted through bags of hand-me-down clothes. We would bag up the things that did not fit us and say proudly, "These clothes are for those less fortunate than ourselves at this time."

Surely there were others less fortunate than ourselves at that time, but we didn't seem to know them. My family struggled. My father's salary as a teacher supported our family of eight, and later ten, as two cousins came to live with us. We lived in a working-class neighborhood, where most of the fathers were New York City police officers, firefighters, or sanitation workers; truck drivers; or construction or factory workers. Some of the mothers worked outside the home as secretaries or in retail jobs when their children got older. We often paid our mortgage as the bank closed on the day it was due, and tensions rose at home when we were later than that.

After paying the mortgage and taxes, we didn't have enough for food *and* fuel oil, so we spent most of each winter without heat, which also meant we could not run the water for fear the pipes would freeze. We usually wore hand-me-down clothes, and for special occasions, such as a first communion, confirmation, or graduation, we sewed our own dresses. We were often short on food. My father used to joke when visitors came, "Don't rest your hand on the table or someone will put a fork through it." My mother would smile as she passed the serving dishes, whispering, "FHB" to us. We'd smile back as we scooped out tiny portions for ourselves, understanding our family code for "Family Hold Back."

It was not a miserable childhood. We packed for and imagined long journeys in the broken-down cars that littered our yard. "Driving to Ireland" was a favorite scenario for our dramatic play. We made lovely fairy houses in the overgrown grass and set up enterprising mud-pie bakeries in the large patches of bare dirt. We climbed trees, made ice castles, built forts, and tried digging holes to China. We played outside with whatever siblings, cousins, and neighbors were around and didn't have a clue what a play date was. When bags of hand-me-down clothes arrived, we had fashion shows in the living room. One summer the agitator in our washing machine broke, so we took turns putting our little brother and sister in the tub of the washer to dance on the soapy, wet clothes while we blared the radio and sang at the top of our lungs.

For me, the hardest part was keeping this secret when I went outside the realm of my family, when I went to school. When I went from our cold house into the heated classroom, I sweated terribly and my face turned red. In the warmth of school, the mildewed scent of my clothing rose sickeningly around me. How could I begin to explain that the roof leaked, that my bedroom walls were covered in mold, that there was no heat and no running water, that we couldn't afford to go to the Laundromat until payday? I simmered in silent invisibility, aching to be like everyone else, all those classmates who seemed so fabulously normal, so stunningly ordinary. I understood that we would never have the backyard swimming pool or bologna sandwiches in our lunch bags or new clothing from the mall. I knew it wouldn't be appropriate to invite classmates to my house. I just wished I could get rid of that smell.

It was even harder in high school. A task as simple as hair washing was an elaborate production in the winter. My father periodically walked through the house on his way to the basement shouting, "I'm going to turn on the water!" We all grabbed milk jugs, buckets, and pots and scrambled to our assigned stations as the faucets sputtered to life. When we'd hear his shout from the basement, "I'm going to turn off the water!" we'd shout, "Wait!" as the water dribbled to a halt. To wash, we boiled water on the two working burners of the stove. Then we mixed some boiled water with some cold water in a pitcher and gingerly poured it over our heads in the kitchen sink, alternately scalding and freezing our scalps. Sometimes I went to the gym locker room during my lunch period to shower and wash my hair, but then I'd have to run to class late, with my long mop of wet hair. I felt very alone.

When I was about fourteen, I told my mother I thought no one else lived like this. She assured me that there were many others less fortunate than ourselves at this time, but said that if I studied hard and earned good grades, I could win a scholarship to college, where I could live in a heated dormitory and eat cafeteria food. It sounded like heaven. I studied hard and worked part time. I got good grades and the scholarship. I graduated at sixteen and went to Bard College, where I took long hot showers, ate two of every meal, gained fifteen pounds, grew a few inches, and studied diligently.

In college, I started doing internships that brought me to new places, like a public school on the Lower East Side of Manhattan and a settlement house in North St. Louis. I realized my mother was right. There were plenty of people less fortunate than us. There were ghettos full of people struggling to make ends meet. I felt less alone, but I wanted to know why the world was like this.

Eventually I walked away from the scholarship, left college, and became a community labor organizer. When I was organizing in Philadelphia, I developed the habit of listening closely to language, to learn new idioms. I remember being with a group of older African American women. They were commiserating with each other about having to raise their grandchildren, because some of their children were addicted to drugs. Just then, a skinny crack addict hurried down the street. They all watched him in silence, and then one woman let out a long sigh, shook her head, and said, "There but for the grace of God go I." The saying stuck in my head, this very proper, archaic language, so aptly captioning this sidewalk scene in the ghetto.

Like "those less fortunate than ourselves at this time," this old expression, new to my ears, empathized with the suffering of another, while acknowledging how fragile and perhaps temporary our own circumstances really are. It is properly humbling to know that a person who seems to have it all could stumble and slide to the bottom. At the same time, it is inspiring to meet someone who is quite together today and learn that she climbed up from hard times, that she had been a homeless crack addict, living between the streets and jail five years ago. This is not to pose a pull-yourself-up-by-your-bootstraps story as an ideal model. This is just to remind myself to make no assumptions in life and to shed even the smallest drops of jealousy or superiority.

reimagining food drives and challenging stereotypes

So how do teachers find ways to approach this complex sociopolitical realm, to nurture empathy and take action without stigmatizing families who are less fortunate than ourselves at this time? Food drives can be a developmentally appropriate activity for young children when used as a vehicle to do the following:

- Challenge stereotypes
- Teach understanding of the complexity of the causes of poverty
- Introduce local activists and organizers as role models addressing needs and working for long-term solutions
- Empower children to take responsibility in their community
- Remove the stigma of poverty

I always must assume that there are some families in my class struggling economically, even if I do not know who they are. Even knowing the occupations, addresses, and free/reduced-price lunch status of my students and their families doesn't give me the whole story. With the huge mortgages and credit-card debt carried by many middle-class families, sudden job loss can spell financial disaster. Because of the stigma surrounding it, especially in our materialistic culture, great pains are often taken to mask poverty. My point is not to identify or single out low-income students, but to be respectful of and sensitive to economic diversity in my class, the school, and the community.

One way I challenge stereotypes is by telling stories from my own life, stories that focus on creativity, compassion, and problem solving, as well as persistence, conservation, and resourcefulness. For example, I tell them a story about when I worked for a large bookstore chain as a department manager earning minimum wage. I earned so little money that I was eligible for a day care subsidy and $80 worth of food stamps each month. I explain that my take-home pay was about $625 a month and that the rent for the basement studio I shared with my son (and an oil burner) was $600 a month. That left me $25 a month to buy diapers, soap, and gasoline, and use the Laundromat.

One month I lost my food stamps on my way to work. I arrived very upset and planned to ask if I could pick up some extra hours. I was shocked to look at the work schedule and see that I had been cut from forty hours per week to thirty, because the holidays were over. When I explained the situation about the lost food stamps to my boss and asked if I could possibly work more hours, she rolled her eyes and sighed, "Hours are an issue with everyone," then turned away. I spent my lunch hour retracing my route from work to the day care center to home and back, to no avail. When I left work that afternoon, I found two bags of groceries on the front seat of my old car, that some of my coworkers, who earned as little as I did, had chipped in on, because they understood it could have happened to them.

As a teacher, I find it is powerful to draw on and speak from my own experiences: having grown up in a struggling family, having been a community organizer, having been a single mother working a minimum-wage job. Obviously not every teacher has a trunk-load of those same stories to tell. Volunteering with local community organizing efforts is another way to gain more personal understanding of poverty. I also look for good children's stories that address matters of class. Here are some that I use regularly in the course of a year.

The Hundred Dresses by Eleanor Estes is a classic story about a Polish immigrant girl who is teased for saying she has 100 dresses, when she wears the same faded old dress every day. It is told from the perspective of the teaser's friend. I read this story aloud over the course of a week, engaging the children during and after each reading in a philosophical discussion about the ethical dilemma of being a silent bystander.

¡Si, Se Puede! by Diana Cohn is a bilingual story about the Service Employees International Union organizing drive and janitors' strike in Los Angeles. This story was especially useful in responding to my stu-

dents' many questions in the "Why were you protesting in front of the school this morning, Ms. Cowhey?" category during a lengthy job action by our teachers union as we ended a year of working without a contract. Over time, more and more students and their families joined our demonstrations. It is useful to discuss why and how workers form unions, what a strike (or other concerted labor action) is, the importance of community support, and connections between the story of the janitors' organizing drive and local labor struggles.

The Streets Are Free by Karusa is a bilingual story about children in a Venezuelan barrio who organize and protest the lack of a playground in their neighborhood and the eventual community action that builds it. Children can retell and then make captioned drawings to illustrate a story of community organizing told by a "guest activist" visitor to the classroom. These can be displayed, then bound into a class book.

Shingebiss by Nancy Van Laan is an Ojibwe legend about a merganser duck that demonstrates the values of persistence, conservation, and resourcefulness to survive the northern winter. This is a favorite of my students and my own children. *Shingebiss* is an excellent role model to refer to when the going gets rough. Slogging through miles of muddy bogs in the rain during a particularly difficult canoe portage trip, my five-year-old daughter often asked, "Could you tell me the story about that duck again?" I am often impressed by hearing my students exhort each other to be persistent or praise each other for being resourceful in their problem solving. I start to think proudly, "Wow! Did I teach them that vocabulary?!" and then humbly remind myself, "No, they learned it from a duck."

Tight Times by Barbara Shook Hazen is about a boy in a financially stressed family who really wants a dog. Told from the child's perspective, it describes the boy's spontaneous adoption of a stray kitten against the backdrop of the father's anger at his sudden job loss. Children can easily make text-to-self connections with the story as they discuss how a sudden change of circumstances can affect everyone in a family.

The Lady in the Box by Ann McGovern is about two children who notice and then befriend a homeless woman living in their neighborhood. *Fly Away Home* by Eve Bunting is about a homeless boy and his father who live at an airport. I use both of these books to help children see beyond the "shopping bag lady" stereotype of homelessness, to recognize that people of all ages and circumstances can become homeless for a brief or longer period of time, for a variety of reasons, and that shelters are not solutions in themselves. Especially for older students, these discussions can be a springboard for mathematical investigations (using the classified pages of the local newspaper and the phone book) into the take-home pay of minimum-wage workers, the cost of a doctor's office or emergency room visit without health insurance, the cost of rental housing, the location and availability of subsidized housing, and the cost and availability of public transportation. Even for younger students, who find it meaningful to collect survival items such as lip balm, hand lotion, socks, blankets, and warm jackets, organizing a "job interview clothing drive" can help them understand the idea of helping people help themselves.

• • •

My first graders worked hard and enjoyed making the pumpkin pies and cookies for the Thanksgiving dinner. Not only did they know where the food was going, but they were committed to delivering it themselves, come hell or high snow. They and their families learned about how people can become homeless and what can help prevent it (affordable housing, higher-wage jobs with health care benefits, reliable public transportation), what services exist for homeless people locally, and different ways we as individuals, families, classes, and schools can help. In a small way, they learned that although donations are good, it means even more to volunteer. One family went back the next day to serve dinner, and others helped with delivering meals. My daughter wanted to bake cookies and bring them down herself, and this has become a family tradition each Thanksgiving. My son's fifth-grade teacher, Margie Riddle, does a similar apple pie project, integrating science and math curriculum. As a follow-up activity, she asks her students to bring in different ingredients each month throughout the winter so the class can prepare a meal for a shelter kitchen.

the giving tree

Around the holiday season each year my school has a Giving Tree project. A large leafless tree is set up in the lobby, with a "Giving Tree" sign. Families bring in nonperishable food items and winter clothing and leave it beneath the tree. Smaller items, such as mittens, hats, and scarves, are hung on the branches. Families who need hats or boots or snow pants can take them from the tree. Traditionally, on the last day of school before the December vacation, our principal or a parent volunteer loaded all of the items and drove them to the Northampton Survival Center.

After our Thanksgiving effort, my students were eager to do more. They began by making posters advertising specific items that were needed for local shelters and homeless people, such as, "Please donate lip balm and hand lotion to the Giving Tree." We invited the director of the Northampton Survival Center to visit our class. Before she came, I told the children a story about when I first moved to Northampton. Because of a change that occurred in the law just before I moved, I was denied food stamps and a child care subsidy. I appealed my denial, but in the meantime, I was running out of food and money. Because I had no child care, I could not work. I called the Survival Center, and they told me I could come get some food. It was more than a mile away, but I didn't have a car or money for a taxi, so I pushed my son in the baby stroller and walked there. They filled up my stroller with food, including fresh vegetables such as zucchini and tomatoes. When I asked where the fresh produce came from, they said that gardeners at the Northampton Community Garden donated it.

I explained to my students that I hadn't thought I would need to ask for help with food, but when I did, I was treated with respect. After that, I realized how important it was for me to do my part to make sure the Survival Center continued to be strong in our community, so it will be there when someone else needs it. The following summer, I became a gardener at the Northampton Community Garden, riding with my son on the back of my bicycle and my vegetables in the front basket. I volunteered to coordinate the deliveries of gardeners' donations to the Survival Center. Nowadays, I continue to plant, water, and weed the Survival Center garden plot, which is right next to my own. Whenever I see zucchini growing there, I always think of the zucchini I was given the summer I had none.

The director of the Survival Center talked about reasons families and individuals sometimes cannot afford groceries and need to come there for food. She explained how some families and individuals earn such low wages, or have such a small disability or pension check, that they have an ongoing need for food. These people can sign up to receive food on a monthly basis and can receive other items such as bread and produce on a weekly basis, to help stretch their food budgets. She talked about the kinds of high-protein foods that are especially needed, such as peanut butter, tuna fish, and beans. She also explained how their clothing distribution program worked. Again my students set to work, making more posters around the school, asking for specific items: "Can you please donate tuna and peanut butter to the Giving Tree?" One student wrote an announcement about the Giving Tree drive for the school newsletter.

The donations began to come in. Each week, my students went to the Giving Tree for math and language arts activities. They categorized, inventoried, weighed, and graphed the donations. They wrote reports for the newsletter and made announcements about the drive's progress.

We began to discuss how we might, as a class, bring the items to the Survival Center. During our study of simple machines, we had discussed the importance of the wheel and axle. Sadie said, "I remember your story about going to the Survival Center with your stroller to get some food. We can't drive cars, but we're strong. There's too much food for us to carry, but maybe we can get some baby strollers and *push* the food over there!" In my weekly family letter, I appealed for wheeled vehicles of all kinds.

The day of the delivery came. We assembled a convoy of garden carts, baby strollers (some with younger siblings riding along), bike trailers, wheelbarrows, and wagons. The children set aside all the donations appropriate for the homeless shelter and loaded our wheeled vehicles with food and warm clothes for the Survival Center. We bundled ourselves against the cold and set off.

Now, you must consider that young children rarely walk straight anywhere. They much prefer to zigzag or twirl, leap, run, or dawdle. I had planned that it would take us about thirty minutes to push and pull about 600 pounds of food and warm clothing nearly a mile to the Survival Center. Perhaps it was the cold, or the importance of their mission, but the teams cooperated, taking turns pushing and pulling our vehicles across icy patches, over snowbanks, and along the slippery sidewalks; we arrived in less than fifteen minutes. We played cooperative games outside until the director arrived to open the center for us. She gave us a tour and explained how the center worked.

Several children looked around and proudly said they knew this place, that they had come here with their families before. The children helped unload and weigh the food. On the way back, I noticed one very shy student skipping along beside her mother, who was pushing a baby in the stroller. She asked, "When can we go back there to get some food, Mom?" Her mother said, "I'd heard of it before, but I didn't know where it was. Now that I know where it is, I will come back on Thursday."

While pushing my stroller, Gabriella and Magda hit a chunk of ice and the front wheel snapped off. Jehann El-Bisi, a graduate student volunteering with my class, saw the girls looking down at the broken wheel and assured them it would be okay, that it was an accident. Gabriella looked at her calmly and said, "We *know* it's okay. Ms. Cowhey won't be mad. She'll forgive us. She tries to be like Gandhi." They resourcefully tipped the stroller onto its back wheels and pushed it to the school, where we warmed up with hot cocoa.

The Giving Tree drive continued through January, with other classes continuing the math activities and deliveries. The drive brought in far more donations than it ever had in the past. The children had learned a lot about nutrition, and used criteria to sort what would be useful to the homeless shelter and what would be useful for the Survival Center. They met with the mayor, activists, and organizers in our community. They applied their counting, sorting, weighing, recording, graphing, and reporting skills for authentic purposes. They worked hard, knowing that this project could benefit their own families, or a classmate's, now, in the past, or in the future. They were resourceful in their problem solving to overcome the challenges of weight, distance, and weather. They respectfully learned more about conditions of poverty in our own community. They collected and volunteered not out of pity, but out of understanding and empathy. They learned to transform their compassion into action.

routines: a day in the life of the peace class

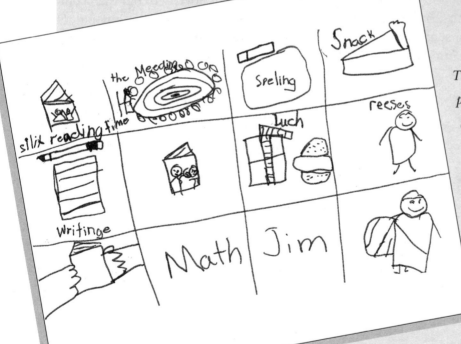

The best laid plans of mice and men often go awry.
—Robert Burns

One autumn day I was being observed by a visitor. It was after lunch recess, and Jasmine raised her hand in response to a math question I had just posed. "I want to share now." I reminded her that when I had asked her during sharing time if she wanted to share, she had said no. She said she had forgotten. I said that we were trying to focus on math just then, but that I would let her share at our closing circle. We continued the mathematical discussion.

It was a hot afternoon, so the windows were open. I noticed one airborne milkweed seed drift by and then another. Sadie got out of her seat to chase "the fairies." I told her to sit down. They continued to waft about. I started to demonstrate a new math game.

Jasmine was easily distracted, and I noticed she kept fooling with a bag under her table. I paused and asked her what was in the bag. "My sharing," she said. I told her to put it in her backpack until later. She said she'd forgotten her backpack. I told her to put the bag on the windowsill.

Seamus, still red faced and dripping from football at recess, complained, "I'm sweating." I turned on the fan and continued playing a demonstration round of the game with Ann, who was seated up front. Sadie was out of her seat again, chasing more fairies. Again I told her to sit down. Now there were at least a dozen wafting milkweed seeds. Gabriella pointed out that a fairy had landed on my head. The visitor had a hard time keeping a straight face.

I looked toward the windowsill and noticed Jasmine's crumpled paper bag. Sticking out of the open end was a dried stalk of milkweed, with a pod that had burst open: the source of the fairies. I laughed. The visitor and all the children laughed. I took a deep breath and thought fast. No one had paid any attention to the math game. Everyone was thinking about chasing fairies.

"We're changing our plan," I announced. I told the leader to take the box of draft notebooks and another student to take the pencil basket. I told Jasmine to close her sharing bag and carry it. I told everyone to line up. We went outside, sat under a shady tree and listened to Jasmine share how she and her mom had found this milkweed stalk, and how milkweed is a favorite food (a host plant) of monarch butterflies. We discussed the milkweed plants we'd seen on our nature walk in early September, before the pods were bursting, and the brown velvety cattails we'd seen in the marsh, the seeds of which would later become fuzzy airborne "fairies" like this. We talked about some ways plants distribute their seeds. I thanked Jasmine for sharing. Then I stood up and said, "Now we'll chase fairies."

With Jasmine's permission, I held the stalk high above my head and walked fast in the autumn breeze like the Pied Piper, with a steady stream of

fairies escaping from the burst pod, chased by delighted, laughing children leaping to catch them. We walked through the field and around to the butterfly garden on the other side of the school. There, the tired children rested on the grass, and the observer (a good sport who had been pressed into service to carry the pencils and draft notebooks during the fairy chase) distributed the materials. The children wrote poems and scientific observations about the milkweed seeds. After awhile, children who wanted to do so shared what they'd written. Then we gathered up the draft notebooks in the box and the pencils in the basket and walked back inside. We played the math game for a shorter time and skipped that day's planned science lesson.

• • •

I was able to change gears because my students know certain things by October. We know how to line up and leave the classroom and stay together when we go outside. We know how to sit under a shade tree to have a discussion. We know how to follow the leader. We know how to pretend, imagine, and have fun. We know how to use draft notebooks. We know, at least roughly, how to write scientific observations and poems.

Without the flexibility our routines gave us, what would my options have been? I could have stuck with my original plan. I could have been tough as nails. I could have gotten really angry at Jasmine for completely sabotaging my math lesson. I could have yelled at Sadie or tried sending her to the office for continually jumping out of her seat to chase fairies. I could have tried blaming the boring math lesson on Jasmine's disorganization and inattention or Sadie's defiant behavior. I could have yelled at the children who were laughing. I could have tried clawing the tenacious fairy out of my hair. I could have tried to make the children play the math game that they hadn't paid attention to when I demonstrated it. When they failed at it, I could humiliate them for not having paid attention. Frankly, those options would have been pretty ugly. On the other hand, if the children didn't know any of these routines, the milkweed walk could have been total chaos and commotion, equally ugly.

structures and routines

Children need a predictable structure and a routine they can learn so they can become more independent learners. When a class has a predictable structure and can do routines with confidence, it can have more flexibility (to accommodate more spontaneous child-centered learning) and can do more elaborate projects and ambitious work as students transfer familiar skills to novel situations.

Then again, there's Murphy's Law—"Anything that can go wrong will go wrong"—which operates very efficiently in my classroom. As a teacher, I can have several nervous breakdowns a day, or I can take deep breaths, laugh, rethink things fast, change my plan, and keep the thread.

Routines need to be taught explicitly, step by step. I didn't know this secret when I first began teaching. I had little patience for this idea of explicitly teaching routines, wanting to dive headlong into everything. I thought up all kinds of hands-on discovery-oriented activities. I would plunge ahead into great adventures with my students scattering in my chaotic wake.

It was all very exciting, but as I reflected on each day, I could see that some activities worked in terms of student learning, and others didn't really work at all. I would feel puzzled and frustrated, thinking, "Why do they punch each other and cry when I say to get the crayons? Why do they fight about getting pencils? How come they get up in the middle of my math lesson to grind away at the pencil sharpener? Why are they fooling with each other's hair when we sit on the rug? Where did a quarter of my class go? Could they all be out at the bathroom at once? Why can we never find all our draft notebooks at the same time? Why do I have to pick up a dozen pencils off the floor every afternoon?"

My second year, my principal was kind enough to provide me with a copy of *The First Six Weeks of School* by Denton and Kriete, a Responsive Classroom book that fosters community as it teaches social and academic skills and routines. On my first attempt, with my usual impatience and enthusiasm, I tried to cram it all into the first week of school. There was some improvement. Each year, having seen the fruits of my investment, I would lengthen that by another week. I've now internalized the teaching habit of guided discovery and focus on it for the first six weeks, but that practice extends throughout the year. If I can teach the children exactly how I expect them to hold a new chick safely, I can relax more when they hold the chicks. My students become more nurturing and responsible. I still champ at the bit, wanting to jump right in, but I've learned the value of breaking things down, practicing step-by-step with explicit modeling and expectations. This kind of work increases academic time on-task in the long run by improving efficiency and civility. It is well worth it.

During my first year of teaching, I estimate I lost twenty to thirty minutes of instructional time each day dealing with postrecess conflicts, long tearful renditions of who did what to whom, fraught with passionate contradictions and denials. Even at that, I knew I wasn't dealing with the conflicts effectively, because they would be repeated the next day like a very bad soap opera. The following summer, I took a workshop in Second Step, a "violence prevention curriculum." On the one hand, it was "teacher friendly" to the point of being scripted, and that didn't thrill me. It felt so explicit, so overly obvious, to teach children to identify feelings. On the other hand, I was so sick of the conflicts and high drama that I decided to reserve my usual criticism and just do it.

I was surprised when some students really couldn't identify emotions such as *disgusted, scared,* and *angry* in photos of children. Before I began teaching Second Step lessons, I observed a couple of boys "joking" with some other children. They didn't notice when one of the other children became upset, and continued "joking" even when the other child began to cry. When I intervened, the jokers said, "We were just having fun." I asked if they thought Patrick, who was crying, was still having fun. They said yes.

I had a second grader who came to my class with a reputation for being mean, for making put-downs and causing other children to cry on a regular basis. His parents said they wanted him to learn empathy. In our first Second Step lesson of the year, we watched a video about a boy who gets lost on a hike with his family in the woods. I showed a large photo from the video of the lost boy looking very scared. When I asked this student how the boy might be feeling, he hesitated for a long time. Finally he shrugged his shoulders and guessed, "Disgusted?" Although this boy was very bright and was able to read books above grade level, he clearly had not yet learned to read emotions. I began to see the purpose of having lessons that explicitly teach children to read facial expressions, body language, and tone of voice to name the emotion being expressed, to recognize cause and effect, and to realize that two people can have very different feelings about the same situation. I was amazed when the angriest boy in my class said, with complete sincerity, that he couldn't think of a time he felt angry.

There is some overlap between the Second Step and Responsive Classroom; they complement each other. After teaching through the entire Second Step curriculum a couple of times, I got more creative with it, integrating it much more into language arts with poems, songs, picture books, and personal writing. The half hour I spend on that lesson each week is also time well invested. I've learned I can greatly reduce bul-

Figure 3.1 Peace Class schedule

8:00 A.M.	Arrive and prepare
8:50 A.M.	Greet arriving children and families. Children do morning and helper jobs.
9:00 A.M.	Sustained silent reading
9:15 A.M.	Morning meeting
9:45 A.M.	Handwriting or spelling/word study
10:00 A.M.	Snack
10:15 A.M.	Writing workshop
11:00 A.M.	Share writing from writing workshop
11:15 A.M.	Reading workshop
Noon	Lunch and recess
12:45 P.M.	Read-aloud
1:15 P.M.	Math
2:15 P.M.	Science or social studies
2:45 P.M.	Closing circle
2:55 P.M.	Cleanup
3:00 P.M.	Dismissal

lying if I can nurture empathy in those who lack it. The result is a safer, kinder classroom, where we all can spend more time on learning.

Obviously, my sense of teaching routines and my classroom management style are evolving. I know I'm not finished yet, because I could be a lot better at this than I am. That said, Figure 3.1 is a schedule for a typical day in the Peace Class.

8:00 A.M. When I arrive, I write the message and prepare my materials for the day. As I do this, I jot down lists of "helper jobs" on sticky notes or on the chalkboard that students or parents could help out with, so I can make these assignments quickly. The ability to delegate work is an important skill. It multiplies the amount of work my class can accomplish. I also check in with my student teacher about lesson plans, particular training objectives, or special assignments. For example, if I need to gather authentic language samples from our English language learners for an oral English language assessment while she is leading the morning meeting, I will talk with her about how to elicit as much spoken language as possible from those particular students.

8:50 A.M. I greet students, parents/guardians, and siblings. Students do their morning jobs: hang backpacks and jackets, put homework or signed

Figure 3.2 Helper jobs

Arranging and salvaging cut flowers, washing vases
Sharpening pencils
Feeding or watering chicks, insects, etc.
Writing thank-you notes for donations, guest visitors, etc.
Writing notes with suggestions or requests to the custodians, nurse,
    secretary, principal
Watering plants
Writing notes with questions, requests, or suggestions to local city
    officials, professors, businesspeople, scientists, or other experts
Straightening the classroom library
Putting notices or homework assignments in student mailboxes

Helper jobs for parents might include the following:
Listening to a struggling reader one to one
Teaching a child how to repair books
Photocopying
Hanging student work for display
Putting photos in the class album or making a poster display
Sending out book-order forms
Returning leveled texts to the literacy closet
Assembling and mailing packages of letters to pen pals

forms in the work basket, write names on lunch and milk tickets and put them in appropriate cups, take down chairs at their tables, and begin silent reading. The leader takes my daughter to her kindergarten class on the other side of the building, like a big brother or sister. Students make quick observations of classroom science experiments: crickets, caterpillars, chicks, and so on. They take a quick look at the message and mark the survey if there is one on the easel. Some early children or parents with a few extra minutes do "helper jobs." Figure 3.2 lists helper jobs.

I'm available for brief conversations with parents and guardians. This includes lots of logistical transactions about play dates, rides, appointments, home and family issues, illness, and so forth, or small things related to homework assignments or curriculum. Sometimes a parent offers to help out with something related to our work, or wants to schedule a time to volunteer. If a parent wants to discuss a more confidential or lengthy matter, we schedule a time to speak privately without the morning distractions and interruptions. Some parents allow time in their schedules to help out briefly during this transition time, which frees me up to be available for families.

Some parents also collaborate during this time. For example, one parent, Laurie, noticed that during the winter, the children were getting agitated first thing in the morning as they struggled to shove their backpacks, snow pants, jackets, hats, mittens, boots, and lunch boxes into our very tightly packed closets. Laurie's son accurately described this phenomenon as "an avalanche of overwhelmingness."

I myself had noticed this problem with some disgust, because inevitably much of their gear ended up on the floor, spilling out of the closets, which were too full to shut, so we couldn't even hide the mess. Every transition to snack, lunch, recess, physical education, or dismissal was a crisis waiting to happen. I had tried sending smaller numbers at a time to the closets, but it was still chaotic and distinctly uncivilized. I really hadn't dedicated much time and energy to resolving the problem.

Laurie and another mother, Cate, discussed the problem of what they called "The California Closets." They first proposed that we construct cubbies in the hallway outside, but our principal said that proposal had been turned down already because of the fire code. A few days later, they proposed a radical solution, to reconfigure our whole storage scheme. I agreed to try it, though I sincerely doubted it would work. It sounded like an invitation to more confusion, especially for my organizationally challenged students. We hashed out a few minor changes, and then I explicitly taught the children the new routine, step-by-step.

We set up "boot-changing" chairs in the hallway where children sat down to take off their boots and put on their sneakers. They lined their boots up in a neat row along the wall and came inside. They put their lunch boxes in a big tub near the door. They put hats, scarves, and mittens in their sleeves and hung jackets and snow pants on their hooks. Then, after delivering signed papers, homework, notes, and milk and lunch tickets to their appropriate places, they lined up their backpacks in a neat row under the chalkboard.

I modeled the entire routine. Then we had a guided practice. Within two days, we'd mastered it. Passing teachers would pop their heads in to say, "I just want to compliment you on your very neat lineup of boots out in the hallway." The children said thank you with pride. The "avalanche of overwhelmingness" was history. Present and caring parents solved the problem. Calm civility was restored.

9:00 A.M. Students engage in *silent reading* either at their tables or in the classroom library area, on rugs and pillows. We develop this routine over time. When the children enter the classroom on the first day, they find stacks of books, ranging from early easy readers to chapter books,

both fiction and nonfiction, on each table. I invite them to sit down, find a book, and read until the morning meeting begins. At first, it is pretty loose. Sitting or lying down are okay; walking or running around are not. Silent or soft-voice reading and even whispering to a friend as you read or look at pictures together are okay; talking and fooling around are not. At first, anything with words and/or pictures at any level will suffice for reading material. Even this is hard for some children who might need some help with the stillness, the silence, the being with books.

To help with this, I make notes in my initial home visits about what students are interested in. For example, a boy with autism was very interested in wolves; a girl who had just arrived from Ukraine loved princesses. I pull out books to match their interests and leave these in their workboxes for them to discover on the first day of school. After I read aloud a picture book, I put it on a display shelf. These are very popular for students to look at and read. When silent reading is over, I clear the books off the tables and put them on the windowsill or back on the display shelves.

Each day, I explicitly model some particular teaching point about silent reading. I show the children a stack of bookmarks (strips of used paper) that I've left under the reading lamp and show them how I mark my place in a book I haven't finished before putting it in my workbox. Another day I take groups of about four children at a time into the classroom library to show them how it is organized. I also show them where to find *National Geographic* magazines; children's nature magazines; favorite author collections by Dr. Seuss, Beatrix Potter, Eric Carle, Kevin Henkes, Patricia Polacco, and others; field guides; encyclopedias; nonfiction collections about Native American nations, inventions, ancient civilizations, biographies, baseball, and horses; boxes of chapter book series such as *Magic Tree House, Junie B. Jones, Little Bill, Encyclopedia Brown, Nate the Great, Cam Jansen,* and others; and spinner racks of easy readers at various levels. Many of these books are old and well worn, discarded by libraries, donated by families, and bought at tag sales and used-book sales. I get some new books with the bonus points I get through the book clubs. I explicitly teach the children how to return books where they found them, spine side showing and right side up.

During that first week I observe which children are actually reading and which ones are just looking. I home in on the lookers and introduce an easy, appealing text, which I ask them to read with me. If I have information on their reading level at the end of the previous year, I use that information to guide me. Some children will have suffered "summer setback" from a complete lack of reading, and others will have advanced. This gentle guidance and getting-to-know them as readers helps these children get on-task and provides me with useful information as I prepare to do my first round of Developmental Reading Assessments.

I begin to organize reading folders, starting with the struggling readers first. I make sure they have about five books at their independent reading level. I often have to remind them to pull out their reading folders. Once I feel confident that all students have ready access to books at an appropriate level (which typically ranges from kindergarten through third grade), I introduce a reading log. I try to keep this as simple and pain free as possible, listing title and pages read under the day and date. I do this so students become more focused on how they use their silent reading time. Parents and guardians are introduced to the reading logs at open house and can look at them whenever they want, to see what and how much their children are reading. I can look at the logs to get a sense of whether children are selecting and reading books at an appropriate level of challenge and prioritize my check-ins with those whose entries seem unrealistic.

As I get guided reading groups up and running (by about the fourth week of school), students may keep books from their groups for rereading. I circulate and praise on-task behavior, looking for the table that has everyone settled into reading first. For children who have a hard time reading independently, I ask them to read with a student teacher, parent volunteer, or me individually, or I may hook them up with a reading buddy. I monitor what children are reading. If it is too hard or too easy, I invite them to the library area with me to find books that might be a better match. I know students' special interests, so I often bring in or dig out books that connect with their favorite topics. I might show Wendy a British chapter book about fairies, give Lucy a book about sharks, give Neil a book about inventions, or show Tom and Joe a book about rockets. I might ask Astrid to finish the final draft of her letter to the supermarket manager about removing his store's shopping cart from the swamp, so that it can go out in the morning mail. I might check in with Drew to see what he thinks about the depiction of Native Americans in his *Tintin* book. I have a couple of students who are very slow producers, and on occasion I give them work to complete during silent reading, like finishing a pen-pal letter before we mail off the package or getting a news article in by the deadline, but I prefer to keep everyone reading.

9:15 A.M. We gather on the rug for *morning meeting.* (See Responsive Classroom's *Morning Meeting Book* by Roxann Kriete.) I take attendance as the children settle onto the rug. We often start with a greeting, which is most often "peace" or "hello" in another language. The morning message starts in a routine way:

"Good morning, friends. Today is Thursday, September 22, 2005. This is the thirteenth day of school. Miguel is our leader. Physical education is our special. Today is the autumnal equinox. Can you think of any words that start like *equinox*? What might be special about this day? We'll learn a new song today, called 'Turn, Turn, Turn.'"

The message is usually followed by our written schedule for the day. We do a choral reading of the message. We pause at the date, and the leader makes 22 cents with coins to put in the calendar pocket; the leader then calls on classmates who offer various ways of making 22 cents, hoping to guess his way. We make some of these combinations with Velcro-backed coins on a chart. We also pause for the number of the day to think about that number in terms of place value and consider various ways to make it, such as 10+3, 8+5, 5+5+3, and so on. We place a straw in a pocket for each day and bundle groups of ten straws as we accumulate them. The leader counts lunch tickets and takes the attendance sheet to the office.

We continue reading the message. This sample message has a focus on science, culture, and language, with the equinox. Otherwise, the message might have contained a mini-lesson in relation to punctuation, grammar, or phonics. The ending part of the message might have been about a current event from the radio news or a news clipping. It might also be an anniversary of some historic event or the birthday of a particular leader. I might bring in a photo or picture book related to that person or event to support the discussion. The Syracuse Cultural Workers Peace Calendar is a great source for this kind of date-related historical and cultural information. Instead of introducing a song or singing a familiar one, I could also introduce a short poem or quote.

We discuss recognizing words or parts of words in words, such as *autumn* inside *autumnal,* and brainstorming other words we know such as *equal, equator,* and *equation.* I would show them the Latin root *aequalis,* which means "equal." Please note that I don't know Latin; I got interested in it when my son began to study it. I look up words in the dictionary and find the roots. Children who speak Spanish (as well as French, Portuguese, and Italian) can have an advantage in this kind of wordplay, because many Romance-language words have Latin roots. For example, Jorge was able to quickly figure out that *solar* must mean "about the sun" because *sol* in Spanish means "sun," and *lunar* must mean "about the moon" because *luna* means "moon." It is useful for all students to learn to become language detectives and look for cognates, roots, and patterns, both to develop their cognitive academic language proficiency in English and to learn additional languages. This wordplay is another routine, a habit of mind.

We discuss what might be *equal* about this day, getting to the idea that this day, and the vernal equinox, have roughly equal portions of daylight and darkness. I introduce a chart with words for the new song, which we sing along with a Pete Seeger recording. I show them the illustrated picture book *Turn! Turn! Turn!* which I will read later. (The book includes the Pete Seeger recording on CD.)

If there is any time left (depending on how lengthy the discussion was), I play a quick math game with the group. Since we'd been discussing the length of days, I take out twenty-four cubes. (I could also use twenty-two for the date or thirteen for the number of days we've been in school, depending on which number is most elegant for my mathematical purposes.) If I want to focus on fractions, I use twenty-four cubes. I show my fraction blocks for halves and ask a student to divide my set of twenty-four cubes into two equal halves, which I relate back to the equinox. I repeat this process with my quarters and thirds fraction blocks, having the student line up the divided set of cubes with the corresponding fraction blocks, saying, for example, "Six is a quarter of twenty-four," or, "You could divide twenty-four cookies into four equal piles of six each."

Another quick math game I often include at morning meeting is "cube stick." I take a stick of snap cubes, maybe thirteen, hold it behind my back with mysterious fanfare, break off three to show in front, and continue to hide the ten behind my back, asking the children to figure out how many are hidden. In all math games, the point is not just to give an answer, but, more important, to explain your thinking. If your answer is wrong, you will likely self-correct during the course of explaining your strategy. I like to ham it up while playing this game as I try to "trick" the children with one too hard for them to solve. The routine, fun, low-stakes nature of these quick morning meeting math activities helps reduce math and/or performance anxiety. It also lets me informally assess students' developing math skills. During silent reading time, before the meeting, I often pull students with intense math anxiety or weak math skills to preview the activity individually so they can be successful in the group setting. This way, anxious children don't have to waste time worrying about whether they'll be called on, whether

they'll know the answer, and when they should plan to escape to the bathroom.

The children learn to refrain from shouting out, making disparaging remarks such as, "That is so *easy!*" or laughing when someone makes a mistake (lest they temporarily be banished to "sit and watch" off the rug). More than just points of polite behavior, they learn that shouting out an answer is what we call "stepping on someone else's words." It may be especially difficult for English language learners to organize their thoughts about their mathematical strategies into English words. When someone shouts out in the middle of their trying to say it, effectively "stepping on their words," it can mess up the whole idea they had carefully put together, so it is especially rude and hurtful.

Students learn quickly that what may be easy for them may be hard for someone else, and vice versa. I may feel ashamed if you mutter, "That's so easy" when it is challenging for me, and that might make me give up trying to figure it out and just wait for you to give the answer.

The worst offense is laughing at someone's mistake. We all have to feel safe enough in our classroom to make mistakes without fear or shame, or else we'd never take risks, and we all know that you have to take a lot of risks to learn. I point out my own errors, so that perfectionist children can loosen up. The children and I make encouraging "coaching" remarks such as, "Good try. Keep working it through."

I like these games because they are open ended and many students can offer solutions. I refrain from saying, "Correct," but always try to respond with, "And how did you figure that out?" or "Please explain the strategy you used." These games allow for lots of participation and afford English language learners a lot of supported "airtime" during which they can use the calendar, number chart, blocks, snap cubes, coins, the number line, or other manipulatives to explain their thinking.

Other morning meeting math activities include interpreting class survey results, skip counting, and using a Judy clock to review our schedule for the day, with students setting the hands to match the times listed. I also do math fact games such as "Ways to make ten," in which I give a student a number such as six, and she has to figure out what to put with it to make ten. I usually focus on just one family of math facts in a given meeting, like doubles (3+3), or doubles plus one (4+5).

9:45 A.M. This is the time to make the transition to table seats for some quick *word work*. During silent reading time, I ask a student helper to leave a stack of whiteboards, dry-erase markers, and erasers on each table so students can take their materials as they sit down. Each week we focus on five new "no excuses" spelling words from the high-frequency word list. Although some words are not too hard to spell, usage can be very tricky (such as *to, too,* and *two*). We explore the role of accents in causing confusion for us, like knowing when to use *our* and *are,* because many of us pronounce these words the same, as in, "Are you coming to our house?" Sometimes we practice Kenyan, Australian, and British pronunciations of words such as *been, again,* and *said* because those pronunciations make the spelling patterns more obvious. We remind ourselves in this way that everyone speaks with an accent, which must be respected and can be understood with some listening practice and appreciation.

I also give five "challenge words" related to our content area each week. For example, this week our challenge words might be *autumn, equinox, daylight, darkness,* and *season.* They might also be related to math, like *shapes* and *attributes,* comparing words, words for writing story problems, words for explaining strategies (*tried, counted, left over, pennies, flew*), or related to science or social studies content.

I try to keep this word study period short, low risk, and fast paced, with lots of participation. By glancing at their whiteboards, I can guarantee success for students who struggle with spelling, calling on them when I know they have the correct answer. We draw on our developing language detective skills to look for patterns, cognates, roots, prefixes and suffixes, synonyms, antonyms, homographs, homophones, and rhymes. Early in the year, several of these periods are devoted to handwriting each week. Roughly every other Monday, I teach a specific phonics lesson and then revisit it briefly on the remaining days of the week.

10:00 A.M. *Snacktime.* Sometimes students share their work on a high-interest "family homework" assignment, such as the stories of their names, ancestor stories, maps of their bedrooms, moon journal entries, and so on. If we are not sharing, I sometimes squeeze in a short read-aloud during snacktime. On this day, it might be the picture book *Turn! Turn! Turn!* The pictures and discussion provide further support for students learning new vocabulary.

10:15 A.M. I begin *writing workshop* by gathering my writers on the rug for a short (ten-minute) mini-lesson. I think aloud, draw, and write as I explicitly model a particular teaching point, such as making a picture plan. In response to yesterday's discussion about bike safety after the accidental death of a bicyclist in our city, I tell the students I decided to

write about what my family did about bike safety when we decided we would all commute by bicycle. As I write my name and date, I point out that the end of the paper with the big space is the top, because I've noticed many children using the lined paper upside down. I draw a line halfway across my chart paper, above which I will draw. I am also explicit about this, because I've noticed that some children use nearly the entire page for a picture, then seem puzzled about having so little room to write their words.

I make a quick sketch showing my stick-figure family and me in a bike store (which I label). On the wall I draw helmets, reflective vests, flashers, and headlights. I am explicit with the children about why I include certain details in my drawings, like the helmets, vests, and flashers, which I plan to write about, and why I don't bother with other details, like our hair and clothing, because I won't be writing about that. For my perfectionists, I emphasize that this is a sketch to plan my story, not fine art for display, so I don't have to worry about drawing the bicycle (which is hard even for an adult to draw) with perfect accuracy. I write only the first sentence of my story, but point out that the rest of it will come from the details in the picture. I ask the children to close their eyes to picture a story they could write about, then describe it to a neighbor.

Each table has named their writing group after scouring bird field guides, much discussion, and eventual consensus. Each writing group has a table monitor who wipes the table after snack, then brings the group's writing folder box to the table after the mini-lesson. He or she distributes the folders around the table, and the children move to their seats to begin writing. They have three choices: to continue work on a story, to revisit a story to add details to the words or pictures, or to start a new story.

Early in the year, our focus is on writing stories about our own experiences. I'm not generally one to quash imagination, but I just can't stomach tons of alien battles with laser guns and princesses getting scorched by dragons anymore. I find the quality of writing vastly improves when I limit our topics to the realm of reality. A focus on story also keeps us out of the "I like skateboards. Skateboards are cool" formula rut. I can confer with the child, look at the picture, and say, "Tell me what is happening in your picture. Who are you skateboarding with? What is happening over here? What happened after that? Great— please write that part down."

For the most part, I expect students to stretch out the words and write the letters for the sounds they hear. They can refer to a "spell-check" card at their table or the word wall for standard spelling of high-frequency words. I circulate and confer with children.

I used to pressure myself to publish all of their stories. This required recruiting parent volunteers to help me with word processing on the computer. I often had a backlog of students "waiting" for conferences or "waiting" for stories to be published so they could illustrate them. This was especially true when children were writing in draft notebooks. Once they started a new piece, they never went back to an old one, because there was no more room there. Since I switched over to writing on lined, dated paper kept in a writing folder that serves as a portfolio, I have let go of that pressure to publish every story. I am happier, and the children spend a lot more time actually writing independently, with much richer detail. Because they are on-task, there are fewer behavioral problems. Every six weeks or so, children can select their best pieces of writing from their portfolios for publication.

11:00 A.M. We conclude writing workshop with ten or fifteen minutes of *sharing*. We gather on the rug again with our writing folders in front of us. The incentive to share with the group motivates a lot of writing. Students share their work, which might be a finished piece or a work in progress. I keep track of who shares what story, to make sure we hear from each writer at least twice a week. I say thank you to each author after he or she reads. Occasionally I allow a brief question, but I do not encourage discussion of each piece during sharing. For example, Brian wrote a story about working on the baling machine at his uncle's ranch in Colorado over the summer. Many children asked, "What's a baler?" When he said, "It's to make bales," many asked, "What's a bale?" I said, "Thank you, Brian. It sounds like many of your readers are interested in more details about hay and baling because most of us have never been to a ranch. Can you write more about that?" At the end of sharing, children return their writing folders to their writing group boxes, which table monitors put away.

By the end of the year, writing workshop sometimes feels hectic to me, like a three-ring circus, but sometimes I look up and realize (to my surprise) that everyone is on-task, engaged in some literacy activity. Sometimes an observer whispers, "What are they doing?" My gut response is to say, "I have no idea; it's their work," but then I think that would make me sound totally clueless or careless. I explain that they are doing about twenty different things. I am not together enough to have a clipboard with a list that says what everyone is working on every minute, but I have a good sense of it.

That girl is writing a news article about the bear that came into her yard yesterday. That boy is writing a letter to the mayor about sewage. Those two guys are the last two to finish up letters to their Swiss pen pals, which will be mailed this afternoon, come hell or high water. That girl is writing a nonfiction piece about how to build fairy houses. That boy is writing haiku. That girl is writing a letter to a haiku poet. That boy is illustrating his story about a camping trip. That kid is writing a piece for the newsletter about how to make a root-beer dispenser.

11:15 A.M. Children take out their reading folders and logs; they settle in at their tables to begin *reading workshop*. I begin to call them to come to the library area or meeting area for guided reading groups. My below-grade-level groups meet daily; my goal is to get all students reading at or above grade level as quickly as possible. Those at and above grade level meet about four and two times each week respectively. My student teacher leads one of the above-grade-level groups. During this period, if I am not doing a guided reading group, I can do running records or more formal Developmental Reading Assessments, which I also train my student teachers to do.

I always feel stretched during reading workshop as I try to lead reading groups and do assessments. What are the children doing? Those two are researching rockets and trying to design a probe to explore Mars. That girl is reading her third nonfiction book about sharks. That girl borrowed Joe's *Eyewitness* book about mummies because she has decided she wants to be an Egyptologist like him. The five laughing children in the library are reading *The Cat Who Wore a Pot on Her Head* with the student teacher. That kid is reading a *Hardy Boys* book, and the kid next to him is reading a *Berenstain Bears* book. Everyone is busy with his or her work. It all has something to do with literacy.

In the past, sometimes we got so busy that we forgot to go to lunch, and a student would look up and say, "Aaaah! We are ten minutes late for lunch!" We'd hustle out of the room, but we were smiling because we were all so engaged in our good work. Now I set a timer to ring to remind us when to stop.

2004 was the first year we worked on producing a newspaper, beginning in late October. About twice a month we made our literacy block into the Peace Class Newsroom. Then we'd devote two full hours to brainstorming articles and features, making assignments, researching, interviewing, and writing. A parent and professional journalist, Jo Glading-DiLorenzo, came in to help us with this and recruited a grandmother and several other parents to help.

We also participated in a Newspapers in Education project with our local newspaper, the *Daily Hampshire Gazette*. We received copies of the paper each Wednesday, with a Kid Scoop page geared to elementary students. We found that many parents objected to the idea of their kids reading the entire newspaper, which on any given day might contain disturbing stories (and images) about kidnappings, rapes, natural disasters, murders, bombings, terrorism, and so on. I began to preview the paper, and when I found articles useful for discussion, I had a student tear them out and put them in a pile for whole-class reading and discussion. We'd also pull out all the Kid Scoop pages and put those in a pile, for a choice during reading workshop on Thursdays. The Kid Scoop page included a weekly call for submissions on certain topics. On about a monthly basis, we'd write on that topic and send our submissions to the newspaper. In the course of the year, about half of our students got published on the Kid Scoop page.

Noon *Lunch,* followed by recess. I use this time to eat lunch, reflect, and plan with my student teacher. I can also connect and collaborate with other colleagues, because we have overlapping lunch periods. I can spend the first thirty minutes of my lunch period with first-grade teachers, or the last thirty minutes with third-grade teachers, or the whole period with second-grade teachers. We also prepare for our afternoon lessons.

12:45 P.M. Children return from recess. We calm and cool down on the rug with a *read-aloud* of either a picture or chapter book by lamplight, with the overhead fluorescent lights off. The story may be connected to a content-area topic, or the focus may be on using comprehension strategies, or we may engage in a philosophical discussion. In that case it may run an extra fifteen minutes or so, and I'll record the discussion on a chart.

For six to eight weeks each spring, a group of philosophy students come weekly from Mount Holyoke College with their professor, Dr. Tom Wartenberg (parent of a former student) for a philosophical read-aloud and discussion with my class. During those weeks, we juggle our Wednesday schedule to allow a full hour for philosophy, in place of our regular read-aloud. Again, we're explicit about how to have a philosophical discussion; it quickly becomes both a routine and a habit of mind.

Tom and I began collaborating on this project, with Dr. Gareth B. Matthews from the University of Massachusetts, and Susan Fink, a fifth-grade teacher, in 1999. At first, we used question sets developed by

Gareth, published by Wise Owl (now out of print). For example, we read the story "Dragons and Giants" from *Frog and Toad Together* by Arnold Lobel and discussed the nature of bravery. We read *The Bear That Wasn't* by Frank Tashlin and discussed who determines identity. Tom and I collaborated to develop more question sets, such as a discussion about aesthetics and the power of art after a reading of *Matthew's Dream* by Leo Lionni or about the nature of prejudice in relation to *The Sneetches* by Dr. Seuss.

After a few years, Tom developed a community service-learning course about teaching philosophy with children for philosophy students at Mount Holyoke College. They spend the first month or so engaging in philosophical discussion of children's literature and developing question sets on campus. These "philosophy buddies" spend the rest of the semester working in our classrooms to engage the children in philosophical discussions with our coaching and guidance. My students enjoy and benefit from the stimulation of this "philosophers' club," and the teaching profession benefits as some of these philosophy students decide to go into education. (For sample question sets, a DVD, and more on teaching philosophy with children, go to www.mtholyoke.edu/omc/kidsphil/.)

1:15 P.M. *Math* frequently begins with a routine activity, "Ways to Make" the number of the day. I often provide particular constraints, such as "using only silver coins," "using multiple addition of just one number," or "adding exactly four numbers." I include challenges, such as finding out what the halves of that number are (or thirds or quarters), how to make the number by using multiplication, and so on. I make accommodations for students who need to work with smaller numbers and manipulatives. I circulate and jot down names of students who have particularly interesting equations to share with the group. Then I usually demonstrate a math game, which they play in groups, or we might work on story problems, sharing strategies and explaining solutions with the whole group. Occasionally we go to the computer lab to work on math.

2:15 P.M. Of course, a great deal of our *science or social studies* content is integrated into the morning meeting, and songs, poems, read-alouds, writing assignments, captioned drawings, and so on that happen during other parts of the day. In social studies, this is when we might do simulations, engage in debates, make posters, do research, and have discussions.

In this period we might do more organized science experiments or observations and discussions. Children use skills, like measuring and charting the growth of an amaryllis or the weight of a chick. They observe caterpillars, crickets, tadpoles, milkweed bugs, and other critters in their habitats, noting changes in their structures and behavior, asking questions and making predictions.

During this time I might also introduce a new artistic technique, such as the use of pastels or collage, in relation to illustrating an insect poem or their essays about Taíno life before European contact. I'm not talented artistically, so I usually consult with the art teacher for ideas or to borrow prints or materials. I often try to schedule parent volunteers for this time of day, as the projects and experiments often get lively and messy, requiring more preparation, cleanup, or extra help. If I have a crafty parent volunteer (oh, to have a Brownie leader!), we might come up with a project related to our content area, like making recycled paper with pressed flowers in it, and work on it at this time of day.

One day each week during this period I teach a Second Step social curriculum lesson. These include relaxation techniques, problem-solving strategies, exploring emotions, reading facial expressions, and body language. These lessons usually involve using the new skill in various role-playing situations. I often do literacy extensions from these lessons, such as read-alouds or making a class book about a certain feeling, such as, "I felt sad when . . ."

Another day each week I bring my class to read with our kindergarten reading buddies. Each week students select a book to read aloud with their buddies and practice reading them during silent reading time. I encourage them to connect with their buddies' interests, as well as to introduce them to new genres. We often connect with our buddies for special celebrations, like the hundredth day of school or Dr. Seuss's birthday.

2:45 P.M. *Closing circle.* We try to have a closing circle at least a few days each week, although it is often rather rushed and raggedy. The closing circle is the afternoon counterpart to the morning meeting, a transition to end the day. Sometimes we go around the circle, giving each child a chance to say his or her favorite part of the day, or share a bit of news. This is also a good time to introduce or practice a new song or poem. Sometimes we do a community-building activity we had planned for the morning meeting if we ran out of time earlier.

2:55 P.M. *Cleanup.* We clean up our messes and materials, put up chairs, and get our mail, jackets, lunch boxes, and backpacks.

3:00 P.M. *Dismissal.* I walk the students out, which gives me the chance to talk and network with current and past student families.

. . .

We also have weekly specials in art, music, and physical education. My class participates in the Language Sharing Network, which includes a Friday morning meeting and weekly lesson in Spanish. I then reinforce the content of the Spanish lesson (through songs, games, quick activities, meeting messages, and so on) throughout the week. I usually do some art or cooking project about every two or three weeks, more often during the cold, wet winter weather. We have an average of three visitors or field trips per month. In the fall and spring, when the weather is good, we go on a lot more field trips, by foot and public bus. We also go out in the schoolyard more often, to observe in the butterfly garden, exercise our chicks, plant bulbs, look for simple machines, and so forth. In winter, we have more visitors come to see us.

Some field trips are routine. For example, we go to visit a nearby marsh five times each year to observe seasonal changes: early September (summer, for insects and seeds), mid-October (autumn, for changing leaves and migrating birds), late January (winter, for tracks and animal signs), early April (early spring, for migrating birds), and late May (mid-spring, for wildflowers and insects). The children learn the routines for how to go on a field trip by foot, how to take turns looking at things, how to collect litter with rubber-gloved hands, how to copy down the name of the store that owns a shopping cart left in the woods, and how to write a letter to the manager to remove that cart or the mayor about removing a car tire or other large litter. For other trips, they learn routines like how to bring six quarters, ride a public bus, return a signed permission slip, listen, ask questions politely, and so on.

So, that's roughly what a day in the Peace Class looks like—swirling, rather hectic and busy. Often the children look up in surprise at the end of the day and ask, "It's time to go *home?*"

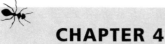

CHAPTER 4

It takes a village to teach first grade

Dear Mayor Higgins,
    My class was on a field trip one day in October going from Jackson St. School to the Barrett St. Marsh on the Bike path, and we saw shoping carts rolled down the bank into the stream It was beetween Adare Place and stop and shop on marsh side, So could you please send some of the towns poeple down to get those shopping carts Out beforthe steam gets clogged and polluted?
    from Tom Forziati-Pliska

    Peace class
    Jackson St, School

When you dream of something, you can begin to take it upon yourself, make it yours, change it. But you have to dream it first.

—Henry Hampton, filmmaker

It was the first week of my first year teaching. It seemed a safe and good idea to start with the theme of pets. I was reading stories about pets, and the children were writing stories about pets. Families were bringing in their pets to share. I nervously thought I looked like a teacher, sitting on the rug with my circle of first graders, reading Ezra Jack Keats's Pet Show or stroking someone's bunny.

One day Carmen announced she was going to be an animal doctor when she grew up. I beamed, silently congratulating myself for holding such high expectations, pleased that this little girl, whose parents had not graduated from high school, was planning to become a doctor. Joaquin challenged her. "How you gonna get to be a animal doctor, Carmen?"

She shot him a withering look, shook her long black hair, and explained, "It's easy. First I'm gonna get a lot of animals. After a while, my animals are gonna get sick. Then I bring them to the animal doctor and listen real good to what he says about how to fix them. Then I'll know!"

Joaquin looked at me and asked me if it really worked like that. I said, "Well, Carmen could have a lot of animals, but she would need a good job to pay for all of their food and their doctor bills . . ."

"You have to pay the animal doctor?" she interrupted, incredulous.

I nodded. "That's how you'll pay your rent and buy your food when you're an animal doctor, because people will pay you." I continued, "Now, Carmen could also read a lot of library books about her pets, and observe them and listen to the animal doctor, but all that wouldn't make her an animal doctor. To be an animal doctor, a veterinarian, you have to go to a school of veterinary medicine, after you graduate from college . . ."

Papo had been leaning forward, listening to this explanation, when suddenly he slapped himself in the forehead, yelled, "College?! I don't know anyone who went to college!" and executed a perfect and dramatic backward somersault off the rug. Many of my students quickly joined his laughter, nodding in agreement about how ridiculous this seemed, graduating from college.

I was temporarily silenced by this reality check. "You know me, and I went to college," I offered weakly after a moment. I graduated from college twenty years after I started, but I still graduated.

Papo looked at me and said, not unkindly, "Yeah, but you're a teacher." Right then I realized that this job was bigger than me.

I talked to my bilingual teaching partner, then called my former Spanish professor at the nearby college and proposed a pen-pal and "reading buddy" partnership between her students and mine. Soon we had college students visiting weekly. By December, every student in my class had a friend in college.

I learned then that good teaching takes more than a teacher with a curriculum teaching her students in a classroom with the door shut. Not only can it be so much more, but to be effective, it must be so much more. That's when I learned that it takes a village to teach first grade.

I considered myself well educated, with a college degree in liberal arts. I felt like I had taken introductory-level courses in nearly everything, from sociology, economics, and ancient Greece to philosophy, art history, and calculus, not to mention higher-level courses here and there. I thought I surely knew everything I was responsible for teaching in first grade. I thought whatever I lacked in content knowledge I could make up for with enthusiasm. Before I started, I couldn't think of a six-year-old child's question I wouldn't be able to answer. I thought the school would give me whatever I needed to teach my curriculum. To top it all off, I thought I'd be a pretty good role model for my students.

Then I started teaching. Suddenly I realized I didn't know or understand that much about magnetism, world religions, navigation, urban planning, or embryology. No teacher has encyclopedic knowledge of the world. Children are naturally inclined to wonder, so the range of their questions is incredibly broad. I staggered through my first year as a first-grade teacher and looked forward to doing a better job of it the second time through. Then I learned I'd be teaching second grade: a new grade and a new curriculum.

Curriculum isn't static either. Districts and states continue to develop and refine theirs, as do the National Science Foundation, the National Council of Teachers of Mathematics, and other national organizations that influence curriculum development. As the drive for standardized testing increases, topics assigned to one grade one year may be assigned to another grade the following year.

I am enthusiastic, even passionate, about some subjects and may not be enthusiastic about, or might even dislike, other subjects that I am required to teach. That bias is often reflected in the classroom. Some teachers resolve this by doing more of "what I like," which means that one class may do a lot of plays and poetry while another does a lot of scientific experimentation.

New teachers often start with nothing. When I started teaching, my principal brought me to my new classroom. "What is this stuff?" I asked, surveying a room that looked to be full of torture equipment. The

principal explained that this was physical and occupational therapy equipment and assured me the custodian would move it to a new location before the first day of school. "How about tables or chairs or . . . books?" I asked cautiously, not wanting to appear pushy. I learned that I could ask the custodian to take me to the attic to find furniture, and that chalk, crayons, and tape were available in the office. There were no textbooks. I asked if there was a curriculum and was told, "Reading, writing, math . . . you know, first grade." It was rather sparse that first year. Generally speaking, veteran teachers accumulate resources over time and new teachers start with very little. Nationwide, we have a huge discrepancy in resources, from classroom facilities and technology to books and other materials.

Still, when I visit schools in other countries, I am struck by the number of resources we take for granted. I visited a rural senior primary school (grades 4–7) in Kwa-Zulu Natal, South Africa, similar in size to my school. There was no electrical power, no running water, and no phone line. There were no computers or copy machines. There were some old textbooks and a small cabinet of science materials. There was no library. There was one latrine. In one area, I saw a pile of brush and a pile of logs. When I asked the principal what they were for, he explained that they were used for nutrition classes, so teachers could teach the children to cook. Being resourceful is part of every teacher's job description.

content resources beyond the classroom

Like the majority of elementary school teachers in the United States, I am European American, native English speaking, and middle class. A growing number of my students, like students across the country, are children of color, English language learners, immigrants, or children of immigrants, from a variety of class backgrounds, including many who are low income. As I taught, I tried to figure out the answer to these questions: How can I learn all the other content-specific knowledge I need while teaching full time and taking additional graduate courses in theories and methods of second-language acquisition? How can I even anticipate what I'll need to know? How can I get the materials and give my students the experiences that will make learning this content relevant and inspiring?

I had to remind myself that I am a capable lifelong learner. I realized I needed to start collaborating with other teachers, at least as much as I expected my students to collaborate with each other. I needed to embrace the idea of being a learner in my own classroom, surrounded by other teachers (the students, their families, colleagues, community members) who share responsibility for teaching and learning.

Just as I am passionate about certain topics and own a degree of expertise and experience, the same is true for people in my periphery (family, friends, professors, fellow alumnae, clergy, activists), others in the classroom community (students' immediate and extended families, and their family friends), and others in the school community (principal, teachers, custodians, cooks, aides, parents, bus drivers, and their families).

I began to take an activist approach to curriculum, always looking for opportunities to make connections, to broaden and deepen, to increase authenticity, build a bridge, and bring it to life with a visitor, a field trip, or correspondence.

I realized that between my students, their families, the school community, and me, we have access to a wealth of resources. I always get more in the long run from asking around for the resource I need than if I had it in the first place. An old organizing adage is that you can organize more off the broken car sitting in front of the office than if you had a working one. We did secretly and constantly wish we had a nice new car, but in the meantime, as we tried to find a volunteer to fix it, we'd find someone who could lend her car, or would volunteer to drive his car, or would donate some gas money, or whose brother worked in a junkyard and could get us used parts, before we finally found the person who could fix the broken car. It is always challenging to work like this, but I always gain more than I expected and more that I can draw on in the future.

Every time I admitted I couldn't answer a question, a new learning opportunity arose. I saw that when I modeled critical thinking and intellectually curious behavior, children imitated these habits of mind.

As much as I might strive to be a role model, I can't be everything to everyone. Children need adult role models with whom they can identify aspects of themselves in both linear and nonlinear ways. For example, when Aneesah, a Muslim high school student, visited our class to teach us about Ramadan and Islam, Michelle raised her hand to say she had a connection with her. Michelle's connection was that just as Aneesah learned Arabic at the mosque to better practice and understand her religion, she was learning Hebrew at her synagogue.

"you can't step on someone else's words"

When I began teaching, all of my students knew some immigrants, just by virtue of knowing their classmates and their classmates' families. About half of my first graders were bilingual Spanish speakers, learning English as a second language. During class discussions, I was often frustrated by some of my impulsive English-speaking students' habit of calling out answers after I had called on an English language learner. I knew, from having participated in community meetings in Spanish (my second language) that it took a lot of concentration for me to follow the gist of the discussion and a lot of courage for me to think I might be able to add something to it. I then organized my thoughts into my "baby talk" Spanish and raised my hand. It was hard for me to continue to follow the discussion while I continued rehearsing my Spanish sentence in my head as I waited to be called on. If I were not called on soon, the window of opportunity for my comment to be relevant would shut. If I were interrupted once I started to speak, I would lose my carefully rehearsed sentence and sit there with an open mouth.

My first graders soon developed our first class rule, "You can't step on someone else's words." Although the native English-speaking children saw their classmates learning a second language (English), they seemed not to appreciate the difficulty of the task, because it was so easy for them, after all. I decided that, just as it was valuable for my Puerto Rican students to know someone who went to college, it was important for my native English-speaking students to know an adult learning English. In retrospect, I realize I wasn't thinking about how this fit into the curriculum frameworks, but I had the sense that it was an important part of oral language development.

I knew one of the parents in my class was taking English classes through the Center for New Americans. The classes were offered at the apartment complex across the street. I called and spoke to their English as a Second Language (ESL) teacher about the idea of a partnership between her adult English learners and my first graders. She was willing to give it a try. The next week, her class came to visit mine.

I wasn't really sure how this would turn out. I vaguely thought we would become pen pals. Her students were from all over the globe—Egypt, Bosnia, Korea, Brazil, China, El Salvador, Poland, Russia—and they were all brand new to English. Their class focused entirely on spoken English; they weren't writing at all. During their first visit, my class gave them a tour of our school. Each student had an adult partner from

black ants and buddhists

the English class. One of my students, Paulo, was a selective mute. He had been in our school for two years of preschool and kindergarten and still did not speak to adults. His partner was a tall young man from Brazil. As we walked down the hall, I was surprised to hear Paulo explaining to his buddy, in English and then in Spanish, about the library. It was the first time I heard him speak to an adult at school.

Later we all ate a snack together in our classroom. The English teacher nodded at a Bosnian couple in their late fifties. She said they'd been her students for months, but that this was the first time she'd ever seen them smile. That struck me. She told me Yusef was an engineer and Fatima was a banker, but their complete lack of English had kept them from finding any work here. I offered that they would be welcome to come and volunteer in my classroom if being around the children made them happy. She asked what they would do in the classroom, and I said I would think of something.

They started coming in on Wednesday afternoons the following week. The children saved all the broken things in the room for Yusef. We showed him our tools, and he showed the children how to fix things. When things were fixed, he played math games with the children. They pointed to the cards, used their fingers, and wrote numbers to show him their answers, and he learned the names of numbers in English.

Carmen was a middle child in a large family. No one at home ever really listened to her read or gave her much positive, individual attention. I asked Fatima to let Carmen read to her. Fatima could not read these little books in English, but I taught her to say, "Good! Very good! Beautiful!" On Wednesday afternoons, Carmen would sit beside Fatima, or on her lap, and read to her. Fatima would look at the pictures, listen intently, and say, "Good! Very good! Beautiful!" story after story after story.

One day we were working on a unit about our families, and the children were showing family photos. Fatima joined the group on the rug, holding her purse, as she always did. I always thought that was a little odd, because she probably had no money beyond her bus fare. Did she think that six-year-olds would bother her purse? She listened to the students tell about their families, and then raised her hand. I called on her. Slowly she opened the purse and took out an old envelope, stuffed with photos. The first graders looked at her curiously. She showed a photo of herself with a bunch of other middle-aged women and a much older woman: her sisters and mother. There was a fairly recent picture of her in an office, dressed in a business suit. Next was a photo of her in a park in the 1960s, standing in pregnant profile. I thought of her husband, Yusef, as a proud father, taking the photo, and thought how her child must be about the age of my younger sister. A student asked where her child was. Copenhagen, she said. She showed them on the globe. Another picture of a young man with two young children: the son and grandchildren. There were tears in her eyes.

As refugees, she and her husband got to come to the United States. Her son's family got to go to Denmark. She took a deep breath, looked down, and stroked Carmen's hair. My students took turns looking at her pictures, and then scrambled to look on the globe for Bosnia-Herzegovina, Denmark, and Massachusetts. Gretel asked if Fatima got to see them, pointing to Fatima, her eye, and the children in the photo. Fatima shook her head. There was a picture of her family in front of a house. Someone asked if that was where she had lived. She said, "Fire" bitterly and made a heavy, crushing gesture with her hands.

I was thinking what it must be like to have a life, a family, a good job, and a nice home and to suddenly get the word that you must go, because you are Muslim. Leave it all behind and get the hell out. Drop everything and run for your life. She had taken this handful of photos to remember she had a life there, before.

My students studied the pictures, as though to make sense of the story, the photos, Fatima's few words. Fatima looked down at the worn, empty envelope in her hands. "How come Fatima's so sad?" Carmen asked me.

"How come they put fire on her house?" Papo wanted to know.

Alfredo shook his head sadly and said, almost to himself, "That's no nice."

I had to agree with Alfredo. "It's not nice anymore in Fatima's country. It used to be called Yugoslavia, and for a long time people got along together there. About five years ago, the country started to break up. That's called a civil war, when people in the country fight each other. Fatima and Yusef are Muslim. A Serbian group made the Muslims get out. It was unfair and dangerous, with fire and shooting. Fatima and Yusef came to our country to be safe from the war in their country. A refuge is a safe place. They are refugees." I wondered how first graders could possibly make sense of that.

Carmen nodded solemnly, and then patted Fatima gently, saying, "Well, you're safe now. You're with us."

Letting Connections Emerge

When I first started teaching, things were often this rough around the edges. The curriculum framework connection wasn't always crystal clear in my mind. It is often a more instinctual feeling—that "some good could come of this"—than a sophisticated rationale. I often make the road by walking, finding books that could deepen the children's understanding of the life lessons we're learning, literature with which they can make strong text-to-self and text-to-world connections. I read these books aloud at story time, and then we discuss them, often using explicit comprehension strategies.

I read *I Hate English!,* a picture book by Ellen Levine about a Chinese girl who loves speaking, listening to, reading, and writing Chinese with her family and in her neighborhood, but hates having to learn English, until she finally sees the need for it. For homework, I asked family members to tell the children their own stories about learning a second language.

I read *Angel Child, Dragon Child,* a picture book by Michele Maria Surat about a Vietnamese girl who gets into a fight with a boy who taunts her. The girl struggles with her own temper, anger about being teased, and sadness that her mother has not yet been able to come join the family. This story of conflict resolution and cooperation inspired a discussion about how we don't know someone's story until we get to know them.

We read some picture books about adult education like *Jeremiah Learns to Read* by Jo Ellen Bogart, in which an old farmer who knows how to "make a table out of a tree or sweet syrup from its sap" decides he wants to learn to read. In *Read for Me, Mama* by Vashanti Rahaman, a boy who loves reading is amazed when his mother asks for help learning to read.

We invited our bilingual teacher to tell us about her previous work as an adult educator. We discussed the kinds of classes grown-ups in our families were taking, and why grown-ups would still go to school. The adult ESL class came to our performances and celebrations. We never had a pen-pal relationship, but I wrote letters on chart paper from my class, and their teacher wrote back the same way.

• • •

I believe teaching is more effective when the teacher is passionate about the topic. Although no one is passionate about everything in his or her curriculum, most everyone is passionate about some things. My school taps into this. Our staff notes and school newsletter celebrate the varied talents, interests, and accomplishments of parents, teachers, and other staff members. A prominent bulletin board in the school lobby features clippings about students, families, and staff in the news. Potluck events encourage families and faculty to get to know one another. Our physical education teacher has a "Jackson in Action" display of "fitness leaders." It features photos and brief write-ups by students and staff describing their favorite fitness activities. The P.E. teacher invited a parent who works as an aide in the preschool to speak to fifth-grade physical education classes about her training to run the New York City Marathon.

Teachers and other staff members often visit other classrooms to share their passions and expertise. I was talking with a fifth-grade teacher, Susan Fink; she said her students had just finished reading *My Side of the Mountain* by Jean Craighead George. I said that was my favorite book when I was a kid. Susan said her students were skeptical because nothing really disastrous happens to the boy. I laughed and said that when I lived alone in the woods as a teenager, a lot of disastrous things happened to me. "You lived alone in the woods, like in *My Side of the Mountain?*" she asked. "I never knew that."

I said that it was only for one summer, not for a year, that I lived in a tent, not a hollowed-out tree, that I was in the Hudson River Valley, not the Adirondacks, but that I had indeed lived alone in the woods. She invited me to visit her class. I told them about the summer I turned eighteen, when I was too stubborn to move home and too cheap to pay rent. (I was saving money for a bus ticket to travel cross-country.) With my meager savings I bought a small tent, a sleeping bag, and a backpack. I selected a site deep in the woods and made my little camp. I worked at a library, which was within walking distance. I also knew of a building on my route that was unlocked most of the time, with a sink where I could fill my water jugs, since I didn't have bleach, iodine, enough fuel to boil my water, or any other way to treat it. I told them how nasty giardia (a.k.a. "beaver fever") is and how easily you can get it from drinking untreated water in the wilderness. Of course, Sam never treats his water in *My Side of the Mountain,* and he doesn't get sick either, but I wasn't taking any chances.

I was rather hungry my first week until I got paid. Having read *My Side of the Mountain,* though, I thought it wouldn't be much of a problem to "live off the land." I squatted patiently on the rocks along the banks of a waterfall, watching the fish struggle to swim upstream. I knew the Hudson and her fish were loaded with PCBs, but I was hungry. I imagined I would pack the fish in mud and cook it in the coals of my campfire. They seemed perfectly still in the water, until I tried to make a quick grab for one. I tried fishing in this manner for hours, experimenting with rocks and sharp sticks too, without success. I had one can of tuna, but not a can opener. I never was able to open the can, but destroyed a couple of ballpoint pens puncturing it.

It was the summer of the cicada that year, and they were everywhere. Partly because they were annoying and partly because I was hungry, I also tried eating cicadas . . . crunchy, but not very tasty. Mostly I ate wild strawberries and sorrel until I got paid. Then I gladly hiked the five miles into town each week and bought granola, powdered milk, bread, peanut butter, rice, and lentils, which were the mainstay of my diet.

The fifth graders wanted to know how I had started campfires. In fact, I never made a single campfire while living in the woods because I was afraid of forest fires. Because I didn't have permission to be living there, I was even more afraid that someone might see or smell smoke, come out to investigate, and discover my location. I cooked each evening on a small gas camp stove. They asked if bears bothered me. I told them that I never saw a bear that summer and had only one stand-off with a porcupine, but that I had to be very vigilant about hanging my food to keep it safe from skunks, raccoons, and chipmunks. They asked what I did when it rained. I told them that I left my ground cloth sticking out around the bottom of my tent the first night and got soaked. I corrected that problem, but it was still unpleasant to hang around camp in the rain. Then, less than a mile from my campsite, I discovered a dump full of all sorts of useful discarded items. I found a large canvas tarp and an old Adirondack chair. I rigged up the tarp over the chair and had a fine refuge in the rain.

They asked if I was ever scared. I told them I was very scared at first. After I settled into my tent the first night and waited for sleep, I heard a baby crying in the woods. Who would leave a baby out in the woods? Maybe it was a trick. I listened hard, and it stopped. I started to fall asleep, and then I heard the baby cry again. It was haunting. It began to rain, and the pounding drowned out the crying. I woke up to a persistent scratching sound. Silhouetted in the morning light were dozens of big bugs scratching all over the thin nylon roof of my tent, inches from my face. I came out warily and shivered at the creepy sight of dozens of cicada shells pinching my tent, clinging to twigs and branches, littering the ground.

A fifth grader asked me what happened with the crying baby. It took me about a week to figure it. One afternoon I noticed a tangle of thick vines at the edge of my campsite and tried swinging in them, like a hammock or big swing. It was fun and relaxing, until I heard the baby crying. I stopped swinging to listen, and the crying stopped. I tried to relax and swing again, but the crying started right up. I looked around and experimented. I discovered that when the vines swung in the wind (or rocked with my weight), they rubbed the trunks of the trees high above, causing the soft, high sound. I dubbed those the "crybaby vines."

The fifth graders wrote thank-you letters with still more questions. They were pleased that their hunch about it not being quite so easy to live in the woods was true. They were impressed that the book they had read had inspired a person they actually knew to try such a thing.

organizing to tap community resources

I keep a mental inventory of people I know, their occupations, and what they are passionate about. This, by the way, is a compulsive organizer habit. I cannot remember my phone number or PIN, but when I have a question for an entomologist, a haiku poet, an urban planner, or a pilot, I know right where to go. I start with family members (they don't have to be local), colleagues, and friends. I think about culture, languages, occupations, hobbies, and lifestyles, like this very small sample:

Ellen: (my younger sister) lay missionary, speaks Thai, yoga instructor, knows Asian culture, sponsors a Burmese refugee family, teaches world religion and journalism, formerly worked in publication and wardrobe/costume design for theater and film

John: (retired custodian at school) raises and races pigeons, opera buff, reads *New York Times* cover to cover every day

Tom: (principal's husband) cardiologist, road rally racer, likes music

Aneesah: (works at children's room of public library) high school student, Muslim, fluent in Arabic, likes gardening; mother will make her *hajj* this year

Susan: (fifth-grade teacher) fluent in French and Hebrew, bicyclist, world traveler, lived in France and Israel

Mary: (first-grade teacher) former attorney, dancer, and pianist, fluent in Spanish, experienced at writing grants

Jackson: (friend's son) home-schooled teenager, raises exotic chickens, sells fertile eggs

My next step is to get to know my students and their families. A home visit is an excellent way to start. About two weeks before school starts (as soon as I can get a class list), I send a letter to all of my students' families. I introduce myself and say I would like to meet them, listing the days I will be making home visits. I give them my e-mail address and phone number so that they can contact me if they'd like to schedule an appointment. Some people call and ask to schedule a different time if they will be on vacation then.

I phone all the families I haven't heard from, to ask if they'd like to schedule a visit. I always find some phones disconnected, so I try to just drop by those homes when I am in the neighborhood. Some families do not want a visit because they are in the middle of a stressful situation (such as moving, divorce, or a serious illness in the family), so I ask if they'd like to just talk a little while on the phone. I know some families are self-conscious about their housekeeping. I let them know that I am not a great housekeeper myself (heck, I'm out visiting families, not home vacuuming my blinds or cleaning out my refrigerator, so who would I be to judge?) and ask if they'd like to sit on the stoop or the porch. One way or another, I connect with most students and their families before the first day. (For more on home visits, see Chapter 11: Building Trust with Families and Weathering Controversy.)

Not only do I know the names of all my students and their family members on the first day of school, but I also gain priceless insight as I learn about each child and his or her family. Although it takes more time and logistical effort to go out and visit at home, I learn so much more: meeting neighbors and members of the extended family, and noticing their photos, instruments, art, and artifacts. I always ask families about their work and their schedules and what skills they might like to share with us as I invite them to volunteer and visit our class. Here's a brief sample:

Tim: Navy corpsman, also trains marines in survival skills (will teach about topographical map and compass)

Ligia: cook at Smith College, trained to be an elementary teacher in Panama, mother-in-law and sister-in-law are also teachers, can volunteer early mornings, and would like to bake with kids

Donna: psychologist, Brownie leader (willing to teach/organize crafts projects), owns South African art and artifacts and has traveled to South Africa, also willing to speak on family diversity issues (adoption, etc.)

Mark: real estate attorney, does work for Habitat for Humanity, pilot (willing to teach about aeronautical navigation charts)

Norma: (friend of Angela's family) retired chemical engineer, Native American (Oto nation), has adopted daughter from

Zimbabwe, good with technology (digital camera, computer, etc.), gardens at Community Garden, going to teach in South Africa, will organize pen-pal exchange between her school and ours, has dog named Gandhi

Throughout the year, I keep families posted on curriculum and continually invite participation through a weekly family letter. Writing this takes me about one hour every weekend. It gives me a chance to reflect, and I'm more disciplined about writing a weekly letter than a daily journal. I make a point to talk with family members at drop-off and pick-up times, performances, field trips, and potlucks, and welcome them to morning meeting. We have a large Peace Class Family and Friends Potluck in December and another in June each year. This is a good time for students to reflect on who we consider "family and friends" of our class and invite them. For example, Seamus wanted to invite "the guy who brought the white pigeon the first time we raised the peace flag" (John, the retired custodian) to our potluck picnic a year and a half after he released the pigeon.

If I do this family and friend work well, I am able to draw on these resources for years to come, long after the children they love leave my classroom. Mary McKitrick, whose son was in my first-grade class four years ago, continues to volunteer on our seasonal nature walks to the nearby Barrett Street Marsh. Mary is an ornithologist who can identify most birds by their calls. My students call her Mary Ourbirdlady. They write her notes about what we're doing, especially as it relates to birds (like hatching chicks) or nature. Now Sadie wants to become an ornithologist.

Answering Questions with More Questions

I have found that the best response when I can't answer a question is to say, "I don't know, but how can we find out? Where could we look? Who would know more about that?" Several years ago, as we were studying the water cycle and the environment, I read my class *A River Ran Wild: An Environmental History* by Lynne Cherry. It is a beautifully illustrated story of the Nashua River in New Hampshire and Massachusetts, from prehistoric times, to its earliest Native American inhabitants, to European contact, to the Industrial Revolution, to increasing industrial and sewage pollution, and to its eventual death. It goes on to tell the story of how activists organized cleanups along the river, lobbied for protective legislation, including the Clean Water Act,

Figure 4.1 Student drawing of Connecticut River ("This is a picture of the Connecticut River when it was a sewer.")

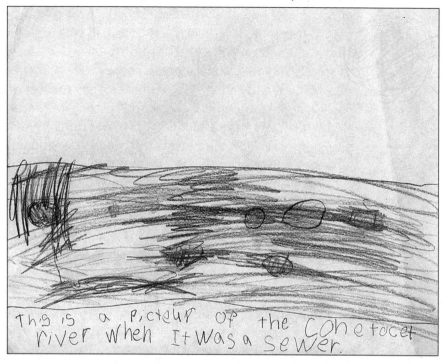

This is a pictchur of the river when It was a sewer. Conetocet

and how the river was saved. Of course, *sewage* was a new vocabulary word for most of my first graders. When one asked what it was, another student quickly answered, "That means poops." The children were shocked. Their eyes popped out of their heads. "They put poops in the river? On purpose?"

I explained that sewage was put in not only the Nashua River, but in most rivers, including our local Connecticut River, for many years. More shock and disgust. "They did that *here?* They put poops in *our* river?" Indignation—then came the big questions; "How did they get the poops out of the river? Where do the poops go now?"

Of course, I've read *The Magic School Bus at the Waterworks* about Ms. Frizzle going to the waterworks more than a few times, so I provided a brief but authoritative lecture on the topic of water treatment. The students nailed me, saying I was off-topic. They didn't want to know about the *drinking* water. They wanted to know where the poops went. And the toilet paper, while I was at it. Okay. I launched into a more vague but no less enthusiastic rap about wastewater treatment. This was briefer, since Ms. Frizzle hadn't been there yet. I was in way over my head. It was time to say, "I don't really know, but how can we find out?"

We wrote to a parent of a former student who works at city hall; she sent us diagrams of city sewer systems. She put us in touch with a city councilor who was the retired director of public works. He sent us a video called something like *The Fabulous Flush.* Soon we knew more about wastewater treatment than most grown-ups know in a lifetime. My students wanted to make sure no poops were going in the river now, and wouldn't in the future. We went to city hall to meet with the mayor. The other grown-ups and I were surprised to learn that in fact our city did not have a water treatment plant to treat drinking water, that it was simply piped out of the reservoir with a few drops of chlorine and out the tap (so much for Ms. Frizzle). But we were reassured to learn that the town was planning to build one in the next five years. We learned more about the city's wastewater treatment plant (unfortunately not as accessible by public bus). As the school year ended, we were still looking for some aging environmental activists who might have been involved with cleaning up the Connecticut River in the 1970s. (Contact me if you are or know one.)

All of this investigation and follow-up takes a lot of talking and writing. If our expert agrees to visit us (or to let us come visit), we prepare interview questions on index cards (individually) or on chart paper (collectively). I talk with the expert/guest beforehand, to let her know what the big ideas in our topic are, what the children already know, their particular question, and how their attention goes. We discuss ideas for props or activities to keep engagement high; additional work I should do to prepare for the visit, like preview content-specific vocabulary; and other ideas for follow-up. As the teacher, I have the best knowledge of how this visitor's expertise connects with our curriculum, what is developmentally appropriate for students, and the feasibility of the activities. I want my students to be engaged and respectful.

There are hundreds of opportunities to bring the curriculum to life. In our first-grade math curriculum, we use quilts as a vehicle to explore two-dimensional geometry. After I realized that some children thought quilts were made out of crayon and paper (like our math designs), I started inviting quilters to visit. Some quilters have set up sewing centers and helped the children make individual quilt squares and a class quilt. Alfredo gave me a warm hug one day, saying, "Ms. Cowhey, you are my most favorite teacher. I never had another teacher who taught me how to sew!"

One year, a local author, Jeannine Atkins, came in to read her new book, *A Name on the Quilt,* about a girl whose family sews a panel for the AIDS memorial quilt in memory of a beloved uncle. We read lots of picture books about quilts. Because I had a pet chicken as a girl, I've got a soft spot for chicken stories like *The Josefina Story Quilt* by Eleanor Coerr, about a pioneer girl who insists on bringing her old pet hen, Josefina, in the covered wagon when the family goes West. To pass the time in the wagon, her mother encourages her to sew quilt patches, which is how she records their adventure.

The Quilt Maker's Gift by Jeff Brumbeau is a fanciful story about a magical quilt maker whose generosity changes a stingy king. *The Keeping Quilt* by Patricia Polacco is a personal favorite. It tells the story of an immigrant family that sews its worn-out clothes from the old country into a quilt that is passed down from generation to generation, used for picnics and play forts, as a *huppa* for Jewish weddings, to cuddle new-born babies, and to warm the elderly. As Polacco revisits the traditions in each new generation, she repeats what is the same and mentions what is different. For homework, I invite families to tell their children about mementos or traditions that are passed down from generation to generation.

In our second-grade math curriculum we use flags as a way to explore fractions. One student's parent had a coworker who is an amateur vexilologist (flag expert). Who knew such people existed? He agreed to come visit our class. The following year he dropped by in December with hundreds of donated (only slightly outdated) "flags of the world" posters in the trunk of his car, enough for every teacher and student at the whole school to have one. He comes back again every year when we do our flag lessons in math. He's a great resource for my whole school.

While we were studying maps, I put a note in my weekly family letter asking parents how they use maps in their lives, asking if they would be willing to share with the class. A conservation biologist showed us global computer maps. A pilot showed us the control panel of a cockpit and explained visual and instrumental navigation and how to use pilot's charts. A marine survival specialist showed us how to use a compass to navigate with a topographical map of the school neighborhood.

the yogurt cup experiment

It takes time to build a network of people resources in a community. Good communication with families has often brought experts to my classroom door. Back in that first year of teaching (by now you are probably thankful that your child was not in my class that first year) we had what became known as the Yogurt Cup Experiment. I used to eat yogurt for lunch, wash the plastic cups, and stack them up for eventual recycling. In the meantime, I used them to pass out math manipulatives like beans and dice, or for watercolor painting. They were part of the messy landscape of my classroom.

One day in January Ana Mari filled up a yogurt cup with water and brought it outside at recess for some purpose. She forgot to bring the cup back in; it was left out on the stoop outside the classroom door. Ana Mari found the cup the next day and discovered it no longer contained water but ice! When the children came in from recess, they were all crowding around her, jostling to see the yogurt cup, to touch it, like this was the greatest miracle ever. I thought that was weird. I mean, by the time you're six, you've seen ice cubes, and in Massachusetts, you've seen plenty of frozen puddles. I didn't get the mystery.

Ana Mari asked me if she could share. I said sure. The studio audience could hardly contain its excitement. She rose with confidence and told the story of the yogurt cup being left out and then brought in. For her finale, she dumped the yogurt cup and gave it a dramatic whack. Voila! The wet round ice slid onto the rug, and the children all oohed and wowed. "How'd you make it do that?" Papo asked.

Ana Mari said, "I just left it on the step yesterday. I got this today!" More wows. This was as magical as leaving your tooth under the pillow for the Tooth Fairy. I thought to myself, "Could they not know that the cold temperature turned the water to ice?" I was waiting for some smart-aleck to contradict Ana Mari, but instead, Carmen asked if she could have a yogurt cup at lunch recess. I said sure. In the next minute, every other child asked too. I said sure.

This went on for days, weeks. Every time I'd pick them up from recess, they'd be all lined up, carrying these old yogurt cups in their mittened hands, asking if they could share. We put names on the cups, to reduce fighting, and began to keep a chart of our observations. We'd go around the circle, and they'd all dump their cups on the rug. Eventually, I got hip and started to spread newspaper on the rug before they came in. The first day that the water in the yogurt cup froze, it was sunny, clear, and cold. The whole week was like that, until Friday, when it was cloudy and warmer. At the end of the week, I asked them what they thought was happening. The initial idea that some fairylike creature was busily switching their water for ice (like a tooth for a quarter) was nixed because sometimes the dumped cups revealed a piece of ice *and* a splash of water. They began using the word *freeze* consistently to describe the change.

The next hypothesis was that the sun was freezing the water. This hypothesis was bolstered by Friday's evidence that the water was not frozen on the cloudy day. Many times I was tempted to just tell them that water freezes at 32 degrees Fahrenheit and proceed to static electricity or whatever science topic was on our curriculum. Something told me not to rush it. Because I wasn't required to teach about ice, I didn't feel any pressure to "cover it" and move on. The experiment continued for another week of soggy mittens and soaked rug. I left some thermometers out. When I observed Paulo covertly trying to break one, I pulled him aside and showed him how to use it. He watched me and said nothing. By the end of the second week, my first graders had figured out that it was the cold temperature that made the water in the yogurt cups freeze.

Gretel, a very quiet little girl, had told her mother a great deal about the Yogurt Cup Experiment. Her mother asked me about it. She knew a chemist and said she once saw him make ice cream out of liquid nitrogen. She offered to invite him to class for a visit. His visit was cool and exciting. He wore a white lab coat, goggles, and large safety gloves. He froze lettuce leaves and balloons. There was lots of fog tumbling off the table. I took photos; my students wrote captions for the photos to make a class book about it. Later, states of matter became part of the second-grade science curriculum. Gretel moved out of the district about a month after the chemist's visit, but eight years later, he still comes to make ice cream with liquid nitrogen.

mystery math guests

Another visitor idea that I got from *Family Math* by Stenmark, Thompson, and Cossey was to invite a "mystery math guest." Basically I look for people (especially women and people of color) with cool jobs that require math. I especially look for people with occupations that challenge gender stereotypes. Although I sometimes invite former parents, I don't ask current parents in my class to do this, because some classmates are already likely to know their jobs.

The mystery math guest arrives in some neutral outfit (for example, not a police officer's uniform) with a bag of hidden "props." I play the part of the emcee. The guest reveals one prop that relates to math on her job, such as a calculator. She identifies it but does not explain how she uses it. Then the students guess a bunch of jobs, which I record on chart paper. When the students have made all their guesses, the guest reveals another prop, such as a metal triangle. Now the students have an opportunity to refine their initial guesses. I record those ideas. We repeat this procedure for a couple more props, such as a date book, a tape measure, and a blueprint, before finally revealing the mystery math guest's occupation. To wrap up, the guest explains how she uses each of the tools on her job and how math is important in her work.

Mystery math guests have included a female carpenter/contractor, a bilingual midwife, a female veterinarian, a documentary filmmaker, and a male nurse. The first time I did this was at a Family Math Night. The next day, a parent named Raquel stopped me outside the school. She had tears in her eyes as she thanked me for the mystery math guest. "I never thought math was important. I dropped out of school. I work nights in a factory now because that's the only job I can do. I want my daughter to do good in math. Tell me anything I need to do to help her. I want her to get a good job like that lady had."

In addition to bringing guests in, I often take my class on field trips. We tend not to do the same trips every year, although most of them are free and local, reachable by foot or by public bus. We do more in the fall and spring, and everyone brings a few quarters if they can. Different aspects of our local college (greenhouse, art museum, botanical garden with frog pond, Japanese teahouse, Foucault pendulum, machine shop) are frequent destinations. We usually go to city hall and other downtown locations. We visit the marsh near our school every season. The field trips always have a curricular focus, such as "How did they get the poops out of the river?" or "Have the beavers made more changes in the swamp?"

It is important to prepare children for the field trips: what to bring, how to dress. I keep a collection of rubber boots (donated by families over the years) in various sizes, because not all children have them and shouldn't need to worry about getting their new sneakers dirty. We talk about what kind of behavior is expected, how we'll travel, and what we'll do there. On walking field trips, we always bring rubber gloves and trash bags so we can collect litter on our way back. Once the children spied an old tire dumped in a stream. They wrote to the mayor and got it removed.

Some trips don't work out according to my best-laid plans, but it is fascinating to see a field trip through their eyes. I often ask the children to make captioned drawings (first grade) or write about our trips (second grade). Once we went to a beautiful photo exhibit at Smith College. The students wrote about their fascination with the variety of state quarters used to pay for the public bus, recognizing skunk cabbage in a small wetland we passed on the way there, the way the bus elevator worked and talking with another passenger who used a wheelchair, noticing a

William Carlos Williams poem displayed on the bus, and eating lunch at round wooden tables in our student teacher's dining hall. Honestly, I was disappointed that this beautiful multicultural photo exhibit didn't inspire them to write about issues of identity and community, as I thought it would.

Instead, they wrote a thank-you note to the college dining hall workers for the Popsicles they kindly gave us. Some of them wrote notes to our principal about how nice it was to eat lunch at round tables in the dining hall, suggesting that we try that. (Two years later, she replaced the rectangular cafeteria tables with round ones.) We located the patch of skunk cabbage on a city map. Two students borrowed a wheelchair from the nurse and surveyed the school building for accessibility. They wrote a report on it, noting that although there were ramps, an elevator, and an accessible toilet in the building, it was impossible for a person using a wheelchair to hold the heavy front door open while simultaneously pushing him- or herself inside.

We marked a U.S. map with sticky notes for all the state quarters we had used on the trip, and noticed they were all on the East Coast. We wrote and solved story problems about quarters. I shared more of William Carlos Williams's poems, and they wrote more poetry. They didn't follow my plan at all, but they wrote letters, poems, and reports. They explored a college campus, rode a public bus, thought about accessibility issues, and used maps and quarters. It was not a brilliant triumph of masterful curriculum framework planning. It was more like squeezing and sucking all the juice out of a crushed orange, but that's how real learning often happens.

Occasionally the Cultural Arts Committee gets grant funding or the PTO provides funding for special grade-level trips to a particular performance, science museum, or restoration village with a single topic-within-a-subject focus. These trips are more expensive because of admission prices and the costs of hiring school buses. They are less spontaneous, often planned at least six months in advance. Although these trips are also enriching, the children usually play a more passive role: ride there, watch a show or see an exhibit, ride home. I think of the more institutional, funded field trips as supplementary and the cheap or free local trips (on foot or by public bus) as more organic and authentic, more closely connected to what children are wondering and wanting to learn.

Bringing guests in, or taking the class out, feeds children's imaginations and their language. I often have students who lack developed language in English or any other language, and children with severely lim-

Figure 4.2 A partial list of visitors and field trips over the years

A Partial List of Visitors Over the Years

This list of visitors does not include parents who volunteered to help out with regular classroom activities such as baking, field trips, art projects, sharing pets, celebrations, performances, and exhibitions, or visits by mentors or observers.

- Adult ESL class from Center for Americans
- Umoja African Dance residency
- David Bickar (chemist) to make ice cream with liquid nitrogen
- Professor Sylvia Berger and Spanish students from Smith College for literacy partnership
- Aneesah Uqdah (high school student) re: Islam and Ramadan
- Karen Bellavance-Grace (parent/activist) re: AIDS Memorial Quilt Project
- Michael Doherty (building inspector/parent) re: building materials
- Mary Ellen Casey (parent/artist) re: how to make quilts
- Aida Rivera (grandmother) to explain how sunflowers turn their heads toward the sun
- Jeannine Atkins (local author) reads *Get Set! Swim!,* talks about writing process
- Dr. Taietsu Unno re: Japanese calligraphy
- Mary Harrington (parent/scientist) lesson re: magnets
- Dr. Ellie Shelburne (veterinarian) to present her findings on the "mystery tooth" we asked her to help identify. It was the tip of a deer antler.
- Jim Croft's presentation about flags of the world, in relation to our study of fractions
- Mari-Jon Adams re: Habitat for Humanity and affordable housing
- Dennis and Emma Francis (visitors from South Africa) shared history, taught anthem, some Zulu, and gum boot dance
- Jackson Mansfield (high school student) re: raising exotic poultry
- Alice Unno re: growing up in Japanese American internment camp (after a reading of *Baseball Saved Us*)
- Angel Martinez (parent/aide) re: Puerto Rican flag
- Ednerilda Lopez (parent) re: Puerto Rican folk songs
- John Davis (astronomer) re: moon journals, eclipse, objects in the sky
- Bill Newell (grandfather/activist) re: experience in civil rights movement
- Karen Sohne and Marshall Hryciuk (haiku poets) re: haiku reading and poetry workshop

A Partial List of Field Trips Over the Years
- Barrett Street Marsh every season
- Smith College Museum of Art
- Forbes Library: children's room and art exhibits
- Smith College exhibit re: Black inventors
- Botanic gardens
- Japanese teahouse
- Farm at nearby vocational and agricultural high school
- Machine shop
- Studio of parent/artist Katy Schneider to see illustrations for *Painting the Wind* and meet children's book author Patricia MacLachlan

Figure 4.2 A partial list of visitors and field trips over the years *(continued)*

- City hall to meet with Mayor Higgins and various other officials to discuss issues including wastewater treatment, homelessness and affordable housing, urban planning (specifically expanding and improving bike paths and lanes), voter registration, civil rights
- Supermarket (for unit on nutrition)
- Theater at Williston Northampton School to see stage set for James and the Giant Peach constructed by Amy Putnam (parent) and her student crew
- Florence Savings Bank to view and cast votes for maquettes in competition for Sojourner Truth Memorial statue selection, and to view future memorial site
- Eric Carle Children's Book Art Museum
- *Daily Hampshire Gazette* to meet reporters and staff, and to see presses running
- Foucault pendulum
- Buddhist monks making butter sculptures

ited vocabularies and experiences. By meeting real people and doing interesting and exciting things that connect with their own learning, by conversing and corresponding with them, children can begin to identify with others and imagine themselves in the future.

In 2004, Seamus used an old race-car calendar he found in the classroom to write a story about a car race. It was a little tedious: "The Porsche zooms ahead. Now the Lamborghini goes . . ." Ramadan thought this was a cool idea and started to write a similar story, using the same calendar. When I asked to see his plan, he hesitated and said he didn't have one. We talked about the importance of starting with a plan. I asked him what he knew about car races. He had never been to one or seen one on TV. He had ridden in cars, but his family didn't have one. I asked if he knew any race-car drivers. He said no, but his eyes got big as he asked if I knew any. I suggested that he write a letter to Tom, our principal's husband, because I knew that he liked to drive in road rallies. He wrote a lengthy letter (much better than his race-car story) with lots of questions. Tom wrote back promptly, answering his questions and offering to visit the class if Ramadan thought his classmates would be interested. Ramadan immediately asked the others, then wrote back and invited Tom to come. All of the students wrote interview questions for Tom on index cards, such as, "Do you ever feel scared in a race?" "Were you ever in a crash?" and "What is the fastest you've ever driven?"

Tom's presentation featured European maps, photo albums, a story about his car getting kicked by wild horses in the Pyrenees, the importance of teamwork and communication, the importance of mathematical accuracy over sheer speed (you are fined points for getting to a checkpoint early or late), and bilingualism (the detailed instructions for the Monte Carlo rally are all in French). Ramadan wrote a thank-you note to Tom, and a story about the road rally. Ramadan stretched his written and oral language capability tremendously with the motivation and responsibility of hosting this special visitor.

* * *

It takes a village to teach first grade. As a somewhat clueless, brand new teacher, I was willing to admit that I couldn't do the job alone. The other teachers had their hands full too. As a former organizer, I know it never hurts to ask. Most people are flattered to be considered a resource and respond positively, even when they have little or no personal connection to the class or the school. Usually it costs no more than a few phone calls and some personal thank-you notes from students. If I manage to scribble the contact information on a sticky note and stick it in the file for that unit, I can draw on that resource for years to come. It can be spontaneous, messy, rough around the edges, and not run according to plan and still result in very powerful learning. It doesn't have to be sophisticated or brilliant. It just has to be relevant and real.

As teachers, we have to make our village, to actively and deliberately build it and recruit the circle of family and friends who will inhabit and sustain it. That village will support the teacher as a learner and nurture students and other "villagers" as teachers for years to come.

CHAPTER 5

talking about peace

People have a right to not have their homes blown up and lose all their belongings to someone else.

The way it should be

The way it shouldn't be

PEACE

War

I am only one, but still I am one. I cannot do everything, but still I can do something. And because I can not do everything I will not refuse the something that I can do.

—Helen Keller

I n January 2002 I was teaching my unit on activism. (If you are wondering where that fits in the state curriculum frameworks, I locate it under social studies: "Civics and government" and "Laws and rules keep us safe.") Vocabulary words such as strike, organize, boycott, protest, and ally are hard for first and second graders to wrap their heads around. I like to start the unit with good children's books such as Swimmy by Leo Lionni and Farmer Duck by Martin Waddell. I recently added Click, Clack, Moo: Cows That Type by Debra Cronin to my collection. In the story, some cows find an old manual typewriter in their barn and teach themselves how to type. They type a letter to the farmer, asking for electric blankets because the barn is cold. The farmer refuses, so they write another note telling the farmer they are on strike until they get their electric blankets. When the farmer refuses, the chickens join the strike, refusing to lay eggs until they and the cows get electric blankets.

My first graders had a lively discussion about demands, strikes, allies, negotiations, and solidarity. As the children made the transition to snacktime, I told my new student teacher, "You have to be careful when you read a book like this in class."

As I often do, I sat down at a table of students to have my snack. They were excitedly talking among themselves about the idea of going on strike to demand more recess at school. I detected a note of nervousness among them, about whether they should keep this plot secret from me. Perhaps figuring their cover was already blown, they decided to ask my advice. David, an outspoken boy, asked me loudly. "Would that work, Ms. Cowhey? Can kids strike?" I said that was a good question, and thought about it. I told them about 15,000 South African students in Soweto who went on strike in 1976, how they refused to attend classes and demonstrated to protest having to learn Afrikaans, the language of the White minority that ran their country. The South African police fired without warning, killing and wounding many children.

Curtis looked over at a poster of our pen pals at a rural school in South Africa. He said, "I think our pen pals would think we were crazy. They have to pay money to go to a school with hardly any books and no toilet, and we get to go to school for free. I'd be embarrassed to tell them we did it."

John added, "I think kids in Afghanistan really want to go to school too, and they don't have any." Another student agreed, and David reconsidered, saying that maybe getting more playtime wasn't such a great reason to strike.

A shy, thoughtful boy named Allan had been sitting quietly at the end of the table throughout this animated exchange. Very quietly, with his cracker near his mouth, he said, "Maybe we could do it to stop the war."

Figure 5.1a and b Student writing in response to *Click, Clack, Moo* (top) and *Farmer Duck* (bottom)

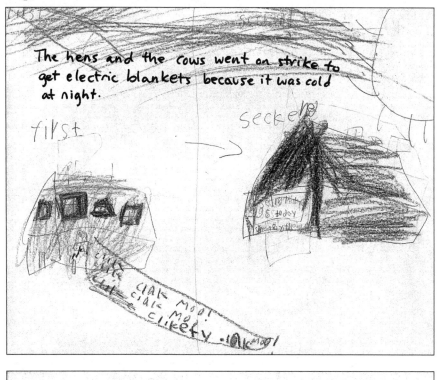

The hens and the cows went on strike to get electric blankets because it was cold at night.

first   seckend

clak moo! clak moo! clikety-clak moo!

I hate this

The farmer treated the duck bad and made him work hard.

David yelled, "What do you mean, stop the war?"

Still looking intently at his cracker, Allan said softly but clearly, "Maybe kids could go on strike to stop the war in Afghanistan." That took my breath away. In this brief dialog, these first graders moved from a perspective oriented toward their own desire for play and pleasure to a consideration of real political reasons that people, including children, might strike.

forgiveness and reconciliation

Returning from the United Nations World Conference Against Racism in South Africa, I flew into New York on the morning of September 10, 2001. I had spoken with many South Africans who had been involved with the Truth and Reconciliation Commission process. After a sleepless night on the plane, I was more convinced than ever that peace was the harder, less familiar road, but that it nonetheless was the only road to take if we care about humanity's survival.

I was also convinced that racism would not be ended by global declarations, but through face-to-face human dialog. I was struck by the power of the arm's-length work we engaged in at the NGO (non-governmental organization) forum of the World Conference Against Racism. I was very affected by several United to End Racism workshops I participated in using the process of Reevaluation Counseling. In a single day, I tried to understand the perspective and experience of an Aborigine elder from Australia, a Dalit (untouchable) from India, a Palestinian mother, an Irish Traveler teenager, and a Zulu schoolteacher. In one workshop on healing the scars of racism we did what seemed like a simple, even silly, exercise. We were to hold the hand of a partner and take turns for a minute, each saying, "I welcome you." My partner was a South African Xhosa man named Lucas, about sixty years old. Lucas held my hand and looked into my eyes and said, "I welcome you, Mary." I was deeply moved. It suddenly felt okay for me, a White American, to be in South Africa, like I was welcome there. When it was my turn, I realized that this wasn't my place to welcome Lucas to, so I welcomed him into my life. The whole exercise was two minutes. By the time we finished, Lucas was crying. He said that in his whole life, he had never held the hand of a White person in a trusting way. (For more about United to End Racism and Reevaluation Counseling, see www.rc.org/uer.)

*Forgiveness and reconciliation are not cheap, they are costly . . .
Forgiveness is an act of much hope and not despair. It is to hope in the
essential goodness of people and to have faith in their potential to
change. It is to bet on that possibility . . . Ultimately there is no future
without forgiveness.*

—Archbishop Desmond Tutu, Nobel Laureate and chairman of the
South African Truth and Reconciliation Commission

The South African Truth and Reconciliation process was flawed and
inadequate to the magnitude of its task of repairing generations of brutal violence and abuse. The fact that a significant number of South
Africans used it anyway impressed me greatly. I remember hearing
Miriam Makeba speak before singing at an antiracism concert in
Durban. Makeba is known as Mama Africa for her anti-apartheid music
and protest activities. Makeba said, "Our leaders ask us not to forget, but
to *forgive.*"

I was stunned by the weight of her words. How could anyone ask a
South African of color to *forgive* generations of apartheid, decades of
oppression, centuries of theft and brutal exploitation? *Forgive?* Yet didn't
Gandhi forgive his assassin? I struggled to make sense of this. I stayed,
listened, cried, and learned. I visited schools in Durban, in the Black
township of Inanda, and in the rural areas of KwaZulu Natal. I listened
to the stories of the people I met.

There had been tremendous bloodshed there, especially during
intense Black-on-Black fighting between members of the Inkatha
Freedom Party (IFP) and the African National Congress (ANC), causing
a huge number of deaths in the years leading up to the changeover. The
Inkatha Freedom Party had cooperated to some extent with the white
regime in return for certain privileges, the major ones being sovereignty
over those areas known as Zululand and the building of Ulundi as its
capital. The IFP saw itself as the leadership of the Zulu nation, although
in fact at least as many Zulus were supporters of the ANC. They struggled for political control of the province once the changeover occurred.
The Black-on-Black violence was a result of the White regime trying to
divide the Blacks by granting privileges to a few, in a bid for Whites to
hold on to power as long as possible. Zululand and the rest of Natal were
later reunited in the province of KwaZulu Natal.

When I saw the scars of that fighting on the hands, arms, and faces
of teachers and in still-broken windows and charred, hacked portions of
their schools, a part of me wanted to ask, "My God, who cut you? Who
burned your school?"

But I was a White American, without a phone or a car, in the heart of Zulu country, a two-hour drive over rocky dirt roads from Durban. My life was in the hands of these teachers and principals who arranged a patchwork of rides for me and welcomed me into their schools. Curious as I was, I knew I should not ask. The answer was not my business. If they said they were on the side of the Inkatha Freedom Party, then what would I do? Stop trusting them? Walk back to Durban alone? The reality was that they could have been on either side, perhaps because they were pressured to be. They could have suffered cruel tragedies *and* done unspeakable things. They could have kept fighting forever, but most important, they had agreed to stop. It was not my place to judge.

Just as my future that day in the rural villages of KwaZulu Natal depended on trusting, listening, and moving forward, I began to understand how a peaceful South African future depended not on forgetting, but *forgiving*. I found the huge sacrifices so many people made for the sake of peace staggering, realizing how costly forgiveness and reconciliation are.

As a White, middle-class American, my sacrifice for peace is not usually to forgive. Even as an antiracist, living what I perceive to be a community and environmentally oriented nonmaterialistic lifestyle, the privileges and advantages I receive (and take for granted) are astounding. Of course, I was left to struggle with the question, "What would I sacrifice for peace?"

It is a lie to teach that peace is easy. Young children already know that it is easier for an aggressive child to get what he or she wants in the immediate by hitting and grabbing rather than using words. Making peace is hard, hard, hard, but that's the price we must learn to pay for living on this planet.

A week after the *Click, Clack, Moo* discussion, Allan's mother stayed after school and volunteered to help pack and ship books we'd collected for our pen-pal partner school in South Africa. I told her the story about Allan. "Maybe that's where he was coming from," she mused. "Last week at dinnertime, he started asking me these questions. I'm a nurse, and he knows I absolutely *hate* smoking. He hates smoking too. Last week, he asked if I knew that it would end all wars in the world forever, would I smoke then? That really made me think. We talked about it for a long time."

Not only had Allan learned this big idea that making peace is hard and usually requires significant personal sacrifice (even doing what you would really rather not do), but he had taken the initiative to teach his family about it at dinner. Allan was trying to figure out what's more important, or which is worse. In probing this, he got his family members and teachers to consider the same.

"Getting It" in the Long Run

We teach, but how do we know what our children are learning? Surely we can take running records of their reading, look at the mathematical strategies they use in problem solving, check their drafts in their writing folders for mastery of mechanics and spelling high-frequency words, and so forth. But how can we assess their critical-thinking ability? How do we know if they are making sense of the stories we tell and the things we do? I wonder if the social justice element of my teaching carries over beyond my time with my students, whether first and second graders do "get it" in the long run.

At the beginning of the 2002 school year, one of my colleagues, Susan Fink, a fifth-grade teacher, stopped me in the hall and said, "I think I got one of yours." I asked how she could tell. She told me about a writing activity with her class. She asked them all to write about their dream summer vacation, not what they did, but what they wished they could have done. "Did you by any chance have Nancy?" Susan asked. (I did.) She told me Nancy wrote, "I would have gone to Afghanistan and tried to stop the war." Susan asked her to elaborate, how exactly she would have done that. Nancy continued writing, "I would bring Gandhi, and a lot of food."

In my first year of teaching, a colleague from another school had introduced me to a literacy activity she called "pocket poems." These were short poems, which the children cut out, word by word, mixed up, and reassembled, referring to a printed copy of the poem on an envelope as needed. I had been looking for some meaningful literacy activities to engage my students while I worked with guided reading groups, so I gave it a try. One day, as I observed children working on the activity, I noticed that most of them were softly reciting the poem to themselves as they worked. The poem was something about snow-covered bushes looking like popcorn balls. I thought, "*Yuck!* I am filling up their valuable brain space with poems about bushes looking like popcorn balls!" I felt terrible and puzzled over what to do.

I decided the activity had some literacy value, if I could use more substantial content. I used some short poems I found in *The Dream Keeper and Other Poems* by Langston Hughes, like "Color," "Poem," "Winter Moon," and "My People." Soon my students were easily recit-

ing Langston Hughes's poetry. Then I decided to try some quotes. I started with Gandhi: "If we are to reach real peace in this world, we shall have to begin with the children." I was struck by how the children took to that quote, how it resonated in their lives. I made a poster with that quote and Gandhi's picture. Years later, it was still relevant for Nancy.

Gandhi's words were particularly relevant for students in 2001 given the events of September 11 and the ensuing "war on terrorism." I read the students *Gandhi,* a picture book by Demi. It describes Gandhi as a shy and fearful young man. It follows him through his legal studies in England, his unsuccessful attempt to practice law in India, and his move to South Africa, where he was physically thrown off a train for refusing to move from a seat in a White section. That experience motivated him to begin organizing against apartheid. The book tells the story of Gandhi's eventual return to India and his nonviolent movement for independence.

One student, Linda, had a variety of special needs. Math facts and literacy were difficult for her, but she loved social studies and related to the stories in very personal ways. Throughout the year, she never could remember Gandhi's name, but she always referred to him as my "friend." She would say, "You know, Ms. Cowhey, what your friend always say?"

"What friend?" I would ask.

Linda would elaborate: "You know, your friend with the no hair and glasses. Your friend that don't own nothing. That man who gots sandals who said about the children and peace. You know, your friend."

One of my students was Ann, a girl who began first grade with me as a selective mute. On my home visit, I learned from her mother that she had attended kindergarten on a military base down south. After her teacher yelled at her on the first day of school, she decided she would never speak in school. When I called her name for attendance on the first day, she did not say, "Here," or raise her hand or even make eye contact. She crawled under the easel and hid. She happened to be the class leader on Gandhi's birthday (October 2), so she had the honor of helping to raise a new world peace flag on our school flagpole. We sang "Give Peace a Chance." Mr. Benoit, our custodian, released a white homing pigeon; we didn't have a dove. After two years of intensive work with Ann and her family, she completed second grade as an avid reader, prolific writer, and active participant in class discussions and projects. Her father had been transferred back to the base down south, and they moved away. Her mother continued to keep in touch by e-mail, and

black ants and buddhists

Ann began to write me pen-pal letters. She wrote me a letter about third grade; "Yesterday, my teacher asked hoo new about gandie and, I was the only one that raised their hand!"

Each spring there is an art display by young children downtown, celebrating the Week of the Young Child. As a theme for our artwork one year, we reflected on Gandhi's words, "If we are to have real peace in this world, we shall have to begin with the children." I asked the children two questions:

- How can children make peace in this world?
- What would real peace in our world look like?

One of the most interesting answers came from Allan, the boy who had proposed that children go on strike to stop the war in Afghanistan. Allan said that real peace would look like "no cars."

David objected loudly, "No cars? I don't *think* so! We need cars. How would no cars make real peace in the world?"

Allan is a boy of few words. "It takes lots of metal and rubber and stuff to make cars, and then cars use gas and oil, and people fight over stuff like that."

"Yeah, but how would we get places without cars?" Curtis challenged.

Another student who had been listening closely took up Allan's argument. "We could be like Adam's family. They ride their bikes everywhere, with baskets and backpacks and a baby seat for his little brother. It could work."

The Peace Book by Todd Parr is a boldly illustrated book appropriate for young children (ages four and up) that is good for helping young children imagine, write, talk, and draw about what peace is. *What Does Peace Feel Like?* by Vladimir Radunsky explores the concept of peace through the senses, as young contributors describe what peace looks, feels, tastes, smells, and sounds like. Spare and poetic, this book is a good springboard for creative writing about peace. Ellen, a second grader, wrote this:

Peace
Peace smells like tulips, Spring, and the morning
Peace looks like a dove flying through the air, a winter day, and friends
Peace sounds like a bird chirping, sheep in a field, and the ocean
Peace tastes like water, pine branches, peppermint
Peace feels like air, climbing a tree, riding a horse
Peace moves like the river, the trees, and the sea

letting children lead

Teaching peace takes more than preaching it. From before I can remember until the day I left home after graduating from high school, one of my sisters and I fought constantly. My long-suffering mother must have said (or yelled), "Stop fighting!" 5,000 times. We were immune; we fought tooth and nail, over everything and nothing. We rarely fought with our older and younger siblings, preferring instead to save our energy for each other. When we weren't actually fighting, we thought it was fun to *pretend* we were fighting, just to rile our mother. If I told my sister to be quiet because I was trying to read, she would start yelling, "Ouch! Ow! Mary! Aargh! Mary, stop hitting me!"

Singing songs about peace didn't make me a peaceful child either. As young teenagers, my sister and I were recruited to be lectors at the 7:00 A.M. Mass on alternating Sundays. For safety's sake, we walked together the two miles to church and then back again, each resenting that we had to go with the other on our "off" week. Our parish regularly sang a hymn called "Let Peace Begin with Me." The soloist who led the parish had a funny habit of slowly cocking her head from left to right and back again while shaking it in a strange vibrato. When it was my sister's turn to be the lector, I dutifully sat in the front row, slowly and subtly shaking and cocking my head ever so slightly from side to side, mouthing the words to "Let Peace Begin with Me," just to make her crack up while reading. She tortured me in the same manner. Then we laughed and bickered all the way home, told on each other, and fought some more. Although we get along fine now, we were terrible then.

I figure if children today are even half as contrary as I was in my youth, a different approach is clearly required. Although there is no magical solution, I think dialog is the key. Critical thinking and dialog go hand in hand.

Patient, thoughtful engagement in dialog can be hard to imagine, when the "dialogers" are six or seven years old, are only beginning to acquire English, are shy or guarded, or have language-based learning disabilities. Surely there is a challenge here, but when it is well met, the results can be powerful. It is one thing to have your most privileged, articulate, and entitled children speak up in a dialog. They may be used to being listened to or demanding attention. For me, the real test is to have the least-empowered children, the least articulate, take a leading role in that dialog while the more articulate children thoughtfully listen and consider things from their classmates' perspectives before they comment or question.

One day Angela shared a very short story she had written. She used to write lots of stories that fit this pattern: "I went to McDonald's. I like McDonald's. McDonald's is cool." They were boring. At most, other children might say, "I like going to McDonald's too," but the connections lacked depth or feeling. I asked Angela to take a break from that pattern, to write how she really felt about something that happened to her. She wrote this story, called "Baseball."

> I am going to little league. I have not played baseball before. I think it will be fun like soccer, but . . . I hope I am not the only African American girl on the team.
>   That would be silly.

As soon as she finished reading it aloud, students began raising their hands. Jasmine, a biracial girl, said, "I can definitely relate to that. When I started school, I was worried I would be the only one."

Samuel said, "I have a connection, Angela, a text, a text, a text-to-self connection." Then he looked directly at Jasmine and said, "I'm like you. I . . . I'm stuck . . . I'm stuck with two cultures. Like I'm Christian." He paused, not having found the precise word he wanted.

"Catholic," I whispered.

"Yeah, I'm Catholic. That's why I go to CCD, to make my first holy community soon, but I'm something else too . . . Hindu?" Again he paused, searching for the word. Krish, who is Indian, has similarly dark skin, hair, and eyes, and is a devout Hindu who often explains aspects of his spirituality to the class. Samuel related to him, knew he had something in common with him, but was confused. Samuel looked at me. "You know that Pakistani one?" Samuel's father is Pakistani.

"Muslim," I said softly.

He nodded vigorously and stood up. "I'm that too. I'm Muslim. . . . Then I'm Spanish. . . . What's that island?"

"Your mom is from Panama," I said.

"Yeah, I'm Panama and . . . and . . . ," Samuel paused. A small, soft-spoken boy who usually avoided eye contact, Samuel now stood tall, with his arms outstretched, his large, beautiful eyes alert and searching the face of each classmate. "And, and . . . I think I'm some Ireland too," he said, taking a big breath. The intensity of his gaze held us all.

Samuel's stepdad's side of the family is Irish. The children don't specifically know that, but they accepted this important testimonial

from Samuel about what it is like to be "stuck" between cultures, how complicated, hard, yet necessary it is to sort out and say to your world all the pieces of who you are. He nodded to himself, satisfied that he had said it all correctly, and then sat back down on the rug.

Som Jet spoke next. "I . . . like Samuel too! I stuck by two cultures too. Only this one," he touched the rug with his left hand, "it's America . . . and . . ." he stretched his other hand far to the right, "and it's Thai."

Gabriella is Puerto Rican and African American. "Yeah," she began, "I know what you guys are saying, in two cultures. I know what you mean too, Angela. When I started kindergarten here, I was so worried I would be the only brown-skinned child. Then when I saw Jasmine, I was so happy and we made friends." Gabriella smiled across the rug at Jasmine. "Then I knew I wasn't the only one."

Sadie rose to her knees. "You're not the only one *now!* We have *three* African American girls in our class!" She waved three fingers in the air for emphasis.

"Four," corrected Jasmine. "Don't forget Michelle just 'cause she's absent."

Sadie looked perplexed. "But Michelle's skin isn't *brown* like yours," she protested.

"Michelle is biracial like Jasmine," I clarified, "with one African American parent and one European American parent. Her skin is lighter because she has less active melanin than Angela, Gabriella, and Jasmine. She is proud to be African American too."

Samuel spoke up. "And I have brown skin and I'm *not* African American, and Krish too. He's brown like me, and he's Indian. I'm . . . I'm Panama . . . and Pakistan." He nodded to himself, as though sorting it out. I agreed with him that not all people with brown skin have African ancestors.

Sadie sighed. "I don't have much melanin," she said, squeezing her pale arm.

Calvin shyly raised his hand. He had been listening and watching, lips pursed, body hunched forward, blue eyes peering out from a cloud of thick blond curls. He's a reserved child, on the anxious side. He looked directly at Angela. "I have a text-to-self connection with your story. In the fall I signed up for soccer, and I was worried I would be the worst player on the whole team." He blinked, swallowed hard, bit his lip, and continued, "Then I went and played and it was fun, but I know what you mean about the worrying."

Angela looked at him, smiled, and nodded. She had written and shared just four sentences, yet she had connected with her audience in profound ways. Her simple story inspired a discussion about the intersections of multiple identities: race, ethnicity, and religion, about melanin, confidence, and differing abilities. They didn't do all that because it was in a lesson plan. They did it because they are used to learning through and engaging in dialog. Clearly, the children trusted each other to share their feelings, these inner stories of their identities. Except for the few times when Samuel turned to me for word-finding help (because he remembers when I visited his home and knows I know his family and his story), the children were all speaking directly to each other. They were not answering a teacher's questions or seeking a teacher's approval.

Tom Wartenberg, the philosophy professor with whom I collaborate, once commented to me after observing a discussion, "These second graders are doing what I struggle to get my undergraduates to do: they are talking to *each other,* not just the teacher." This dialog reminded me in some ways of the workshop dialogs in South Africa, people speaking honestly about their own experiences and perspectives. It brought to mind a quote from Albert Einstein: "Peace cannot be kept by force. It can only be achieved by understanding."

• • •

Freire contrasts critical thinking with naive thinking. He writes that for the naïve thinker, it is important to accommodate to the "normalized today." Freire believes it is important for the critical thinker to transform reality (1970, p. 73). I think back to Allan, who at six was rejecting the "normalized" state of an ongoing "war on terror." Allan had not single-handedly solved the issue of world peace. His children's strike for peace did not seem particularly practical. His question of how much his mother would personally sacrifice for world peace (with smoking being the hardest and most disgusting thing he could think of) was more hypothetical than realistic. Yet I was impressed that Allan, who was painfully shy, chose soft-spoken, provocative dialog to engage his friends at snacktime and his family at dinnertime in thinking critically about the present state of war and what it might take to change it.

Retelling this story about Allan reminds me of Gandhi's quote, "Whatever you do may seem insignificant, but it is most important that you do it." Didn't Allan's ideas and questions seem relatively insignificant in the grand scheme of things? I didn't run out that afternoon and organize a children's strike for peace in Afghanistan.

The next day, in response to David's question, "Can kids strike?" I showed them photographs of child laborers from *How the Other Half Lives*, by Jacob Riis. I taught them a lesson about Mother Jones and the children's march she organized in 1903, when at least 10,000 of the striking textile workers in Kensington, Pennsylvania, were children. They marched through New Jersey to Oyster Bay, New York, to see President Theodore Roosevelt. They carried banners saying, "We want time to play." The president refused to see them, but Mother Jones wrote, "Our march had done its work. We had drawn the attention of the nation to the crime of child labor" (Zinn 1980, p. 338).

Later we studied the United Nations Declaration of Human Rights, which Eleanor Roosevelt helped craft in 1948. We read aloud *For Every Child: The United Nations Convention on the Rights of the Child in Words and Pictures*, with text adapted by Caroline Castle. The students then made their own captioned drawings about the rights of all children.

In reading, we began to explore text-to-text connections between picture books on the topic of war and peace. We read *Land of Many Colors*. A class of preschoolers wrote this book, about different groups of people (blue, green, purple) who each think their group is the best and fight for supremacy. After much injury and destruction, a small dust-covered child shouts at them all to stop, that fighting doesn't make sense. They stop fighting and patch up the people and animals with Band-Aids and fix their broken houses. They mix up and share all their blue, green, and purple food.

One of my students, who was a refugee from Kosovo, listened to this story with interest, then pointed out, "It's not like that in real life. It's not so easy to stop." Since then, whenever I read this book, I make a point of telling my students what she said, and we discuss why this book might have oversimplified that idea. Allan said he had a text-to-text connection with a picture book by William Steig called *Rotten Island*, a place where awful creatures enjoy fighting with each other relentlessly, until something happens that threatens to change all that. He brought that in for a read-aloud. We made a Venn diagram to compare the stories and their different outcomes (peaceful resolution versus utter destruction). Then we read *The Butter Battle Book* by Dr. Seuss. In this allegory about the arms race, two groups engage in an escalating war with increasingly sophisticated weapons to demonstrate the correctness of eating toast with the butter side up (or down.)

We continued to struggle in our classroom community with questions about whether children could go on strike, what they would go on strike for, whether they'd ever done it, and what people would sacrifice

Figure 5.2 Children's picture books for peace discussions

The following children's picture books are especially helpful for opening conversations about peace:

The Butter Battle Book by Dr. Seuss
Land of Many Colors by Klamath County YMCA Preschool Staff
Rotten Island by William Steig
For Every Child: The United Nations Convention on the Rights of the Child in Words and Pictures, with text adapted by Caroline Castle
The Peace Book by Todd Parr
What Does Peace Feel Like? by Vladimir Radunsky
Peace Begins With You by Katherine Scholes
Gandhi by Demi
Swimmy by Leo Lionni
Click, Clack, Moo by Debra Cronin
Farmer Duck by Martin Waddell
The Big Box by Toni and Slade Morrison

in exchange for peace, but we took no immediate action. Still, these questions were threads that my class pursued for the entire year. The power of Allan's idea stuck with me. The following year, the United States was planning a massive invasion of Iraq. Many in our community cried out against the drumbeat of war, which continued to pound louder and louder. At the weekly peace demonstration downtown in early March, Claudia Lefko, a local peace activist, invited me to participate in an upcoming International Day of Action.

There was word that Smith College students would stage a walkout. There were rumors that students at Northampton High School would walk out at noon and join them for a demonstration downtown. The high school administration said that any student who walked out would receive a suspension. Students and parents debated over dinner tables whether participation was worth the consequence. Personally, as a peace activist, I wanted to be on the street that day too, but professionally (and ethically), I would not "walk out" on my young students. I contemplated how I could keep these personal and professional roles separate and balanced. Maybe I could go to the demonstration at lunchtime, or after school. I thought of Allan saying that maybe children could go on strike to stop the war. I spoke with my principal about the idea of organizing a Children's March for Peace. We agreed that, being political in nature, it would not be a school-sponsored event, but a community event. Very quickly, I found some parents of current and former students to help me send e-mails and make phone calls and posters to organize a Children's March for Peace after school, at 4:00 P.M.

I hurried downtown after school that day and left thermoses of hot water, cans of cocoa, and hot cups with the demonstrators at the courthouse and told Claudia Lefko we would march down the sidewalk to join them. I hurried on to our meeting place on the steps of city hall. It was a bitter cold, gray New England afternoon. I hung up the beautiful "Peace Class" banner my students had made with Angela's mother and our school's peace flag. I began to unpack the poster-making materials I had brought. I was feeling a little lonely. Then Angela came, with her family. Next Jasmine arrived with her family. Emily, a student of mine from the year before, showed up with her mother. My family arrived. Some families began to arrive from my son's school. One of my former students, now in middle school, came with his family and shyly said hello. My principal arrived, along with other teachers and aides from my school. More and more families and teachers joined us. Sadie's big sister and her friend, who had walked out of the high school earlier, joined us, with their pink hair, Goth attire, and peace signs. The children finished a banner saying "Children's March for Peace."

There may be times when we are powerless to prevent injustice, but there must never be a time when we fail to protest.

—Elie Weisel

We set out marching. For most of these children, and for many of their parents, it was their first peace demonstration. As I looked over my shoulder, I saw our large band of small marchers and their families, proudly carrying their handmade signs, banging drums and tambourines, stretching a half block behind me down the sidewalk and across Main Street as the end of our group left the steps of city hall. Pedestrians stopped and watched, clapped, and encouraged the children. "Good for you! Wow! Kid power! Thanks for being out here!" When we arrived at the courthouse, we got a rousing reception from the demonstrators there, many of them senior citizens. The children did not want to stop for cocoa. They wanted to keep marching. We continued, making a large loop through the downtown. Seamus, with his boundless energy, shook his "Honk for peace!" sign and waved at every passerby. Drivers slowed down to wave and honked their support. The children, tired and very cold, felt proud that they had joined the International Day of Action for peace. Later, they drank cocoa on the snowy sidewalk in front of the courthouse under the glow of streetlights, chatting with activists who had been working for peace since the bombing of Hiroshima.

Our Children's March for Peace did not stop the war, but it was important that the children marched anyway. It was important that they wondered if children could go on strike to stop a war, and they tried as hard as they could, marching bravely in the cold until dark. The children talked with their parents about what they would sacrifice for peace. For many parents it meant arranging to leave work early, or bundling up a younger sibling, or having dinner later that night. For the children, it meant giving up a Brownie meeting, gymnastics, television watching, or playtime. For all of us, it meant marching and standing, singing, chanting, and clapping in the cold for two hours, to try to stop a preemptive war from starting. For the drivers and pedestrians the children encountered, that brief engagement caused them to consider where they stood on the question of war, perhaps made them ask whether war really was inevitable and unavoidable, or if they were accommodating to this "normalized today."

Sometimes people ask me, "When you teach this way, do the children really get it? Does it make any difference?" In the gathering dusk, seeing this collection of students from every year I have taught, and their families, my colleagues, and other families and teachers I had never met, I thought, "Yes, some of them really get it." Allan got it. Allan understood that people could do something (and that children can strike and march) to try to stop a war if they think a war is wrong. Like me, he did not know exactly what his sacrifice, or his mother's would be for peace, but he knew that at some point, peace might require him or her or me to do something hard, because peace is not easy.

It does make a difference, although it is not a headline-making difference. I think back to the dialog that began in the classroom, sparked by the discussion of *Click, Clack, Moo,* when I learned that children were thinking not only about stopping war, but what *they* could do to stop war. From my conversation with Allan's mother a week later, I learned that not only did Allan grasp the big idea that achieving peace is hard and requires sacrifice, but he took the initiative to continue the dialog beyond the classroom, with his family at home.

In anticipation of the Children's March for Peace, many more children who heard of the march and wanted to participate had to initiate that dialog in their homes with their families. On the day of the march, the children interacted with pedestrians and drivers, sparking more dialog in the community through their thought-provoking action. At the courthouse, they talked with older activists. The next day in school, they continued talking, with classmates who had come to the march and with those who hadn't, about what they did and how they felt about it. Like the rings that ripple around a rock thrown in a pond, rings of successful dialog that begin in the classroom can ripple outward in ever-larger circles into homes and out into the community.

out of the big box

Later that spring, my principal and I played host to a delegation of visitors from the Baltic States of Estonia, Latvia, and Lithuania. Participants in an Institute for Training and Development program, they had come to learn about how teachers and schools might help reverse the status quo of corruption in their countries. I found myself talking with these visitors about teaching critically and about the kind of classroom community and school culture that support it. They were intrigued and asked to return to observe two days later.

The Baltic visitors came in the afternoon, when I was reading aloud *The Big Box* by Toni and Slade Morrison. The children in the story have "made the grown-ups nervous" by failing to conform to expectations. The grown-ups conclude that the children "can not handle their freedom" and have sent them to live in a big brown box outfitted with everything from Legos, Nintendo, and Barbies to pizza and Pepsi.

We discussed what it would take to get them to give up their freedom. A few children willingly named their price, saying, "You would have to give me a basketball and Gameboy *and* pizza all the time and as many videos as I want." Angela frowned and shook her braids, saying, "Nothing. You couldn't give me anything to make me go in the box. I wouldn't give up my freedom." The discussion shifted as the students began to think about how the children in the book could escape from the box. Sokong suggested spilling Pepsi on the floor to soften the cardboard, then making something strong and sharp out of the Legos to poke through the box and tear open a hole. Michelle suggested organizing all three children to stand against one wall of the box, stretch their arms out, and run as fast as they could to simultaneously push the opposite wall and knock the box over. Gloria pointed out that the cool furniture like their water bed and TV set could slide across the floor and crush them. Michelle said that on the one hand, they could push the heavy furniture up against the wall they planned to push, to keep it from sliding down to crush them, but on the other hand, "You have to

black ants and buddhists

take some risks to change things, to get freedom. You can't just do it if it's going to be easy and quit if it's hard."

The next morning, in recognition of the fiftieth anniversary of the *Brown v. Board of Education* decision, National Public Radio was running a story about Brenda Johns. In 1951 she was a shy student at a segregated African American high school in Farmville, Virginia. She led a walkout of her school's 400 students, who marched downtown. The superintendent wasn't in, so they met with a minister, who brought them to the office of a lawyer from the National Association for the Advancement of Colored People. He thought their demand for integrated equal schooling would lose, but he didn't have the heart to tell them. The African American students were on strike for two weeks. There was never a single photo or story in the papers, on the radio, or on television.

Their action must have seemed insignificant at the time. The only indication that anyone noticed was that Brenda Johns's life was threatened, so her family sent her down south to live with her uncle, the Reverend Vernon Johns (who was dismissed by Dexter Street Baptist Church for being too radical with regard to civil rights—a young minister named Martin Luther King Jr. replaced him). Brenda Johns's case lost in Virginia's highest court, but it was one of the seven school desegregation cases combined in the historic *Brown v. Board of Education* decision in 1954. It was important that those students staged the walkout after all.

I told the story of Brenda Johns to my students at the morning meeting. Michelle said it reminded her of our discussion of *The Big Box* the day before. "See? If that girl Brenda didn't take a risk, nothing would have changed. You have to be willing to risk something for freedom." Jack said that reminded him of what Gandhi said: "Maybe it seems like what you do doesn't matter, but it's important that you do it anyway."

A week later, I got a note from Elaine Ulman, the director of the Institute for Training and Development, thanking my principal and me for working with the Baltic visitors. She said that one of the Baltic educators said of the visit to our school, "I saw what is prevention of corruption *in essence.*" Elaine wrote, "But perhaps the greatest testimony to the value of your work was the action plan developed by Diana, the principal of a large school in Estonia, who intends to write a children's book in Estonian that can be used to teach school children ideas of ethics and personal responsibility in a thoughtful, open dialogue."

Does it make a difference? Are these fragments of history, current international struggle, children's literature, and daily community activism related? Does children's participation in a dialog about responsibility for personal action, which might involve risk or sacrifice but might still seem insignificant in the eyes of society, make a difference? I think it does, if that dialog is authentic, powerful, trusting, and thought-provoking enough to resonate, if it changes the perception of reality from static entity into something that can be transformed, if that dialog has the power to continue into homes, into the community, into a school across the ocean. It makes enough of a difference to keep doing it. But without dialog, without truly listening or connecting, we might not have known that.

learning through activism

Get blank voter registration cards in English and Spanish from City Hall.

VOTER REGISTRATION

with the cards here I come

registra NOW

cards

We shall over come today

Powerlessness and silence go together. We . . . should use our privileged positions not as a shelter from the world's reality, but as a platform from which to speak. A voice is a gift. It should be cherished and used.

—Margaret Atwood

As a second-grade teacher, I receive samples of glossy weekly publications for children, promising to be on grade level and tied to curriculum frameworks. In August 2004 I received one with photos that showed the presidential candidates and told the names of their dogs. Weighing budget cuts and educational value, I hadn't ordered them.

With Election Day only weeks away, I struggled to find a developmentally appropriate, authentic, and meaningful way to teach my students about the election process. I thought about the voting debacle in the 2000 presidential election. Fear paralyzes, but hope inspires action. I decided to teach the history of the struggle for voting equality, starting with abolitionists and women suffragists such as Frederick Douglass, Elizabeth Cady Stanton, and Sojourner Truth. We moved on to the civil rights movement to learn about the march to Selma and Sheyann Webb, a third-grade girl who marched and sang for voting rights there.

When I teach history or civics, I try to teach it so children will care. Many seven-year-olds are too young to understand the complexity of all the presidential campaign issues, but I don't want them to think it is about the name of a candidate's dog. They are old enough to understand that thousands of people fought for the right to vote for years and that many died in that struggle because the vote is powerful and because exercising it en masse does threaten the status quo. When these kids grow up, I believe they not only will register to vote when they turn eighteen, but will be more active in the democratic process than the kids who just learned the name of Bush's dog.

After discussing what we could do in relation to the upcoming election and the importance of the right to vote, my class decided to organize a voter registration drive. One morning before school, my students buzzed around under their big "Voter Registration Drive" banner. They excitedly asked all approaching adults if they were registered.

A woman came up to me with an intense look on her face. I wondered if she'd been asked four times. "This is a subversive activity, you know." Her finger pushed the stack of voter registration cards. I felt defensive for a moment, thinking, "Wait, we got an okay from the secretary of state to do this." Then I felt protective of the dozens of completed registration cards and wanted to pull them closer.

"Do you know what would happen if every school did this?" she asked. I was still trying to read whether her expression was hostile or supportive. She leaned toward me and said, "It would change the entire country!" She gave the registration cards a satisfied pat, said, "Thanks," and walked away.

I thought about the literal meaning of subvert, *"to turn from beneath." The voter registration drives of the civil rights movement certainly were subversive, but was this? These children will grow up with the staggering weight of a huge national debt and the ramifications of a preemptive war and occupation. This election was about these children, and they had a right to speak up about it. I looked at the handmade signs hanging crookedly around their necks, with their slogans: "Voting is your right. It's your responsibility." Tom's said, "It's free. It's easy. It's your destiny!"*

Rachel approached me and said, "Ms. Cowhey, I think we should sing now. You know, like they did." She cocked her head knowingly, in reference to the civil rights organizers. We gathered and began to sing "Oh Freedom." A blind woman walked into the lobby just then, with her guide dog. She did not see the banners, table, or registration cards, or the children of all shades, with serious faces or proud smiles, but she heard their voices. She stopped and sang with us. People came out of the busy office to listen. Everyone in the lobby stood still. The children ended their repertoire with a Jane Sapp song called "Vote for Me." And for a few minutes, struck by the power of the children's brave voices, the grown-ups stopped and listened.

learning through activism

Learning through activism is powerful because the need to use vital academic skills for social justice motivates their acquisition. These skills include reading, writing (reports, letters of thanks or inquiry, news articles, speeches, etc.), speaking, singing, listening, researching (asking good questions, finding people with answers), gathering and representing data, noting observations, making posters and banners, raising money, getting to know political leaders and how to access them, or more specific skills, such as how to organize a voter registration drive. The most important skill that can and must be developed through activism is critical thinking.

Learning through activism also helps children develop a sense of social justice, a sense of fairness and equity that begins with personal and community experience and extends globally and historically. It also empowers children and their families in concrete, authentic, replicable ways. It is not just about feeling good in the moment. Learning through activism recognizes and honors "everyday activists," which in turn cultivates more activism among students.

My students studied the history of voting rights and criteria for U.S. citizenship, including the abolition of slavery and women's suffrage (see Figure 6.1).

They studied the civil rights movement, with a focus on the participation of "everyday activists," especially children such as Sheyann Webb, and young people such as Bernice Johnson Reagon, a teenage

Figure 6.1 Essay by Yulia, a recent immigrant and English language learner

Elisabeth Cady Stahton worked for women to vote. She was really old, but she still tried to vote, even though the men threw her vote in the garbage. She got women to help her. Later, more women helped her. She said when this girl grows up, she will vote! When she died a lot of women were still fighting so every single woman could vote. When I grow up, I will vote.

civil rights activist and freedom singer who became a founding member of Sweet Honey in the Rock, an African American female a cappella group. I enjoy using the interviews conducted by children in the book *Oh, Freedom! Kids Talk About the Civil Rights Movement with the People Who Made It Happen* by King and Osborne. They also learned about the important role of music in the civil rights movement, for inspiration, courage, and solidarity. They learned to sing several songs from that movement, including their favorite, Jane Sapp's "Vote for Me." Students made their own posters and banners to hang in the school and neighborhood. They wrote announcements for the school newsletter, to publicize the drive.

One goal of the project was to increase student and family understanding of the right to vote, which is too often taken for granted and ignored. I focused on teaching the history of the struggle for the right to vote, with the realization that without the abolition of slavery, women's suffrage, the opportunity for immigrants to gain citizenship, the civil rights movement, and the Voting Rights Act, three-quarters of our class (girls, African Americans, immigrants, and Native Americans) would have been denied the right to vote as adults. Students were indignant about the injustice of that and were eager to educate others.

We also wanted to educate voters about their rights, so they would not be turned away from the polls. We did this by inviting an attorney to explain the Help America Vote Act. We learned how to register voters from the registrar, and in turn taught others. We publicized the deadline for voter registration and informed people who needed to reregister (i.e., those who had moved or had not responded to the city census). We also educated people about how to ask for and use a provisional ballot, if there was a problem.

Students who were not citizens got interested in how to become citizens. One student wrote a note to his mother, an attorney, asking her to explain how classmates adopted from other countries become citizens.

We got voter registration materials from the city registrar. Our class parent volunteers sent home a notice to the families and scheduled the family volunteers. We ran the voter registration drive at a table in the school lobby for a half hour on each of three mornings and afternoons, as staff and parents were coming and going. Each table had an average of four parent volunteers. A total of twenty parents volunteered; some volunteered two or more times. One parent would supervise a group of children wearing sandwich-board posters outside the school, inviting people inside to register. Our principal, and other adults who direct traffic in the parking lot, also wore posters.

Students politely approached adults to ask if they were registered to vote. If not, students asked if they were U.S. citizens, older than eighteen. If they were, they invited them to come to the table to learn how to register to vote. In addition to the twenty-two students from our class, three other first- and second-grade sisters volunteered regularly at the tables.

Juan's mother, Eneida Garcia, works at Casa Latina, a local organization that advocates for Latino community members. Between getting four boys out to school each morning and working full time, Eneida was unable to volunteer at the table, but she recruited Evelyn, a volunteer from Casa Latina, who came each morning. It was especially important for us to have a bilingual volunteer and registration materials in Spanish. One parent volunteer was so enthusiastic that she took voter registration forms to work and signed up three coworkers.

We wanted to reach parents of students at our school, as well as citizens of Northampton and surrounding communities. We were particularly hoping to register people of color and others who may have felt disenfranchised. We made posters in Spanish and English and posted them around the school, at the two apartment complexes across the street from the school, and at neighborhood stores. Of the thirty-six voters registered, about half were people of color and/or bilingual.

Some additional people took forms home to register a relative, neighbor, or coworker, but we did not count those unless they returned a completed form to us. More of those forms were probably mailed in. Hundreds of adults who were already registered to vote thanked our students for reminding them how important it is to vote. One student, whose mother had not registered to vote in twenty years, convinced her that this was the year to register and vote again. Dozens of people thanked us for holding the drive right in the school, because it was so convenient.

After completing the drive, the students rode the city bus downtown to deliver the completed voter registration cards to the registrar's office at city hall. Students were asked to prepare an exhibit for the mayor's office and wrote captions for a collection of drawings they had done titled "How to Register Voters." The registrar of voters, the mayor, and her staff were supportive. The evening before Election Day, students organized a reception at city hall to open the exhibit, followed by a candlelight vigil on the steps to encourage voter participation. The local director of the American Friends Service Committee assisted with the candlelight vigil, one of more than eighty nationwide that night, by providing candles and sending out a press release. About fifty people

Figure 6.2a and b Excerpts from the voter registration guide written by students

participated in the vigil. After the election, the students analyzed the results using the local newspaper, with a particular focus on understanding the arithmetic of the Electoral College.

Another goal of the voting rights project was to empower students and their families as active citizens participating in the democratic process by inviting lots of parental participation for the voter registration drive (volunteering at the tables), the field trip to city hall to meet the registrar and visit the mayor's office, the art exhibit reception and candlelight vigil. Most students and many parents have never been to the mayor's office. After visiting there twice, having their artwork exhibited there, organizing a vigil there, and receiving letters from the mayor and her staff, my students feel like they belong there, that they have access.

In addition to increasing interest in the election here in the United States, this project increased student interest in elections worldwide. That September and October, we had a Swiss teacher working in our classroom for three weeks and a British teacher in our classroom for a week. Our students were very interested to learn more about voting rights and participation in those countries. One of our students was Australian, and we learned from her mother that voting in Australia is compulsory. Those who fail to vote are actually fined.

Ripple Effects

Local news coverage of our voter registration drive got our students interested in newspaper reporting. With the volunteer help of parent and journalist Jo Glading-DiLorenzo, several other parents, and a grandmother, we launched a class newspaper called *The Peace Class News* (see appendix). The first issue had a story about the voter registration drive. The second had a story about the candlelight vigil on Election Eve. Our third issue had stories about the contested elections in Ukraine and the recount in Washington State. Students' work on the voter registration drive got them "tuned in" to voting and elections in an effective and ongoing way.

A favorite line from Jane Sapp's song "Vote for Me," sums it up when I hear my students sing, "Voting is more than a right, you see. Voting is your responsibility to ME!" My students are passionate about voting rights. Many parents told me stories of how their second graders would politely ask adult friends and relatives if they were registered to vote and if they were planning to vote—ready to meet any negative replies with instructions for how to register and a pep talk on the importance of voting.

Our voter registration drive was strictly nonpartisan. At this age, students' views most often mirror the political views of their parents. I encouraged families to engage in discussion of political topics with their children. From our discussion of current events in our morning meetings, it was clear that many of the students were engaging in lively political discussions at home. Students did come to understand that although it is good to engage in political debates with others, no one can tell someone else how to vote, and that all people have the right to keep their votes and their political opinions private if they so choose.

Students and their families came away from this project with the belief that social studies classes are very relevant. These students aren't looking at civics as some dry and dusty topic. They understand it is their duty as citizens to keep informed, think critically about issues, and participate actively in the electoral process, that democracy is not a spectator sport. Many parents said they wished they had learned social studies like this when they were students.

Students, families, and community members also came away very impressed at how effective our second graders were. In fact, many commented that the budget override vote in our city was defeated by *one* vote the previous spring. That story was very motivating to the students, who understood the difference even one vote could have in an election. The students also felt very empowered at how much they were able to do as seven-year-olds. They all said they would vote when they became old enough, and many were looking forward to participating in voter registration drives and political campaigning in the future.

These children and their families learned lessons about citizenship, democracy, and voting rights that will not easily fade or be forgotten, lessons that have changed their lives forever. These children learned not only important lessons about American history and civics, and rules about the Electoral College and recounts, but also how to make an effective poster, how to politely approach an adult and engage in effective dialog, how to speak to reporters and write their own news stories, how to talk to local politicians and attorneys, and how to target and reach particular constituencies in our community. Although they may not think of it in these terms, they know from their own experience what is possible. They have the skills, motivation, and confidence to be active citizens for life. Our voter registration drive was one of six school projects in the country to win an award from the national League of Women Voters for increasing parental and community involvement in the national election.

real-world recycling

One year my first and second graders were working on a science and technology unit about materials that can be recycled. We read *Just a Dream* by Chris Van Allsberg, a picture book about a futuristic dream through which a boy learns the importance of taking care of the environment.

We read other books about environmental activism, including *Hey, Get Off Our Train* by John Burningham, a great participatory read-aloud picture book, suitable even for preschoolers. The dreamy illustrations are delightful. Children love to join in on the refrain. It is dedicated to rain-forest activist Chico Mendes. His name, and the habitat-loss issue, led us to a book about the rain forest, *The Great Kapok Tree: A Tale of the Amazon Rain Forest* by Lynne Cherry, in which rain-forest animals attempt to persuade a tree cutter not to cut down their home. Cherry has another great book about water pollution, which I use for this unit as well as for studying the water cycle, *A River Ran Wild: An Environmental History,* also mentioned in Chapter 4. It focuses on the story of the Nashua River in New Hampshire and Massachusetts and how the river changed over hundreds of years, the eventual death of the river through pollution, and how it was revived and reclaimed through environmental activism and the passage of the Clean Water Act. *She's Wearing a Dead Bird on Her Head!* by Kathryn Lasky features Harriet Hemenway and Minna Hall, rather proper ladies who became passionate activists for the protection of birds and helped found the Audubon Society.

My goal for this unit was to change student as well as family behavior in relation to reducing, recycling, and reusing. However, I did not want all the families to end up cursing me for nurturing new obsessions in their children. I learned from my son that first graders are capable of quoting their teachers verbatim in the most annoying way, repeating, "But Miss Blahblah *said* . . ." Over the years, good-natured parents have informed me that I have unwittingly become an authority on subjects ranging from hand-washing protocols to sugar content in breakfast foods.

I had one student in particular, an intellectual, articulate boy named John, who would argue until he was blue in the face but do very little. John was in the habit of bossing his parents around, telling them, for example, "Carry my backpack!" I decided that role playing might be an effective way to go. To prepare, I spent a couple of days picking through the classroom trash and the recycling bins in my neighborhood to gather my props.

First, I chose a student to be the parent while I role played a child who was bossy, lazy, and self-righteous about recycling. "Mommy, you should compost those banana peels, you know. And you know it's dumb to waste all those paper towels when you clean up the juice I spill. You should use a rag or a sponge so you don't kill all those trees." I asked the student playing the parent how she felt. She said, "Like *Why don't you do it if you're so smart? Don't boss me around. Do it yourself!*" I asked the children if they thought that this parent's habits would change because of what I said. They thought they wouldn't.

I invited John to be the child in the next role play. As the parent, I pretended to pour him a glass of milk, then threw the plastic jug in the trash. He stood up all agitated. "There's a recycling symbol on that jug, you know."

"Oh yeah?" I replied, pretending to wash dishes.

"We could recycle it," he said.

"I guess so, but I'm busy. I have to go to a meeting tonight," I answered.

He scratched his head and nervously shifted his weight. "Just do it, John," a student whispered.

John took a deep breath and a resolute step toward the trash can. He pulled out the milk jug and walked to the pretend sink. "Excuse me, Mother. I'd like to rinse this out." I stepped aside while he made lots of *Pisssshhhhh* sound effects and then shook it out. "Uh, where's our recycling?" he thought out loud. He brought it to the recycling bin and dropped it in. "Oh, right! Crush it!" he told himself. He pulled it out, stomped on it thoroughly, and put it back in the bin. He nodded, looked at his classmates, and took a bow. As the parent, I said I felt inspired by his example and appreciated his help.

The role plays became a favorite activity as we continued the unit. They were often interspersed with problem-solving brainstorms. We debated the advantages and disadvantages of cloth versus disposable diapers, weighing laundry-water consumption against landfill use. We investigated the cost saving and environmental benefit of buying in bulk (yogurt, juice, snack foods) and repacking in washable plastic containers. We examined products and packaging to find out which companies used recycled paper to make their boxes or paper products, realizing it wouldn't do much good to recycle your own paper if you didn't support companies that used recycled paper. I sent home a family letter about the investigation and asked families to work together on three homework assignments about how the students could help their families reduce, reuse, and recycle. Here are some of their ideas:

"Carry our compost to our neighbors' compost pile."

"My brother can reuse some of my stuffs, like Step 1 books and baby toys."

"We can reuse plastic containers in lunch boxes."

"In the food store, do not ask for something that is wrapped in nonrecyclable material."

"We recycle clothes when we give our clothes to the Jesse's House." (Jesse's House is a local shelter for homeless families.)

"We can wash out Ziploc bags more."

We went downtown to visit the mayor to discuss local landfill and recycling matters with her. We met with a recycling expert while we were there. The children were shocked to learn that although Styrofoam often has a recycle symbol on it, it does not get recycled in our city.

One morning Maureen and her twin daughters, Eileen and Kaitlyn, came in from the free breakfast program in the cafeteria and said they were disturbed to notice that the school had started using Styrofoam trays instead of the regular plastic ones. They also noticed how many plastic utensils were being thrown away. We decided to ask Mr. Benoit, our custodian, to give our class a "waste tour" of our school. He showed us the trash Dumpster and the paper-recycling Dumpster and talked about how much waste our school produced each day. Eileen and Kaitlyn decided to gather data about waste in the breakfast program. They enlisted Maureen's help and recorded how many trash barrels of waste were produced each morning. Then they estimated how much using washable plastic trays and metal utensils and recycling plastic cereal bowls could reduce trash.

They wrote letters to the assistant superintendent, who was in charge of district purchasing, to find out what the school spends on waste disposal and recycling. They also wrote to the director of food services for the district to find out the costs of items such as Styrofoam trays and plastic utensils. They asked Mr. Martinez, a parent and classroom aide, if he would chat with the cafeteria workers to find out how the dishwasher worked in relation to plastic trays and metal utensils.

We were nearing the end of the school year and still had not received a response from the director of food services. The children asked me to call him. When I did, he apologized, saying he'd never received the letter, but he offered to come visit the class to discuss the issues.

While all of the first and second graders in our class that year had done the role playing, the family homework, and the field trip, this particular "recycling group" of about eight second graders, including Eileen, Kaitlyn, Sorny, John, Beth, and Nancy, had chosen to pursue the cafeteria investigation by gathering and charting the data, writing additional letters, and so forth. On the day of the visit, Nancy and the other members of the recycling group pushed two rectangular tables together to make a conference table, arranging little chairs all around it. They set up two easels to hold their charts and posters. They reviewed their questions and recommendations. A call came from the office, saying that Mr. Fenwick had arrived. I sent another student down to greet him.

Nancy gathered her group around and said quite seriously, "Look, even though we know we're right, we shouldn't scare him." The other students nodded in solemn agreement. A moment later, Mr. Fenwick filled the classroom door. I gulped. He was the size of a refrigerator. Nancy calmly walked over, shook his hand, then held it as she walked him over to the table and offered him a tiny chair beside the easels.

Nancy and the other students presented their data, asked their questions, listened to his answers, and presented their suggestions. Mr. Fenwick was not disrespectful, but he was brusque as he said that children are not careful in the cafeteria, that they dump metal utensils in the trash, that it is too expensive to keep replacing them. My students silently bristled at the stereotype that all children are careless about throwing their metal utensils in the trash, but Nancy promptly offered to organize a silverware drive at the school. He declined her offer. He said that if they used plastic lunch trays and metal utensils in the breakfast program, they'd have to pay someone to put them in the dishwasher and take them back out again. Beth pointed out that that could be a job for a parent who needed work. Besides, he said, he'd just purchased 10,000 Styrofoam trays.

In the end, Mr. Fenwick did not promise to make any of the changes the children suggested, but he said he'd consider them. When he left, Beth said, "You know, Ms. Cowhey, next time your kids do this, we have to try to think of even more what-ifs, like what if he says this or that." They did not feel defeated. In September, I had a new group of students. Mr. Fenwick got a new job somewhere else. The district never switched back to metal utensils or plastic trays.

A part of me felt disappointed. I wanted Mr. Fenwick to say, "Gosh, you're right! I'll return all those Styrofoam trays today! We'll go back to using plastic trays and we'll hire a parent to operate that dishwasher again." I guess I expected him to be kind to my students because they were so sincere, and had worked so hard researching this and . . . I hate to say it, because they were cute. He treated them brusquely, like . . . adults. Well, I supposed, it was good that he didn't treat them like children. He didn't condescend or tell them they were cute. They didn't cry or even take it personally. My students assumed that of course my next class of students and I would pick up the torch and continue the battle against Styrofoam trays the next year. The reality is that we didn't. The reality is that school years, no matter how packed they are or long they feel, ultimately come to an end. If I'm not looping, a new year brings new children and new interests and new projects.

So was it worth it? Yes. James Baldwin wrote, "Not everything that is faced can be changed. But nothing can be changed unless it is faced." My initial goal was to change student, and ideally, family, behavior in relation to rethinking, reducing, reusing, and recycling. By the end of the year, these kids were routinely rinsing yogurt cups and juice boxes to take them home to recycle. Parents replaced plastic spoons in lunch boxes with metal ones that kids brought home to wash. Parents were buying snack and lunch items in bulk, with less packaging. Many families told me stories about starting their own compost piles or arranging to contribute regularly to a neighbor's, as well as stories about children taking a much more active role in recycling and composting.

Were the efforts of the recycling group for naught? No. Our school has been participating in a composting program for about five years now. I think it started because someone at the vocational high school got a demonstration grant, not because of our efforts. Beth Bellavance-Grace, a parent from my class who works at our school as an aide, organized a schoolwide recycling program. Now we recycle paper, milk and juice cartons, yogurt cups, water bottles, soda cans, cell phones, and printer ink cartridges. Although my future classes never did resume the battle against Styrofoam food trays, my current students participate in composting and recycling, just as part of responsible citizenship in our school community.

Nancy and Beth demonstrated important lessons that day about gaining confidence by respecting and caring for your adversaries, instead of fearing or trying to intimidate them. That recycling group learned a lot about how to gather data through observation, inquiry, and correspondence. They learned how to represent data and articulate their arguments. They learned how to listen to an opponent, and they learned the value of thorough preparation. Although they didn't win the specific issue they tackled, they helped make our school a more environmentally conscious place in the long run. They are at the mid-

black ants and buddhists

dle school now, but the new second graders who sit in their tiny chairs today stand up responsibly to recycle our paper and milk cartons every day like it is the most natural routine in the world.

taking it to the playground

Sometimes children use skills developed through activism, such as persuasive letter writing, poster making, petition writing, and negotiation, to resolve conflicts on the playground.

One year I had a class with a lot of athletic kids who were very passionate about football. A group of students played football every day at recess. Inevitably, they came in angry and upset about losing, accusations of unfair team composition, getting injured, and getting screamed at for making mistakes or not knowing the rules. At one point, the boys "in charge" of the game had decided, "Anyone can play, but you have to know all the rules." Several girls and a boy who had just come from India felt excluded because they did not know the rules, although they were willing to learn. We discussed not excluding others and how the kids who knew the rules could explain them at the beginning of each game. After having invested a lot of instructional time to problem-solve this particular issue, I finally said they had to take a break from playing football, and we brainstormed other things they could do at recess. These ideas included wall ball, which could also be contentious.

Jack decided to write a nonfiction piece, which he published as a poster:

Ideas for Making Recess Easier and More Fun

Observation	Suggestion
People are sometimes getting yelled at when they are learning a game.	Teach the person the game if they don't know it.
Some people aren't allowed to join a game.	Let the person join the game and then rule 1.
In wall ball, some people catch the ball a lot.	If you catch the ball a lot, back up to let the other people catch the ball.
People are mad or sad during or at the end of recess.	Try to talk to the other person and compromise.

Jack presented his poster and hung it up in the classroom.

One day Ben brought in a petition he had written at home.

Dear Ms. Cowhey,

I want to know why we can't play football. We are not having too much fun, it's getting boring playing wall-ball, and we never get to work out how to include people in football. Could you give us another chance? I promise that we will include people, have fair teams and not have too much fighting. If you decide after this note that we still can't play football, I will feel very sad. Could you please read this out loud and see who else wants to sign it?

Love,

Ben

I read Ben's petition out loud at the morning meeting, and eleven other students signed it. I then asked students to remember why football playing had been stopped. They were quick to offer, "There was some pushing, and fights about fair teams and winning. Some felt left out and excluded. It was hard to get into the game. People got hurt. There were fights about rules and penalties. Talking about teams was distracting during work times in class. There was lots of crying because of injuries and hurt feelings."

Ramadan said, "*Now* I remember why we don't play football." I said we needed to try again to think of some solutions to respond to the petition. One suggestion was to make copies of Jack's poster and send them home for students to discuss with their families, and to review the poster before going outside. I had recently returned from a trip to visit schools in England and told the children what those playgrounds looked like. My students asked me to develop and bring in those pictures so they could get ideas for fun things to add to our playground for recess.

I told the children that I was not an expert on football because girls were not encouraged to play it when I was little and no one in my family played it, watched it, or went to games. Because of my lack of expertise, it was hard for me to understand, let alone resolve, some of their complicated arguments about rules and penalties. I reminded them that this was the playground, not the Super Bowl, and that we didn't have to play by strict and complex NFL rules. Perhaps we could find a simpler way to play so more people could learn and fewer playtimes would be lost to arguing. We wrote a letter to ask our physical education teacher to teach us a simpler version. I went with my class to the next few P.E.

classes to learn, and that was the football they played for the rest of the year.

Another year there was a dispute between some of my first-grade boys and girls over "the platform." This was a flat concrete slab about five feet square, raised about eight inches from the blacktop. A group of girls began to use the platform to play "baby" (a version of playing house) in which some girls were parents and the rest were babies who crawled around. Then a group of boys decided they wanted to use the platform too. This grew into a daily contest between the girls and boys. The girls became increasingly upset. They said the boys weren't really playing on the platform; they were just sitting there to keep the girls from using it. The girls wanted me to "make a rule" that the boys couldn't chase them off.

I said that I didn't particularly have jurisdiction over the platform, but that Ms. Agna, our principal, might. I said they would all have an opportunity to write a persuasive letter to Ms. Agna, clearly laying out their arguments in support of their proposed solution. The girls wrote letters developing their arguments in detail, describing their play, the advantages of the concrete platform over the wet grass for the crawling required by their pretend play, and so forth. During our discussions, the girls argued that the boys should be prohibited from using that space, but in their letters, they proposed that perhaps the platform could be used for "playing baby" and "relaxing" on alternate days. The boys wrote briefer letters, just saying they liked to relax on the platform, without any particular reasons why they needed that precise space. I noticed the boys looking over at the draft notebooks of the girls at their tables, and then developing their arguments and proposals a bit more. I stressed to them that Ms. Agna would bother to read only legible letters, because she's a busy person. Eventually they submitted their letters. Ms. Agna read them, then came and met with the class to determine an equitable solution.

thinking critically about causes

The question is not "Can you make a difference?" You already do make a difference. It's just a matter of what kind of a difference you want to make, during your life on this planet.

—Julia Butterfly Hill

One day Terrance, one of my second graders, brought in a news clipping about American schoolchildren who were holding a penny drive to buy

the freedom of Sudanese slaves. My students were shocked to learn that slavery still existed in the world. We looked at a map and found Sudan on the continent of Africa. They thought they might want to collect pennies. I told them that there was historic precedent for this. Muslims used to buy the freedom of slaves as a form of *zakah* (charity) during the holy season of Ramadan. Quakers used to sometimes buy slaves, such as Sojourner Truth, and release them. Nancy asked me to read the article again. It mentioned that some people had been captured as slaves two or three times. She said it would be sad if we bought freedom for a slave and then he or she got captured again. Then Beth asked who would get all those pennies. Would we be giving our money to slave traders? One student, sounding a bit like a parent, said that perhaps we shouldn't give money to the slave traders, or "we would only be encouraging them." Beth concluded, "It's bad if Africans buy slaves. It would be even worse if a bunch of Americans started buying them too."

The news article discussion got these first and second graders to think about the economic principle of supply and demand, as it applied to slavery. They were not able to think of a solution to the problem of slavery in Sudan, but they decided that giving money to slave traders could make the problem worse, so they did not participate in the penny drive.

This is an important point for activists of all ages. A critically thinking activist doesn't jump on every bandwagon that rolls into town. Realistically, no one can do everything. Critically speaking, not everything out there is worth doing. That is not to say that the things I decide against doing are "bad" things. Maybe the cause is just but the method is ineffective. Maybe the motivation for the project is dubious. Maybe the idea is good, but I have too many unanswered questions about how the organization operates or who it is affiliated with to feel comfortable working with it. Maybe the project is important, but the issue itself is too disturbing and developmentally inappropriate for the age of my students.

With something of a reputation as an activist teacher, I receive lots of suggestions, requests, invitations, and ideas about all kinds of projects, causes, and campaigns to work on with my students. I can't do them all, and I shouldn't do them all. Sometimes it is hard to sort out or pull back, especially if I have begun the project in some way.

One May our class received a short-notice invitation from the mayor's office to meet with Tony Lake, former national security adviser to President Clinton, about a children's campaign to eradicate land mines. It sounded official and important, and I was flattered that we were invited. Frankly, those factors distracted my critical-thinking process; I jumped on the logistical details, assuming that of course it would be good to go. Because of constraints imposed by the public bus schedule, the school lunch schedule, and the short time frame, I couldn't take the entire class to the 1:00 P.M. meeting. I wrote a letter to the families with a copy of the invitation and said they would be welcome to pick their children up early from class to take them to the meeting, as representatives of our class and reporters for *Peace Class News*.

About five families said they would take their children. Before they left, I did a short lesson about the issue of land mines, using a children's book by UNICEF called *A Life Like Mine: How Children Live Around the World*. I told them I first began to learn about the land mine issue when I saw an exhibit about it at the United Nations in 2001, and that I wondered why the United States had refused to sign the international treaty to ban the use of land mines.

As it turned out, Tony Lake was unable to attend the meeting, but the Peace Class representatives met with Perry Baltimore III, a representative of CHAMP (Children Against Mines Program) and Rosie, a mine-sniffing dog. They were given folders with literature and an informational CD and asked to collect quarters that would be used to purchase and train a mine-sniffing dog named Massachusetts.

When they returned to school the next day, my student reporters gave me the packet of information and told us about the meeting with great enthusiasm. Sophie had asked Mr. Baltimore why kids were raising money for mine-sniffing dogs if the United States hadn't signed the world treaty to ban the use of land mines. Mr. Baltimore said that Mr. Lake had gotten legislation passed banning the manufacture of land mines in the United States. (In fact, the United States still owns one of the largest stockpiles of land mines in the world.) Mr. Baltimore said that the United States wouldn't sign the treaty because "land mines are strategically necessary in some circumstances." I was starting to feel uneasy, like maybe I had made a mistake and rushed into this too fast.

I read through the material and previewed the informational video. The next day we watched it in class. Using our bias-detection skills, we noticed most of the people interviewed were White men in suits. Many of them had American flags hanging behind them. Only one was not American; he was from the United Nations. We noted that one man was from the U.S. State Department Office of Humanitarian De-mining, which is one of the primary sponsors of CHAMP. We noticed that Jody Williams, the American woman who founded the International Campaign to Ban Landmines and won the 1997 Nobel Peace Prize, was

not interviewed or even mentioned. There was a brief clip of Princess Diana visiting a minefield, but she was not interviewed or quoted.

I observed my students' reaction to the video: some were visibly frightened by the explosions and saddened by the land mine injuries. Our discussion demonstrated that some children were especially anxious about land mined African, Asian, and Central American countries where they were born or to which family members traveled, fearful for their safety. Feeling stupid and guilty for having proceeded that far already, I decided the topic of land mines was developmentally inappropriate and downright disturbing for some second graders. I also had a lot of questions about CHAMP, its sponsors, agenda, and purpose. We discussed this as a class and decided not to pursue this quarter-collecting campaign because of the developmental inappropriateness of the topic for elementary students and because we didn't feel like we'd gotten a good enough answer yet to Sophie's question.

One of Sophie's moms, Jo Glading-DiLorenzo, a professional journalist and publisher of our *Peace Class News,* was with us in class when we watched the CHAMP video and was there for that discussion. She and I talked about it when the kids went to lunch. As adult activists, we wanted to pursue it further to get at the underlying contradictions, but it was clear that pursuing it as a class would disturb some children. On the other hand, there were some children, like Jo's daughter, Sophie, who wanted to find out more about CHAMP and why the U.S. State Department was sponsoring this project. After many conversations, much debate, and soul-searching, we made a deliberate compromise. Jo volunteered to work with a small group of interested students to do some investigative reporting about CHAMP. I wouldn't teach about it any further as a topic, and we wouldn't participate in the campaign.

Through our interaction with CHAMP, my students learned that activists have to think critically, that smart activists don't jump on every cause. They learned to use their bias-detection skills to help them think about who is missing, who is talking and who is not, who is providing information and who is not, what information is given and what information is not. Rather than just learn to passively name continents on a world map, they learned to critically read maps and graphs, and to interpret the data on them while considering the source. Because their comprehension skills have been developed through the use of schema, they make connections between what they know and the new information being presented. Because they are used to going to city hall and meeting with community and political leaders, familiar and unfamiliar adults, they are empowered and confident enough to ask those adults challenging questions. Because their critical thinking has been consciously nurtured, they are in the habit of noticing and pursuing contradictions. They ask more questions, by e-mail, by letter, and in person, when the answers they're given don't make sense. They gain experience in investigative reporting and learn the importance of making and revising a plan in writing as their research helps them clarify where the real story is.

All of these are vital academic skills. Although children will not master them in second grade, they are not too young to begin to learn and use these skills. Will all of this raise their math and reading scores on standardized tests? It sure can't hurt. Will it make them more informed, articulate, active, and participatory citizens who know the power of their own voices? I think so. Is it subversive? What do you think?

teaching history so children will care

These are the feet of African slaves packed in the bottom of a ship.

What we do about history matters. The often repeated saying that those who forget the lessons of history are doomed to repeat them has a lot of truth in it. But what are the "lessons of history"? The very attempt at definition furnishes ground for new conflicts. History is not a recipe book; past events are never replicated in the present in quite the same way. Historical events are infinitely variable and their interpretations are a constantly shifting process. There are no certainties to be found in the past.

—Gerda Lerner

One year my students were investigating where racism came from, where people got the crazy idea that Whites were better than Blacks, and why anyone else believed it. We knew this idea had been around a long time, long before Rosa Parks and Martin Luther King Jr. We went back, back, back in history to the beginning of the slave trade. I read excerpts from a very powerful picture book by Julius Lester called From Slave Ship to Freedom Road, *illustrated by Rod Brown. The picture that most fascinated my students was one of rows of feet and tops of heads, slaves chained and stacked on shelves in the hold of a ship. (See work sample "These are the feet of African slaves packed in the bottom of a ship.")*

One day during indoor recess I noticed Jimmy knocking a whole bunch of books off the bottom of the bookshelf. This was unusual, because he often volunteered to straighten up the old nature encyclopedias. I was about to ask him what he was doing when I noticed he was talking to another student. "They did the slaves like this," he said, curling up and jamming himself into the bookshelf. "They did them like they was books!" Jimmy, a Puerto Rican second grader, was able to succinctly articulate the dehumanizing nature of racism.

Another time, months later, a reading group was presenting a lifesize Galapagos tortoise they had made from papier-mâché as part of their study of the Galapagos Islands. The assistant superintendent and several visitors from the State Department of Education had just "dropped in" for an unannounced visit. Jasper was explaining that explorers and pirates learned that the tortoises could live for up to a year without food or water. They stopped by the islands to catch them, and stacked them, live, in the holds of their ships, to provide fresh meat on long voyages. This practice pushed the giant tortoises to the brink of extinction. Jimmy shook his head in disgust at hearing this. He elbowed the kid next to him and said in a loud, serious whisper, "That's how they did the slaves." His neighbor nodded solemnly. The DOE visitors raised their eyebrows and cleared their throats. Jimmy was right, and he remembered.

• • •

On the first day of school last year, I noticed several parents who stayed for our morning meeting taking notes before the meeting even began. I wondered what they were writing, since I hadn't said anything yet. Later, one of them pointed to this Freire quote on the bulletin board and said she liked it so much she copied it down. The other scribblers said they had done the same:

1) The purpose of education in an unjust society is to bring about equality and justice.
2) Students must play an active part in the learning process.
3) Teachers and students are both simultaneously learners and producers of knowledge.
—Paulo Freire

That quote on my wall reminds me every day why I teach. I want to think and learn along with my students, so that they can feel the excitement of lifelong learning. I appreciate their insights, their abilities to synthesize and question, to struggle for truth and reason. I want my students to pursue questions that don't have easy answers.

I want to teach my students history as a contextualized story. I want them to learn a story with rough texture, complete with flaws and conflicts and complexities, not a slick, sealed, sanitized version. I want to share my passion for history and my experience as an organizer for social justice with six-, seven-, and eight-year-olds in a way that is meaningful, challenging, and developmentally appropriate. I hope to teach them to become educated consumers of history and current events, who consider the perspective of the author and the authenticity of the documents referenced. I want them to become confident, critical thinkers, eager to dive below the surface to find deeper meanings and connections. I want them to grow as people who not only can recognize injustice but are willing and able to take an effective, principled stand for justice.

Early in my teaching career I began to develop a six-week social studies unit on the theme of activism, but it developed into a yearlong curriculum. Although mostly related to social studies, the theme wends its way into math, science, art, music, reading, writing, morning meeting, philosophy, current events, and everything else. It is a generative curriculum. Students think critically, recognize injustice, study the words and deeds of activists famous, infamous, and obscure, and empower themselves to address issues of power, perspective, and privilege. As they do so, they begin to assert more power in relation to the curriculum, suggesting activities, events, and research questions. My hope is not that another teacher will attempt to implement the exact same curriculum again (I haven't even done that myself), but will be able to recognize contradictions and teachable moments as springboards for similar and additional lessons.

Usually history is taught from the perspective of powerful White men. We can rest assured that our students will get more than their fair share of that in their educational careers. I try turning history around, telling the story from the perspective of other groups whose voices we don't usually hear: Taínos,* Wampanoags, women, rebel slaves. I introduce them first. That seems like a small point, but it matters a lot. I've noticed that it is hard for student teachers to do that sometimes, that it doesn't feel like "starting at the beginning." In fact, it usually requires starting *before* what we traditionally think of as "the beginning" of the story. If that point is missed, the unit has gotten off on the wrong foot.

For instance, we begin by learning about ancient Taíno culture, the Arawak language, their lifeways, the rhythm of their lives, their spirituality. We develop a deep respect and caring for the Taíno people before I even introduce a single European. I repress the desire to even whisper "story of Columbus" or "Thanksgiving story." This is easier to do because I don't teach about the Taínos in October or the Wampanoags in November.

In teaching our students about Taíno spirituality one year, my student teacher and I decided to show a video about El Yunque rain forest, which was and is considered a very sacred place. The day after previewing the video, my student teacher proposed bringing in a bunch of smooth rocks so the children could make petroglyph drawings on them, like the petroglyphs they would see in the movie. I thought it wouldn't be very authentic, since the Taínos didn't draw with permanent markers but rather painstakingly pecked with sharp rocks. Furthermore, the Taínos didn't make them on pocket-sized smooth rocks but rather on huge boulders or rock faces, where they would watch the people forever. She argued that the kinesthetic experience of touching and choosing the rocks and the artistic experience of drawing the petroglyph motifs would deepen their learning. Plus, she had already dragged in a forty-pound box of smooth rocks she'd collected.

All right, my student teacher had made some good points and had taken some initiative on the lesson. I said she could do it if she and the children discussed how this experience was similar (authentic) to how

---

* The Arawak were the indigenous people Columbus encountered on Haiti, Borinquen (also called Boriken and later renamed Puerto Rico), Cuba, and other Caribbean islands. Archaeologists and anthropologists, tracing a trail of distinctive pottery, believe the Arawaks migrated from Venezuela north into the Caribbean in large canoes that could hold as many as 100 people. They continued to migrate to the northern islands to avoid contact with the hostile Caribs. The Arawak's own name for themselves is Taíno, which means "Good and Noble People." Taínos speak the Arawak language. Many historians prefer to use the term Arawak, or use Arawak interchangeably with Taíno. In my teaching, I prefer to use the name Taíno.

Figure 7.1 Student representation of Taíno life before European contact

Taínos made petroglyphs, how it was different (inauthentic), and our reasons for doing it this way (lack of boulders, and so on).

A few days after we watched the video and drew petroglyphs on rocks, we were wrapping up the portion of the unit about Taíno life before European contact. We asked the children to make captioned drawings about what they had learned. This was in a double class of first and second graders, many of whom were bilingual Puerto Rican students. As I hung up their drawings, I noticed that many of the children, particularly the Puerto Rican children, had not drawn the typical first-grade icon for the sun, a yellow circle in the corner or a yellow ball with rays. Instead, they had drawn the Taíno petroglyph for the sun. (See Figure 7.1.) There was no instruction to include petroglyphs in the drawing, but many children did it spontaneously. They did it because they had come to identify with the Taínos in the story we'd been learning.

In a later assignment to fold their papers in half to illustrate a Taíno perspective on one half and the perspective of Columbus and the Spaniards on the other, several children dictated the caption for the Taíno perspective in the first person or drew in little word bubbles to express how the Taínos might have felt. (See Figure 7.2.)

Figure 7.2 Two perspectives captioned drawing

Students' captioned drawings of Native American life before European contact, like these about Wampanoag life (see Figure 7.3), are rich in appreciation of Native technology and innovation. They also accurately identify the various roles of men, women, and children in society.

Sometimes we don't have access to as much information as we'd like. Our curriculum frameworks for social studies added "first settlements," including St. Augustine. Because we have no textbook, it meant finding materials and creating additional curriculum. My principal was going to travel to Florida, so I asked her to try to pick up any resources she could find about the First People of Florida. She brought back *The Crafts of Florida's First People* by Robin C. Brown, which contained a lot of interesting information about the use of indigenous plant fibers by the Calusa Indians who lived in Florida for 12,000 years before the Spanish arrived. I asked my student teacher, who was preparing lessons on this topic, to visit the plant house at Smith College to ask for samples of the plants so the children could actually see and touch the fibers used to make cord, string, rope, nets, and baskets. She brought in cotton bolls attached to their stems, sabal palm leaves and trunk fiber, palmetto leaves and stems, Spanish moss, and other plants native to Florida.

Figure 7.3 Captioned drawings accurately identify various roles

Wampanoag women are weeding their garden. The children are scaring away the crows.

This is a Wampanoag man killing a deer for meat, clothing and tools.

These Wampanoag fishermen are catching fish in a river.

We didn't have anywhere near as much information about Calusa life before European contact as we did about Wampanoags or Taínos, but we used the same approach to help children relate to the material life and culture. Even though it was a small unit, the children concluded, "It wasn't easy to live in Florida in those days, but the Calusa people figured out how to live there. The Spanish colonists were pretty miserable and could only survive if they had slaves. If they couldn't survive there on their own ability, they should have gone home."

using comprehension strategies: connections and categories

I explicitly teach children how to use schema theory as a comprehension strategy. Using the approach described in Keene and Zimmerman's *Mosaic of Thought,* I encourage children to make connections (text-to-text, text-to-self, and text-to-world) between different parts of the same historical story and between historical stories. This strategy becomes a critical tool for understanding history. For example, upon learning that the powerful Naragansetts sometimes attacked the plague-weakened Wampanoags, a student said, "I have a connection! Remember how the Caribs were fierce, and the Taínos were afraid of them?" This habit of making connections helps children identify patterns and parallels in history. Comparing and contrasting through the use of Venn diagrams is another way for children to grasp similarities and differences between different historical stories. Children began applying their mathematical ability to categorize and represent data in our history lessons.

During a social studies unit about slavery and abolition, we read excerpts from the correspondence between Benjamin Banneker, a brilliant free African American, and Thomas Jefferson. Banneker was a mathematician, inventor, surveyor, and astronomer. He was one of three surveyors who together planned and surveyed the nation's capital, Washington, D.C. He used his reputation to confront the hypocrisy of the White "founding fathers" who owned slaves while declaring, "We proclaim these truths to be self-evident, that all men are created equal; that they are endowed by their Creator with certain unalienable rights, and that among these are life, liberty and the pursuit of happiness."

This activity was a good opportunity to consult primary-source documents such as the Declaration of Independence and Banneker's letters. Here is an excerpt of Banneker's letter to Jefferson, written in 1791,

Figure 7.4 Resources about slavery and abolition

From Slave Ship to Freedom Road by Julius Lester, illustrated by Rod Brown. 1998. New York: Dial Books. A moving collection of paintings with text that includes meditations, provocative questions, and "imagination exercises."

Harriet and the Promised Land by Jacob Lawrence. 1997. New York: Aladdin Paperbacks. A powerfully illustrated brief biography of Harriet Tubman in verse.

Crossing the Danger Water: Three Hundred Years of African-American Writing, edited and with an introduction by Deirdre Mullane. 1993. New York: Doubleday. This useful reference book contains primary-source documents from Phillis Wheatley, Benjamin Banneker, Nat Turner, Frederick Douglass, Sojourner Truth, Harriet Tubman, and many others.

Behind Rebel Lines: The Incredible Story of Emma Edmonds, Civil War Spy by Seymour Reit. 1988. Orlando: Harcourt, Brace, Jovanovich. This chapter book describes the Civil War experiences of Emma Edmonds, who enlisted in the Union army disguised as a young man, served as a male nurse, and took on special assignments as a spy (sometimes disguised as a woman).

But, Sir, how pitiable it is to reflect, that although you were so fully convinced of the benevolence of the Father of Mankind, and of his equal and impartial distribution of these rights and privileges, which he hath conferred upon them, that you should at the same time counteract his mercies, in detaining by fraud and violence so numerous a part of my brethren, under groaning captivity, and cruel oppression, that you should at the same time be found guilty of that most criminal act which you professedly detested in others with respect to yourselves. (Mullane 1993, p. 48)

After lively discussion, first and second graders teamed up and wrote their own letters to Thomas Jefferson. This is a useful activity to encourage children to engage in a dialog or correspondence with historical characters. Although it is not authentic in the sense that they cannot mail these letters, it is a good springboard to writing letters and talking to political leaders about contemporary issues.

Thomas, a second grader, was shocked that Jefferson owned slaves. I told him that I too was surprised when I learned that, but that some historians say it was not unusual for rich White men like Washington

Figure 7.5 Beth's letter to Thomas Jefferson

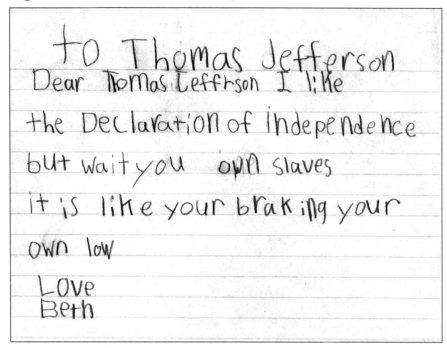

to Thomas Jefferson
Dear Tromas Leffrson I like
the Declaration of Independence
but wait you own slaves
it is like your braking your
own low
Love
Beth

and Jefferson in Virginia in those days to own slaves. He was even more shocked. "George Washington had slaves too?" I told him yes, that Washington let them go when he died. A couple of days later, during literacy workshop, Thomas asked if he could go to the office to photocopy pictures for some "research." Later, I observed him making a poster with a couple of other classmates. Under Thomas's headline "Slave Owners" they had pasted pictures of Thomas Jefferson, George Washington, and Columbus. They asked me to photocopy an excerpt from Columbus's letter to King Ferdinand and Queen Isabella about the Taínos: "They would make fine servants . . . With fifty men we could subjugate them all and make them do whatever we want." Under Jefferson's picture, Thomas wrote, "Wrote Declaration of Independence. And owned slaves."

Thomas hung his poster up. Other students were inspired. New posters were started every day and added to after they were hung up. The next one was "Abolitionists Who Also Worked for Women's Rights." Another was "Activist Schoolteachers," which included Maestro Rafael, a Puerto Rican activist teacher and folk hero about whom Angel Martinez, a parent and bilingual classroom aide, had taught us. They added Prudence Crandall, a White schoolteacher from Connecticut whose schoolhouse was burned to the ground after she refused to stop teaching African American children; she continued teaching even after the fire. Another was Susie King Taylor, an African American nurse who joined her husband's Union Army company; in addition to nursing the wounded, she taught African American soldiers to read every night. One student made a poster titled "Cross Dressers in the Civil War" that featured women who disguised themselves as men to serve in the Union army. According to Seymour Reit, author of *Behind Rebel Lines: The Incredible Story of Emma Edmonds, Civil War Spy,* historians estimate there were more than 400. The class favorite was the abovementioned Canadian-born Emma Edmonds, assigned as a male nurse who took on special duties as a spy; her most successful disguise was to dress as a woman to gather information as she crossed enemy lines to peddle goods in rebel camps or flirt with Confederate officers at southern parties.

A couple of months later we were studying money in math. Thomas was carefully examining coins and bills with other students at his table when I heard him exclaim, "Look at this! I can't believe it!" His table-mates leaned in to get a good look. "They put Jefferson's picture on the money! He got a nickel!"

"So?" a first grader asked. "All the money gots guys on it."

Thomas stood up and said, "But this guy said all men were created equal, and he owned slaves!" After a quick discussion at his table, Thomas and company decided they should protest this. Clearly, there'd been an error. Thomas wrote a letter to the U.S. Treasury informing them that Presidents Jefferson and Washington had been slave owners and should be taken off the money for that reason. He suggested replacing them with other heroes such as Frederick Douglass, Sojourner Truth, Lucretia Mott, and Benjamin Banneker.

These children actively engage with history. They interact with texts, copying photos and quotes to put on their posters. They are hungry for fascinating stories, stories about people who never made headlines, people who made unusual and brave decisions that make us wonder what we'd have done in their situations. Another comprehension strategy from *Mosaic of Thought* that we practiced was "questioning texts." This kind of active engagement leads children to generate their own research questions and ideas for their own nonfiction writing. Some of their questions included the following:

> How did it feel to be taken from Africa, make the trip, get sold at auction, and arrive on a plantation?
> Why were the slaves chained at the neck?

Why did the slave owners give a towel for clothes?

How did it feel to a runaway slave on the first day of running away?

Was Frederick Douglass born in Africa or on a slave plantation?

Why did people choose to have Blacks as slaves instead of Whites?

Where did slaves sleep when they ran way?

How many people were taken from Africa?

The tendency in elementary education has been to smooth over conflict rather than to explore it. This contributes to a general student perception that history is boring. In fact, it is the conflict that is most fascinating. Here is a piece of writing by Sorny, a second-grade English language learner.

Slaves Back in Time, Part 1

Part 1 Long ago, people were sold from their families and called slaves like Harriet Tubman, Sojourner Truth, even children were slaves. They *work* for their master very hard. Some of the slaves runs-aways from their masters to quakers. Because their masters treated them badly. Sometimes the masters would whip them and step on them. People think that Columbus was a hero but he wasn't because he brought 500 Taínos to Spain and when they got to Spain they died, "So he wasn't a hero!"

Sorny includes a lot of historic fact and details gained from read-alouds of picture books, discussion of primary-source documents, and independent reading. She names specific slaves. She knows that Quakers opposed slavery and provided a safe refuge for runaway slaves. She remembers that slaves were whipped and refers to a passage in which a slave-ship doctor recalled going down into the hold, which was so packed with chained slaves he had to step on people because there was no floor space. She pinpoints Columbus's pioneering role in the trans-Atlantic slave trade by reporting his shipment of 500 Taínos to Spain and weighs in on the debate of whether or not Columbus was a hero. In "Part II End Slavery!" Sorny continues,

People ended slavery by using their words. Some people used violence. They had a big meeting for blacks and whites. Finally it ended. (Word bubbles in illustration say "End it!" and "I hate slavery! Kill it!")

Writers and fighters: using debates to sort it out

In this section, Sorny refers to a debate we had in class on the topic "Who was more effective in ending slavery, the writers or the fighters?" We had read excerpts from Banneker's eloquent correspondence with Thomas Jefferson and an antislavery poem written to the Earl of Dartmouth, "No longer shall thou dread the iron chain . . ." written by Phillis Wheatley, a talented poet who was herself an African slave in the United States.

We also learned about violent resistance to slavery and uprisings by Nat Turner, John Brown, Sengbe (also called Cinquez) on the *Amistad,* Gabriel Prosser, and Denmark Vesey. (Gabriel Prosser was a slave who planned to attack Richmond, Virginia, in August 1800 with thousands of followers. He was betrayed. He and many other slaves were captured and hanged. Denmark Vesey was a carpenter who bought his own freedom. Vesey planned one of the largest slave revolts in history in Charleston, South Carolina, in 1822. He was also betrayed and executed with thirty-five other men.) I wanted the children to have some historical perspective in order to understand that when Dr. Martin Luther King Jr. took the path of nonviolence, it was a deliberate choice. He didn't have to choose it, as other activists before him had not all chosen nonviolence. As the debate began, many students said they thought the writers were more effective because "they were nicer" and "they used their words."

John seemed agitated during this part of the discussion, sputtering a lot before finally raising his hand and standing to speak. He was emphatic. "We are not talking about *nice.* The question is about who was more *effective* in ending slavery? *Effective,* that means who had more of an *effect.* Who read Benjamin Banneker's letter? Just Thomas Jefferson, and he probably was embarrassed and kept it a secret, and he still didn't free his slaves, so that wasn't really *effective.* Phillis Wheatley wrote that poem to the Earl of Dartmouth, but that didn't end slavery either. But just think about it. Nat Turner and a bunch of slaves get guns and start shooting White people. I don't *like* that they did that, but I'll bet lots of people heard about it. It got their attention. It had a bigger *effect.*"

Ultimately, they decided that neither the "writers" nor the "fighters" ended slavery. It didn't officially end until the passage of the Thirteenth Amendment, after the Civil War. The primary purpose of the Civil War had been to preserve the Union, not to end slavery.

We read a biography of Sojourner Truth, with a particular passage that described her shock and dismay when she heard her previously pacifist friend Frederick Douglass supporting a violent end to slavery. She stood up at a public meeting (this is probably what Sorny was referring to when she wrote "They had a big meeting for blacks and whites") and shouted out, "Frederick! Is your God dead?" If I had been Frederick Douglass speaking on stage, I think I would have fainted. These were terribly difficult times and choices. Sorny, a second-grade Khmer American girl, was able to capture much of the historical detail and tension in her writing.

Debates are a good way to bring children inside history. I read aloud *Squanto's Journey* by Joseph Bruchac. Then I read the student handout "Native Perspective on Thanksgiving" with information from *Unlearning Indian Stereotypes* (Council on Interracial Books for Children 1997). Next we organized a debate in the form of a hypothetical meeting among Wampanoags to decide whether to let the English newcomers stay or to drive them out. (This lesson idea is adapted from *The Wabanakis of Maine and the Maritimes: A Resource Book About Penobscot, Passamaquoddy, Maliseet, Micmac, and Abenaki Indians,* published by the Maine Indian Program, American Friends Service Committee. The student handout and additional lesson ideas can be found in *Beyond Heros and Holidays,* edited by Enid Lee, Deborah Menkart, and Margo Okazawa-Rey.)

One half thought about the arguments that might have been favored by Epinow (who had been kidnapped and taken to Europe as a slave) opposing any cooperation with the English. The other half thought about the arguments that might have been favored by Samoset (a Wabanaki man from Maine) and Tisquantum (Squanto, a Pawtuxet), both of whom also had been kidnapped and taken to Europe as slaves, and Massassoit, a Wampanoag *sakom* (leader). These men saw some benefit in letting the English stay. Each group brainstormed their reasons, which were recorded on a chart.

The two groups came together to begin the debate, with someone from each alternating side reading one reason at a time. Members of both sides were free to move toward the center or opposite side if they were moved by their opponents' argument and back toward their own side if they were in strong agreement with those. The extent of the movement of the children back and forth across the rug showed how difficult a debate this was. It wasn't a clear-cut "good guys/bad guys" scenario.

Here are some of the captions for student drawings made after the debate:

Figure 7.6a and b Contrasting student captioned drawings

This is a girl canoeing her boat on the ocean. We should let the English stay because they don't know a lot of stuff and Indians could teach them. And also because I am a white person.

We should make the English go away because they brought sickness that made our people die.

Adam: We should let the English stay because maybe they will let us use their guns.

Curtis: We shouldn't help the English or they might trick us into getting on their boat.

Natalie: We should make the English go away because they brought sickness that made our people die.

Mark: We should make the English go away because they started taking Indians as slaves.

Allan: We should not hurt the English or they might push us into the ocean.

Molly: This is a girl canoeing her boat on the ocean. We should let the English stay because they don't know a lot of stuff and Indians could teach them. And also because I am a white person.

Marietta: We should help the English because they're sick. We should take care of them with food.

David: We should let the English stay or else they will starve.

captioned drawings: getting a look inside

History is more engaging to children when they are given many different kinds of opportunities to engage with it. I use captioned drawings as an assessment tool, like a window to see and hear what the children are

Figure 7.7 Nancy's drawing of a Quaker and slaves

Quaker is helping slaves run away.

"getting" out of our studies. At the same time, they are an opportunity for the children to express deeply held feelings and work out aspects of their own identities.

See Figure 7.7 of Nancy's drawing. Nancy, a White girl, had been very upset about the behavior of White slave traders and owners but was encouraged when she learned about the role of the Quakers and other White allies in the Underground Railroad and the abolition movement.

Henry was a boy with a learning disability. He was fascinated by learning that Harriet Tubman suffered blackouts that could last from minutes to hours. The blackouts left her and the runaway slaves she guided vulnerable to the trackers who were always after them. Henry was intrigued that a person with such a serious disability was so brave and capable and that so many people depended on her. (See Figure 7.8.) By identifying with positive, activist role models who were in some way like them, Nancy and Henry were able to put themselves into the story in a very personal way.

Although the drawings of first graders may often be rather scribbled and populated by stick figures, they can still be quite expressive. Children are free to write their own words if they wish, and stronger

Figure 7.8 "These are slaves waiting for Harriet Tubman to wake up from being unconscious."

writers (especially second graders) often do. In this activity I am trying to assess their thinking, not their writing ability, and I don't want the communication of their ideas to be limited in any way by their writing ability. My student teachers and I try to record their words as precisely as possible in English or Spanish, without editing. The captions they dictate are often quite powerful.

Diana's said, "There was a war with the English. If I was Wampanoag, I would die for my people." These children are not bored bystanders in history. They have put themselves into the story and care deeply about the outcome. Jimmy's drawing about the King Phillip's War was simple and his dictated caption was striking. "The English put Metacomet's head on a stick. If that was me I'd be crying in heaven."

Whenever I teach Native American history, I always approach the story in three parts: before European contact, at the point of and soon after European contact, and contemporary Native American life. Although millions of Native Americans did die as a result of slavery, violence, forced relocation, and disease, the misconception that all Native Americans are dead could reinforce acceptance of the status quo and rationalize arguments against reparations and ongoing struggles for justice. I've learned it is equally critical for me to teach about Native American survival, resilience, and continuity. I strive in my teaching to recognize and honor the presence, scholarship, leadership, and participation of Native Americans in our community, region, country, and continent. For example, in our study of the Wampanoag, I use news clippings about Wampanoag linguists teaching and reviving their native language, about Day of Mourning protests and demonstrations, about legal victories, and living traditions. I use a book called *Clambake: A Wampanoag Tradition* by Russell Peters, illustrated with photos, about his contemporary Wampanoag family having a traditional clambake.

I don't teach this entire history curriculum every year, and I never teach it exactly the same way. One reason is that if I taught the same exact thing every year, I wouldn't be taking an active part in the learning process. I would only be teaching. The way I look at it, I'd be doing only half my job.

I hope these stories have let you see students, teachers, and student teachers all working together as "learners and producers of knowledge" as the children take initiative to make posters, write letters, draw, share stories, and ask questions.

I love history because it is about story. When I introduce the subject of history to a class for the first time, I purposely pronounce it *hiSTORY*, emphasizing the word *story* within history. I believe that learning and sharing stories, especially stories that involve conflict, can bring history home for children. Comprehension strategies like using schema theory to make connections or questioning texts to generate research ideas can also help children think more critically about history.

I introduce characters we don't usually see, explore perspectives we don't usually consider, listen to voices we don't usually hear to provide my students with more "ways in" to history. I help them find their own ways to identify with active players in history. Jimmy related to African slaves packed in the hold of a ship in the Middle Passage and Metacomet (King Phillip), the Wampanoag leader. Nancy related to Quaker conductors on the Underground Railroad. Henry identified with Harriet Tubman, who, like him, had a disability. I share powerful images, stories, songs, poems, speeches, artifacts, and other primary-source documents with children. I study their drawings, watch them play, write their dictated words exactly, read their stories, and *listen* to them to see what resonates.

We can teach to bring about equality and justice. We can start by teaching history so children will care.

nurturing history detectives

People always seem to know half of history, and to get it confused with the other half.

—Jane Haddam

About 1000 years ago, the Vikings went to North America. They were tough.

O ne year, in the middle of my unit on explorers, a petite Puerto Rican second grader named Diana stopped me in my tracks. I had made a poster of Bartolomé de Las Casas's Taíno population figures on the island of Haiti, to document the effect of the European contact.* It began with a preColumbian estimated population of 8 million. By 1496, 1 to 3 million Taínos were left alive on the island. According to Bartolome de Las Casas, there were only 200 Taínos left alive in 1542, and by 1555 the Taíno population was zero. We reviewed the shrinking numbers on the chart, looking for patterns. Suddenly, Diana stood up and shouted, "That's not true, Ms. Cowhey! I know it isn't true!"

I quickly checked my reference, Lies My Teacher Told Me by James Loewen, to make sure I had my facts straight. I asked, "What part do you disagree with?"

"The numbers! That zero!" she said.

I touched the zero on the chart. "Why do you disagree?"

Diana slapped her tiny chest for emphasis and shouted, "'Cause there's me! 'Cause I'm alive!"

"Diana, you are so right," I said after a moment. Facts rushed through my mind, that de Las Casas's statistics were for Haiti, not Borinquen/Puerto Rico, but I said, "He couldn't have counted them all. Some hid in the mountains and others escaped, and there were more still living in Borinquen, where some of your ancestors lived. Your Taíno ancestors survived." I thought to myself, "Thank God your Taíno ancestors survived." I teach for moments like this, when students are smart, sharp, and confident enough to question the teacher, to question the books, to pose counter-examples that speak their truth.**

how do you get at the truth in history?

The reality is that much of what passes for history in elementary classrooms would be more accurately categorized as historical myths. These are oversimplified, sanitized, domesticated little stories, at home out of

---

* Bartolomé de Las Casas was a young Spanish priest who came to Hispañola early in the conquest; he owned a plantation worked by Taíno slaves. He later gave up his plantation and became an outspoken critic of Spanish exploitation and cruelty. His extensive writing both documented and criticized the Spanish invasion of the Caribbean.

** This exchange with Diana prompted me to do additional research. I learned that in fact there are isolated villages such as Caridad de los Indios and Rio Toa in remote mountainous areas of Cuba where 2,000 Taínos still live today (Ciment 1996, p. 24).

For more information on contemporary Taíno life and heritage, visit the Web site of the Jatibonicu Taíno Tribal Nation or Boriken at www.taino-tribe.org/jatiboni.html.

context, tidy bits associated with particular holidays in picture-postcard fashion with familiar one-liner captions like, "Columbus discovered America in 1492," "The Pilgrims shared their Thanksgiving feast with the Indians," and "Lincoln freed the slaves." This is the introduction to history that many elementary students receive. It's the history I was taught in the 1960s. I read an article in November 2004 about a first-grade class at a school in a nearby town doing a Thanksgiving play with construction-paper feather headdresses. The myth lives on.

I remember learning that "Columbus discovered America" in fourth grade, obediently reciting the rhyme, "In 1492, Columbus sailed the ocean blue." We learned that Columbus gave "beads and trinkets" to "friendly Indians," but we never found out what happened to all those "friendly Indians." We were not encouraged to ask questions. We were taught that Columbus was smart and brave, that he alone believed the world was round while everyone else thought it was as flat as a table and feared sailing off the edge.

We were taught that Columbus sailed the *Niña,* the *Pinta,* and the *Santa Maria* to the New World. I asked how they got home to Spain. "They sailed, of course," was the answer. I remember asking if the wind blew them *west* from Spain to the New World, how the same wind could blow them back *east* again, because you can't just make the wind change direction. "Well, it did," my teacher answered.

How could the wind blow him home? I was not satisfied. I brought this up at dinner. My father sternly told me not to contradict my teachers. My mother, however, bought me stamps and helium balloons. I began to write stamped, self-addressed postcards and attach them to helium balloons launched from my Long Island home, asking the finders to mail the postcards back to me, saying where they had landed. I got a few postcards back from Connecticut and may have unwittingly choked a few sea mammals in the course of my historical experiment, but I was unconvinced that the wind blew back to Spain. I shared my findings with my teacher, who was pointedly disinterested; we were *finished* with Columbus. October was *so* over. "It was the currents," she said dismissively.

"The *ocean* currents?" I asked.

"Yes, of course," she said, obviously annoyed.

I doubted this as well, because every time I went to the beach, the waves were heading toward me. On the other hand, I had also experienced the scary sensation of being pulled out by the undertow, which was clearly flowing away from the shore. I decided I would test this idea. I wrote more postcards and sealed them up in bottles. It was late autumn. My mother gave me stamps and drove me to Jones Beach. I threw those bottles as hard as I could over the waves, again and again, until the ocean finally took them away. Late that winter I got back a couple of postcards from eastern Long Island. I didn't get any postcards from Europe. I did not bother the teacher with my findings. History was a lonely business for a skeptical nine-year-old.

Whenever I teach about Columbus, I tell my students that story of my early historical experiments. Then I show them how wind and ocean currents are marked on the globe, and tell them that those currents are created by the spinning of the Earth. Together we wonder if Columbus just had to wander around for a while before discovering the currents that would bring him east toward home, because they wouldn't have been marked on a map already.

I also read my students *Captain Bill Pinkney's Journey* by Bill Pinkney, about an African American sailor who circumnavigated the globe alone in 1992. I use this book to help children grow accustomed to tracing routes on maps and globes, noting continents and oceans and looking for the ocean and wind currents along his route. I tell them they can meet him as I did aboard the historic *Amistad,* which he now sails, when it is docked in New Haven, Connecticut.

My point here is that sailing and navigation (which I know relatively little about) is difficult work, requiring a sophisticated understanding of mathematics, geography, weather, wind, and ocean currents. In 2005 we invited Ella's father, Doug McDonald, who grew up sailing, to come teach us more about those currents. He told the students stories about things that had been carried by currents, like a shipping container full of bath toys, including lots of yellow rubber ducks, that washed overboard in a storm. Eric Carle's *10 Little Rubber Ducks* includes a news clipping about the bath-toy container. The picture book explores this idea of how ocean currents move. Using large maps on which Doug and Ella had drawn the ocean currents in red and the wind currents in blue, we predicted and tracked the routes of the rubber ducks, and explorers from the Phoenecians and St. Brendan to Columbus and Magellan, all the way up to Ellen MacArthur, who sailed around the world solo in a record-setting seventy-two days in 2005. Sailing and navigating are not as simple as getting in a car and driving west on a highway. I can respect Columbus for his awesome navigation and sailing ability.

On the other hand, Columbus committed some heinous acts. On his first trip back to Spain, he kidnapped between six and twenty-five Taínos; few of them survived the journey. In *Lies My Teacher Told Me,*

James Loewen describes Columbus's role in beginning the trans-Atlantic slave trade. By 1495, Columbus still hadn't brought back much luxurious loot in the way of gold and spices. Needing to bring some product back for his benefactors, he and his men conducted a huge slave raid on Haiti. They seized 1,500 Taíno men, women, and children. He kidnapped 500 of these to sell as slaves in Spain. Two hundred of them died on the way there. The Spaniards kept another 500 for use as slaves on Haiti. The rest were released. A Spanish eyewitness described the Taínos as so terrorized that women dropped their infants on the ground and ran for their lives, running for seven or eight days' journey, across mountains and rivers, to get away from the Spanish (Loewen 1995, p. 56).

Columbus wrote to King Ferdinand and Queen Isabella in 1496 that he could send all the slaves that could be sold. "Although they die now, they will not always die. The Negroes and Canary Islanders died at first" (Loewen 1995, p. 52, quoted from a 1496 letter from Columbus, quoted in Eric Williams, *Documents of West Indian History*).

In 1496, a religious debate over the enslavement of Taínos was resolved with the decision that slavery was justified if the slaves were prisoners of war. The colonists began to deliberately provoke the Taínos in order to arrest and enslave them. Under this new policy, 300 Taínos were immediately arrested and sent to Spain for sale as slaves (Jacobs 1992 p. 61).

In addition to exporting 5,000 Taíno slaves (more than any other individual), Columbus instituted first a tribute system, in which all people over the age of fourteen in the gold-mine areas had to turn in a certain amount of gold every three months in exchange for a token, to be worn around their necks. Those Taínos without fresh tokens were punished: the Spanish cut off their hands.

When that system failed, the Spanish set up a forced labor system called *encomienda,* in which whole Taíno villages were granted to colonists. Both the tribute and the *encomienda* systems reduced the Taíno population dramatically. As a result of de Las Casas's persuasion, new laws he drafted to protect the Taínos were enacted in 1516. The laws, to free the Taínos, end the *encomienda* system, and provide Christian religious education for the Taínos, were to be enforced by Jeronymite monks. The colonists protested that their farms and mines would not be profitable without forced labor and the Spanish colony would be abandoned. A compromise was reached in 1518: to import African slaves, thus opening the door to centuries of African slavery in the Americas (Jacobs 1992 pp. 88–90).

Posing forced relocation and religious conversion as a kinder and gentler alternative to slavery and murder, the Spanish had constructed thirty villages by 1519. They planned to relocate the freed Taínos to those, but another smallpox epidemic wiped out half of the remaining Taíno population. The Taíno population on Haiti was estimated to be about 8 million before Columbus's arrival. By 1548, fewer than 500 pure-blooded Taínos remained. Bartolomé de Las Casas reported that by 1555, they were gone. Columbus was not only a deceptive and greedy slave trader, but responsible for genocide.

The curricular requirement to teach first graders about national holidays and heroes and second graders about explorers gave my students and me an opportunity to question what we think we know, consider multiple perspectives, and search for the truth in history. Of course, any aspect of American history (early colonization, westward expansion, and so forth) that has been elevated to the pedestal of historical myth lends itself well to this kind of critical study.

To be honest, I don't much like the idea of teaching "the explorers." I was hard-pressed to name my favorite explorer. Then in 2002, I met the Arctic explorer Ann Bancroft and heard about her expedition, skiing across the continent of Antarctica with another woman, Liv Arneson. Now I feel like I have positive and powerful role models to whom I can refer, women who exemplify the positive ideals of exploration.

To introduce the unit on exploration, I read aloud picture books about contemporary and recent explorers and adventurers, to teach and illustrate the vocabulary. I read *Ann and Liv Cross Antarctica,* a picture book by Ryan and Arnesen about Bancroft and Arnesen. They each pulled 250-pound sleds loaded with supplies as they skied and windsailed to cross the continent of Antarctica in 2001. We notice that they did not carry weapons, fight with or hurt anyone, and didn't take anything but data (such as the temperature and notes on the weather) and pictures.

When we do study explorers, I find it more useful to focus deeply on deconstructing the Columbus story than to do a superficial survey of a long list of European explorers. I take some time to have the students consider historical theories of pre-Columbian explorers. Using a table from *Lies My Teacher Told Me* (see Figure 8.1), I mention the date, national origin, destination, and some historical evidence in support of various theories. I ask the students to confer with their table groups and vote whether they think that theory is likely, unlikely, or possible.

For example, my students thought that Afro-Phoenician seafarers may have reached the Atlantic coast of Mexico around 750 B.C., because

Figure 8.1 Explorers of the Americas from *Lies My Teacher Told Me*

Year	From	To	Quality of Evidence
70,000? B.C.–12,000? B.C.	Siberia	Alaska	High: the survivors peopled the Americas.
6000? B.C.–1500? B.C.	Indonesia	South America	Moderate: similarities in blowguns, papermaking, etc.
5000? B.C.	Japan	Ecuador	Moderate: similar pottery, fishing styles.
10,000? B.C.–600? B.C.	Siberia	Canada, New Mexico	High: Navajos and Crees resemble each other culturally, differ from other Indians.
9000? B.C. to present	Siberia	Alaska	High: continuing contact by Inuits across Bering Sea.
1000 B.C.	China	Central America	Low: Chinese legend; cultural similarities.
1000 B.C.–300 A.D.	Afro-Phoenicia	Central America	Moderate: Negroid and Caucasoid likenesses in sculpture and ceramics, Arab history, etc.
500 B.C.	Phoenicia, Celtic Britain	New England, perhaps elsewhere	Low: megaliths, possible similarities in script and language.
600 A.D.	Ireland, via Iceland	Newfoundland? West Indies?	Low: legends of St. Brendan, written c. 850 A.D., confirmed by Norse sagas.
1000–1350	Greenland, Iceland	Labrador, Baffin Land, Newfoundland, Nova Scotia, possibly Cape Cod and further south	High: oral sagas, confirmed by archaeology on Newfoundland.
1311?–1460?	West Africa	Haiti, Panama, possibly Brazil	Moderate: Portuguese sources in West Africa, Columbus on Haiti, Balboa in Panama.
c. 1460	Portugal	Newfoundland? Brazil?	Low: inference from Portuguese sources and actions.
1375?–1491	Basque Spain	Newfoundland coast	Low: cryptic historical sources.
1481–91	Bristol, England	Newfoundland coast	Low: cryptic historical sources.
1492	Spain	Caribbean, including Haiti	High: historical sources.

Figure 8.2 Olmec Indian carving

An Olmec Indian is carving a huge stone head in Mexico. The faces look African.

of the presence of the "Olmec heads," large stone carvings with strikingly Negroid features (see Figure 8.2).

They thought the theory of Viking exploration of North America was likely, because of legends and archaeological evidence of settlements. I told them about the legend of St. Brendan, an Irish abbot, and seventeen monks who traveled for seven years in a leather boat. According to legend, they visited a pillar of crystal and an island of fire and said Mass on the back of a whale. That story quickly got the thumbs-down (unlikely) vote (see Figure 8.3).

I then showed them pictures of Iceland, a volcanic island, and pictures of icebergs, asking if those might look like an island of fire and pillars of crystal. I told them about a small village I had visited on the North Atlantic coast of Canada called Tète á la Baleine (Whale Head) because of a big rock there that looks like a whale rising out of the water. I showed them a 1977 *National Geographic* magazine article by Tim Severin, one of five contemporary explorers who built a leather boat according to the legend's specifications and successfully reenacted the journey. After lively discussion in all of their small groups, my students voted again; many teams decided the St. Brendan story was "likely."

• • •

Figure 8.3 Student depiction of "unlikely" legend

I don't believe the legend of St. Brendan because there couldn't be an island of fire. An island is in water, and water puts out fire.

We talked about why, if even a few of the dozen or more historical theories of pre-Columbian exploration of North, Central, and South America are true, Columbus gets credit for "discovering America." This led to an interesting discussion about the difference between *exploration* for the sake of knowledge and understanding, and *conquest* for the sake of domination and exploitation.

provoking "furious debate"

Loewen defines history as "furious debate informed by evidence and reason" (1995, p. 5). So how do you begin to get at the truth in history? First, I must begin with humility. This is not to say that I have not studied history; it is to acknowledge that the history I studied may have been inaccurate. I had to begin to study history anew, with a fresh mind and new eyes. Many teachers find it hard to let go of authoritatively knowing, but that is the first step, to model for my students how to ask really big and hard questions. I encourage them to do the same. For example, Thomas's list of research questions included "Why did Chris go to get spices for the queen anyway?"

To bring children inside that "furious debate" I structure many activities like these that encourage them to look at a historical incident from different perspectives.

In my weekly letters home to the families, I always write about what we are learning. Shortly after we discussed the Vikings and other pre-Columbian explorers, Calvin brought in an article about a controversy over the authenticity of a Viking map. Other families brought in old issues of *National Geographic* or current news clippings relevant to our studies. This demonstrates to the children that the study of history is collaborative and ongoing. It should not be as passive as listening to a teacher's lecture or as lonely as a little girl throwing notes in bottles into the surf. It should be the stuff of lively dinnertime conversations and excited sharing of news in the morning meeting.

When I introduce any new content-area topic, I work with the students to make charts of vocabulary words we will use. Precise language is important. In a unit on Columbus and exploration, the chart might include *discover, meet, visit, explore, invade, conquer, trade, take, steal, share, bring,* and *capture*. We develop definitions for those vocabulary words and frequently consult the chart to check on the accuracy of the language we read, write, and speak. I describe various scenarios, such as, "Your mom calls your aunt who lives nearby and invites her to come for dinner. That evening, you hear the doorbell ring. When you answer the door, you see your aunt and cousins on the doorstep, and your aunt is carrying a cake for dessert. What is your aunt coming to do?" The children discuss the scenario and vocabulary, and after a bit of arguing about whether or not the aunt already knows you or has been to your house before, or if she is nice, they usually decide the aunt is coming to *visit* and *share* her cake.

• • •

After developing vocabulary and a bit of context for exploration, we focus on the life and culture of the indigenous people, the Taínos in this case, and the landscape before European contact. (See Chapter 7.) Once the children have established a solid appreciation of the people and place, assessed through captioned drawings, writings, and artwork, we move into picture books about Columbus. Here is a description about how this part of the unit unfolded one year with a class of first and second graders. (Also see the appendix for a sample progression of twenty-five lessons and a listing of classroom resources.)

I began by reading a traditional/heroic version of the Columbus story of the "In 1492 Columbus sailed the ocean blue" variety to my first and second graders. Later in the day, I read them *Encounter* by Jane Yolen, which tells the story of Columbus's encounter with the Taínos from the perspective of a fictional Taíno boy. Then I asked them which story was true. The first student said *Encounter* was more true because it was bigger and had a hard cover. One student said *Encounter* must be true, because I got choked up and cried a little when I read it. A bias-detection expert in the group guessed that *Encounter* was true because she thought I liked it better. I asked how they could really find out which book was truer. They suggested looking in more books. I said that most of the books in our school library were like the heroic one. Did that make that version truer? They suggested asking another teacher. I said that some people might know only the heroic story, or that some teachers might only feel comfortable teaching what they were taught. If more teachers knew only the heroic story, would that make it true? (I now use *A Coyote Columbus Story* by Thomas King.)

The children were curious. They wanted to know, "How do you get at the truth in history?" I told them that this was an excellent question, asked by bright historians. We talked about how just reading or listening to history and believing everything you hear is often misleading and frequently boring, and how most people quickly forget about it when they learn history that way. I told them we would be looking for the contradictions and mysteries in history. To solve those mysteries, to try to get at the truth in history, we would look for evidence, in the form of primary-source documents. I encouraged them to question teachers as well as books for the evidence.

We got back to Columbus. "Who would really know what happened?" I asked them. A first grader suggested we "go to the videotape" like they do in football games on television. Another student said they probably didn't have television that long ago. No problem, the first student replied, we could just check the photographs. A second grader pointed out that cameras hadn't been invented yet either. Of course, some first graders ask me if there were cars when I was a little girl, so chronology in general is hard for first graders to wrap their heads around, let alone the history of technology. A student finally suggested we write to Columbus to ask him. Another said that he was dead. Maybe he wrote something down, another wondered.

We began to discuss primary-source documents, which, as history detectives, we would call evidence for short. Videotapes and photographs are primary-source documents, as are letters and journal entries. I told them that Columbus did keep a journal and wrote letters to the king and queen of Spain. I told them that historians who study Columbus actually go back and read his journal and letters. Then a student asked, "But what if he lied? Like what if you did something bad and you knew it was bad, you wouldn't write it down, would you? He probably wanted to make himself look good."

This was indeed perplexing. More discussion. Eventually someone suggested interviewing some Taínos and some of the Spanish sailors. Again the question of lying was raised and that troubling detail about all the witnesses being dead. Another student pressed on, "But if you could ask enough of them, you could probably figure out most of the truth, even if some of them were lying."

I told them about Sonia Nieto's question, always remembering to ask, "Who wrote the book?" We started discussing the importance of historians using primary-source documents.

We paused for a brief historical experiment. I asked three students to act as witnesses by standing in different spots in the room. Then I whispered instructions for another student to walk outside the classroom, reenter, and do a few things as he walked across the room. Next we sent two of the witnesses out and asked the third to report her story. I wrote it on chart paper, then covered it and repeated the process with the other two witnesses. We noticed variations in the stories, with one reporting that our "actor" had stopped near the bookshelf, another saying he had picked up a book, and another naming titles of two books he had picked up. The students agreed that none of our witnesses had a reason to lie, that telling the story a certain way in this case wouldn't make them look good or bad. Then why, I wondered aloud, didn't they report the same exact story?

The students explained that the witnesses spoke in their own words. They were standing in different spots and paid more attention to certain things. For example, the witness who noticed the titles of the two books that the actor picked up was not closest to the bookshelf, but was a good reader who liked books. I explained that historians call this gathering stories from different witnesses "looking for multiple perspectives," just like their idea to interview Taínos and Spanish sailors, in addition to reading Columbus's letters and journal.

To end our experiment, I asked each witness, then the class in general, to think of a reason to explain why our actor did what he did as he walked across our classroom. Some theories were simple: "He was looking for a good book to read." Others were more elaborate: "He heard the sounds of children playing outside. He was walking over to the window to look out to see if the fifth graders were out at recess, because he wanted to see if he could see his brother playing kickball. He just got a little distracted by the books on his way to the window." We talked about theories and how much evidence there was to support them.

Students agreed that there could be more than one theory and that one or none of them might be true.

A week or so later, after we had deconstructed the Columbus myth more thoroughly, we were discussing whether Columbus was a hero and whether he was brave. A first grader said that a hero has to be brave and good, so he concluded that Columbus probably was brave but not a hero. Later in that discussion, a student asked how come Columbus got a holiday, when he had kidnapped and enslaved people. A second grader named Thomas was outraged and thought they should rally to get Columbus Day canceled as a holiday. One student said, "Well, I don't think Columbus was a hero, but I think it's cool we get the day off from school."

Thomas brightened. "That's it! I think we should all come to school in protest!" We had a brief discussion about how teach-ins were used as a form of protest against the Vietnam War in the 1960s.

Then a realist in the group said, "Thomas, the school's gonna be all locked up. It's gonna be closed!"

Thomas's lip began to tremble as he considered the problem. Then he shot his fist up in the air and shouted, "Ms. Cowhey will unlock the doors!"

Over the years since then, inspired by Thomas's confidence, I have worked to build a repertoire of "teach-in" activities that I can use with my students. There's a good song by Nancy Shimmel called "1492," which asks, "How could anyone discover the spot when someone was already here?" My class prefers to replace "Caribs" in the lyrics with "Taínos." The lyrics are in *Rethinking Columbus* edited by Bill Bigelow and Bob Peterson, and the recording is available on a wonderful CD put out by Teaching Tolerance called *I Will Be Your Friend.* The CD and songbook (one per school) are available free from Teaching Tolerance (www.teachingtolerance.org).

simulating an invasion: the students respond

Another one of these activities that I heard about years ago was telling a story or role playing a simulation about an alien invasion. I usually tell a hypothetical story about a spaceship landing. Aliens walk into your house without knocking, eat the food you offer, and then start to take food out of your refrigerator without asking. They play with your toys, give you some little beads and bells, then take your toys to their spaceship, not leaving your house when you ask them to leave, and making

black ants and buddhists

you live in the damp basement because they've decided they like your place.

When I taught this most recently, I decided to make it a simulation, rather than just tell it as a story. I told half the students they would be space aliens and that I was their commander. I took them to our classroom library area (our spaceship), where they twirled their arms and made a whirring sound. I told the other half of the students that they and Sarah, a parent volunteer, would be gentle earthlings. They took out toys from our play area and started cooking food in our pretend space kitchen. My spaceship landed and I led my aliens over to the earthling area. The earthlings greeted us. They fed us and invited us to play with their toys.

I began to pick up toys and food and instruct aliens to "Put this on our spaceship" in a robotic voice. After all the toys and food were gone, I chose a few earthlings and told the aliens, "Put them on our spaceship." A couple of aliens stayed on the spaceship with the earthlings. Although I had not instructed the aliens to take anything themselves, some took the initiative to imitate me. I noticed that at least one earthling, Neil, was not willing to surrender his toy. I briefly interrupted the simulation to remind the earthlings that they were nonviolent. Then I resumed using my robotic voice and told the aliens to move away from Neil, who still refused to give up his toy.

When one of the earthlings, Joe, noticed that some of the earthlings were being taken away, he looked over and saw his twin brother, Barry, on the spaceship. He shouted, "Hey, don't take my brother! I don't know if he can breathe on your planet, or if he'll get sick. He can't understand your language. Don't hurt him!" There was a hint of panic in his voice. I stopped the simulation again.

Barry looked up and said, "Joe, I'm an *alien*."

Joe took a deep breath, looked relieved, and then said, "Well, I was just pretending that Wendy [an earthling captive] was my brother." I asked Joe if he was okay, and he said yes. I announced we were going to stop there in our simulation and return to the rug for a discussion.

The entire simulation lasted less than five minutes. The only physical contact was when I gently put my hand on a few earthlings' shoulders to indicate they should be taken to the spaceship. With the exception of Neil, whose resistance was not contested, the earthlings put up no struggle as the other aliens and I took away their toys and food. I monitored students' emotions closely throughout, stopping when it seemed too intense for anyone. I had observed more emotional reaction on the part of the earthlings and wanted to check in to make sure every-

one felt safe. I first asked the earthlings how they felt during the simulation:

Joe: I was worrying, "Why did they take my brother on the ship? Will they hurt him if he can't understand them or do what they want? Will he be able to survive where they come from?"

Neil: When the aliens first arrived, I wondered, "Why are they here? Are they mean or nice?"

Esperanza: I felt tricked when the aliens turned mean. The aliens were rude to eat and take *all* of our food.

Wendy: When they brought me to the spaceship, I wondered what they would do to me. Would they bring me to their planet? Would I see my friends again?

Ricardo: I felt mad when they took our food, our toys, our family and friends. I got madder when they wouldn't go away.

Ellen: I felt like the aliens were stealing *my* toys.

Although we were just role playing in a brief simulation, the children took the experience very personally. Our props were classroom chess sets, buckets of Legos, and plastic pretend food; the spaceship was only a rug area ten feet away, but their feelings were real and intense.

Next, the aliens shared:

Meena: I felt excited. I started nice, but then I was too rough.

Rachel: I felt the earthlings were my friends, but I had to listen to my commander. I tried to treat the earthlings nice on the ship, like I gave them pillows, but I still didn't let them get out.

Alicia: I felt bad for the earthlings when I had to take their stuff, but I had to follow orders.

Barry: I was excited at first, but it got *more* exciting when we took their stuff.

Alejandro: It was fun, but I felt bad when the earthlings looked scared.

Astrid: I felt my commander was powerful. It was hard not to obey, because I didn't want my commander to make me a slave like the others.

I was struck by the stark honesty of the students as they articulated their complex emotions. I was also struck by the variety of feelings. Although all of the earthlings reported feeling upset by the encounter with the aliens, some felt tricked, worried, mad, ripped off, or confused. Although they were told to play "gentle" earthlings, Neil actively resisted by refusing to give up his toy, and Joe protested loudly when he thought his brother had been taken captive.

Among the aliens, there were some who felt excited by their power in the simulation. Alejandro described the mix of emotions, the fun of being powerful and sympathy for those who were scared of his power. Rachel, Astrid, and Alicia all did not like having to take part in the invasion, but they all obeyed without protest, saying they "had to," citing the commander's authority and power. This was particularly disturbing to me because I was the commander. There was no consequence for not participating. Children were given the option before and during the activity to sit out if they wanted, yet they all participated and "obeyed" in their roles. Rachel described how she tried to reconcile those feelings. "I tried to treat the earthlings nice on the ship, like I gave them pillows, but I still didn't let them get out."

I asked the students if they had any text-to-self connections between these feelings and any of the stories we'd been reading. "Yeah, it's like *Encounter,*" Astrid answered quickly. "We [the aliens] were like the Spaniards, and the earthlings were like the Taínos." In our recent discussions, I had noticed that some students were beginning to lump all Spaniards together as "bad guys." We looked at our earthling and alien feeling charts again. I asked if we could say that all the aliens were "bad guys" and all felt one way or that all the earthlings felt one other way. "We felt some different ways," Meena said.

In our next lesson, I told them the story of Fray Antonio de Montesinos, a Dominican friar, who in 1511 criticized the Spanish colonists, including the governor, from the pulpit about their mistreatment of the Taínos. (See the book *The Taínos: The People Who Welcomed Columbus* by Francine Jacobs.) The wealthy Spanish colonists were so outraged by the friar's impudence that they met after Mass. After much debate, they agreed to give him one last chance the following Sunday to retract his criticism.

The next week, Fray Antonio took to the pulpit again. This time, he not only refused to apologize or retract his previous criticism, but threatened to excommunicate them if they did not free their Taíno slaves immediately. They promptly shipped him back to Spain, where he went straight to King Ferdinand and would not be silenced. He was so passionate and persistent that he persuaded not only the king and his court, but even the colonists' representative. The result of his persuasion was the passage of the Laws of Burgos in 1512.

Some of the "improvements" required by the new law were that Spaniards had to call Taínos by their names and could no longer call

them "dogs," that women more than four months pregnant could not be forced to work in the mines but could perform household chores, and that children under fourteen could not be forced to work in the mines and shouldn't be forced to do anything more strenuous than weeding. At first my students thought the provision for kids was pretty good, until I pointed out that there was no time limit to how many hours a day they might have to work under the hot sun planting, weeding, and picking, and there was no requirement for provision of food or drinking water.

Even with the eventual passage of the Laws of Burgos, enforcement in the distant colonies was weak at best. Bartolomé de Las Casas, himself a wealthy Spanish landowner in Haiti, was eventually persuaded by the arguments of the Dominican friars against the mistreatment of Taínos. He became one of the most outspoken critics of Spanish colonial exploitation of Taínos and worked tirelessly to save them. The efforts of Fray Antonio and Bartolomé de Las Casas were too little and too late to reverse the genocide the Spaniards unleashed on the Taínos, but their work provides us, as historians, with a window into the variety of perspectives among Spanish colonists and brings us a little closer to getting at the truths of what happened as a result of the Spanish/Taíno encounter.

(For a full description of the progression of lessons in the "Exploration and Contact" unit, please consult the appendix.)

separating truths from myths

Why are historical myths still being taught today? Why is American history whitewashed for student consumption? In *Lies My Teacher Told Me,* James Loewen suggests a host of reasons:

> Pressure from the "ruling class," pressure from textbook adoption committees, the wish to avoid ambiguities, a desire to shield children from harm or conflict, the perceived need to control children and avoid classroom disharmony, pressure to provide answers—may help explain why textbooks omit troublesome facts . . . Most of us automatically shy away from conflict, and understandably so. We particularly seek to avoid conflict in the classroom. One reason is habit: we are so accustomed to blandness that the textbook or teacher who brought real intellectual controversy into the classroom would strike us as a violation of polite rhetoric, of classroom norms. (1995, p. 25)

Many people have asked me, "Don't you think these children [first and second graders] are too *young* to hear the truth?" First, I tell them that no one taught me the truth in first or second grade, or in middle school, or in high school. Perhaps I didn't choose the right courses in college, but I didn't start to learn about the truth in history until I began to study it on my own, as an adult. I recently spoke with a university professor who said she asked a class of senior undergraduates to name the first people to live in what is now the United States of America. They told her it was the English. I have my students only when they are young, for a year or two at most. I believe in starting where you are.

I ask these critics what they propose as alternatives: to teach children lies or to teach children nothing? If you teach children lies, you condition them to passively accept and repeat lies. If you teach them nothing, or a superficial, sterilized version with gaping omissions, you turn children off to history, which in turn causes them to ignore current events, which are history in the making. If you do not create citizens who think critically about history and current events in the context of history, then you give tyranny a free hand. Democracy doesn't work as democracy with an ignorant and apathetic citizenry. Critically thinking citizens with a realistic sense of the complexities of history could not be bought by the largest campaign fund with the most television commercials.

I do not believe in teaching young children about every gory detail of every massacre and aspect of slavery, but I think I should introduce these realities. I believe in teaching multiple perspectives and alternative historical theories, presenting what evidence is known and letting students draw their own conclusions. If you are looking for an authentic use for history (in response to all those high school students asking why they should bother studying history), you don't have to look too far. A citizen today needs to listen and read beyond the headlines of a single media source. How tragically have we learned that repetition of a lie doesn't make it true? Haven't we learned that citizens, and especially our representatives in Congress, must demand to see *evidence*?

One year we read *The Real Thief* by William Steig, in which a goose who works as a guard for the king is accused of stealing from the royal treasury. Some of the students were outraged that he could be convicted. We invited a parent who was a lawyer to explain what circumstantial evidence is (the basis of the goose character's conviction) and the rules of evidence in court. One student, Nancy, became zealous in her quest for evidence. Our discussions thereafter were punctuated by Nancy's driving question, "What's your *evidence*?"

Time and again, when children ask me good questions, I must say, "I don't know, but how could we find out?" I must have said that a lot the year Samuel was in second grade, because he ended a note card on the last day of school with, "Thank you for teaching us what you knew and what you didn't." I took that as a compliment.

• • •

I must be humble enough to rethink everything I was taught, committing myself to relearn every piece of history I am responsible for teaching. If I catch myself relying on the story I first learned in elementary school, I am especially cautious. In addition to *Lies My Teacher Told Me*, the other books I rely on most are these:

A People's History of the United States by Howard Zinn
A Different Mirror: A History of Multicultural America by Ron Takaki
    (for later U.S. history)
Rethinking Columbus edited by Bill Bigelow and Bob Peterson

These are good books to own, to keep handy for reference. I read excerpts from them as I teach, and flip to the footnotes to cite the primary sources. I teach the children to try to catch me if I fail to cite the primary source. Why believe me, Loewen, Zinn, or Takaki, for that matter? I teach students to *demand* to know the evidence.

For me, just beginning to read these books raised many contradictions. Freire wrote that many teachers who use the traditional banking approach "fail to perceive that the deposits (of knowledge) themselves may contain contradictions about reality" (1970, p. 56).

I try to tune in to contradictions, knowing that mass media and mainstream history texts tend to gloss over them. When a contradiction is mentioned in the mass media one day, it is usually forgotten the next week. Whether in history or current events, contradictions are opportunities to ask larger and deeper questions. I remember that Beth, a second grader, once asked, "If the slave owners wanted the slaves to forget about their African religions and become Christians, then why did slaves 'jump the broom' to get married instead of having a regular church wedding?" I responded by explaining what it meant to "jump the broom." She insisted, asking *why* they jumped the broom. She puzzled over this, and asked a lot of people what they thought about it.

Eventually our research brought us to the *Remembering Slavery* tapes recorded by the Smithsonian in which an old former slave elaborated on this point. She said that the slave owners didn't want slaves to have a wedding that said, "Let no man put asunder what God has joined together," because they wanted to keep the right to sell off husbands and wives separately and didn't want to feel like they were breaking God's rule. The slave woman also recited the moving words that traditionally accompanied jumping the broom. I had known about jumping the broom for years, but had always assumed it was a different cultural tradition and hadn't considered the contradiction my student noticed. Later, while reading a biography of Sojourner Truth, we learned that she accepted a marriage the master arranged with another slave, but insisted on a legal marriage and refused to jump the broom.

I reflected on the jumping-the-broom contradiction in relation to the recent debate in Massachusetts over gay marriage. Many grumbled that gay activists should accept civil unions and quit pushing for marriage equality. Would civil unions have been another version of jumping the broom, something like, but not quite, legal marriage?

The year I returned to teaching second grade the social studies curriculum included teaching about "Roanoke, the Lost Colony." I didn't know the story of Roanoke, the Lost Colony, so I checked with Loewen and Zinn to see what they had to say about it. Loewen suggests that the early English colonists in Roanoke did not die out but were absorbed by the Croatoan Indians. The English and Croatoans may have later merged with the Lumbees. The Lumbees? This rang a bell.

I remembered that years ago when I lived in Philadelphia, I had known a middle-aged African American man. One summer, he told me he had just returned from seeing his tribe in North Carolina. I thought he was using the word *tribe* to refer to his large family and asked if he'd been at a family reunion. "I was at a powwow," he said. "I'm Lumbee." I had never heard of the Lumbees. I had just assumed this man was African American because he looked and sounded like an African American from the South and lived in an African American neighborhood. When he self-identified, he was very clear about being Lumbee. Still, I assumed he was part Lumbee and part African American. Loewen writes that these "triracial isolates" incude the Lumbees of North Carolina, the Wampanoags of Massachusetts, the Seminoles of Florida, and many other smaller groups throughout the eastern United States.

I had known that for many African slaves in the deep South, running north to escape was more dangerous than it was for a slave in Maryland or Virginia. I knew that a better route for many of these slaves was to run south to join the Seminoles in Florida or west to join the

Cherokees, who adopted them into their tribes. I have friends and relatives who identify as multiracial or as African American, Irish, and Cherokee. I had previously thought of this not much differently than saying that I am Scottish and Irish American or my friend saying that she is Scottish, Abenaki, and African American, or any other of the many ethnic combinations that make most Americans. Often someone will say, "I am part Greek and part Irish," or "I am Irish on my father's side and Greek on my mother's side." We tend to think of our ethnicity as parts or fractions that contribute to the whole of our American identities. What I suddenly understood differently, in retrospect, was that my friend in Philadelphia did not think of himself as part European American, part African American, and part Native American. He was simply all Lumbee.

This Roanoke story was the first I'd heard about English colonists abandoning their colonies and throwing in their lot with the Indians. Jamestown was also part of my curriculum. Jamestown seemed more familiar terrain for my second graders, who quickly shouted out Pocahontas, John Smith, and Flicker. Flicker? "Flicker is the raccoon in the story," my students told me. Raccoon? One student whispered sympathetically to another, "Ms. Cowhey has no TV" to explain my ignorance. Suddenly I realized we were deep in Disney country, where history is even weirder than in American history textbooks. I borrowed the Pocahontas video from the library and watched it at my mother's house. There was a lot of unteaching to do here.

Howard Zinn describes the founding of Jamestown:

> Powhatan watched the English settle on his people's land, but did not attack, maintaining a posture of coolness. When the English were going through their "starving time" in the winter of 1610, some of them ran off to join the Indians, where they would at least be fed. When the summer came, the governor of the colony sent a messenger to ask Powhatan to return the runaways, whereupon Powhatan, according to the English account, replied with "noe other than prowde and deisdaynefull Answers." Some soldiers were therefore sent out "to take Revendge." They fell upon an Indian settlement, killed fifteen or sixteen Indians, burned the houses, cut down the corn growing around the village, took the queen of the tribe and her children into boats, then ended up throwing the children overboard "and shoteinge owtt their Braynes in the water." The queen was later taken off and stabbed to death. (1980, p. 12)

Loewen describes this phenomenon of the runaway colonists.

> As Benjamin Franklin put it, "No European who has tasted Savage Life can afterwards bear to live in our societies." (footnote 42) Europeans were always trying to stop the outflow. Hernando de Soto had to post guards to keep his men and women from defecting to Native societies. The Pilgrims so feared Indianization that they made it a crime for men to wear long hair. "People who did run away to the Indians might expect very extreme punishments, even up to the death penalty," if caught by whites (footnote 43). (1995, p. 101)

As a teacher, I try to synthesize this information. I realize that a textbook statement such as, "Life for the early colonists was difficult" does not begin to capture the degree of incompetence, deprivation, dissent, or hardship that drove desperate early colonists to grave robbing, cannibalism, and murder. I do not describe this in gory detail to my students (although Loewen and Zinn use primary-source documents to do so). Instead I give them each a small paper cup with exactly one-third cup of oatmeal, which I explain is like the barley the early colonists had. We skip snack and eat our cooked portions of oatmeal, and imagine that being food for a whole day, for weeks and months, and then even that food runs out.

Children need to know and feel enough historic details to sense how complex and multifaceted the story is. They need a technological appreciation of what it means to sail, to use wind and ocean currents for power and stars to navigate. They need to know all the characters, not just a single name. I find it ironic that most American adults can readily identify the *Niña,* the *Pinta,* and the *Santa Maria,* but most could not identify the Taínos (let alone tell you about their culture or how their lives were affected by contact with the Europeans). If we are to know and understand Christopher Columbus, we must know and listen to his ally-turned-critic contemporary, Bartolomé de Las Casas. Children need to appreciate the motivation of these historical characters, think about whose story was recorded, and wonder, as Sonia Nieto reminds us, *who wrote the book?*

The questioning is important. Surely I don't own the truth about history. The point is to *seek* truth, to get as close to the truth as possible, knowing even that no single person who was there knows the whole truth. One year, I had a class that pursued this question relentlessly.

During a study of the roots of racism in the United States, I read aloud excerpts from *To Be a Slave* and *From Slave Ship to Freedom Road,*

both by Julius Lester. The students were very impressed by these and referred to them often. Finally Nancy suggested we write a letter to Julius Lester to invite him to visit and ask him how he got his "evidence," and what he thought about this question of getting at the truth in history. Mr. Lester wrote back saying that he usually didn't go to elementary schools, but that because these students seemed so serious and had such a good question, he would make an exception in this case.

When Mr. Lester visited in May, the students just about held their breath when Nancy asked her question, "How do you get at the truth in history?" There was a pause, and then Mr. Lester said, "I think there are many truths in history, and I try to get at them." By that time, they had pretty well figured that out for themselves, but they felt remarkably affirmed by this African American historian and author who took the time to come talk with them about it. Thomas wrote in his thank-you letter, "I like it when you said, 'ways to find the truths in history' because I'm trying to find diffrent perspectives on what happind with culumbus." Thomas's note reminds me of what Carter G. Woodson, African American historian, wrote: "Truth could move multitudes with untutored language."

● ● ●

Part of teaching this way includes letting the students know that not all teachers or standardized tests they encounter will share this perspective. A couple of years ago, the mother of Beth, one of my former students (previously a painfully shy first grader and then a more confident second grader) approached me in the school parking lot. She told me that Beth's third-grade teacher had showed them a video about Columbus. Beth came home and told her mother, "It said he was a *hero*." Her mother asked her what she had done. Beth answered, "Well, I raised my hand and said not everyone thinks he's a hero and what about other perspectives? And Sorny [another former student] asked what about the Taínos?" Her mother asked how the third-grade teacher had responded. "She didn't say anything. She just looked at us. I don't think she knows the Taínos. She just kept talking about Columbus."

I worry about this potentially dulling effect, as critically thinking students sit in classrooms with teachers who do not respond to contradictions. Sometimes I wonder if I ought to teach history at the secondary level, instead of first grade. I wonder if social justice education in the early grades can be undone by later teachers who embrace the status quo. When she was in fifth grade, Beth invited me to see her class play,

black ants and buddhists

The Trial, the product of an artistic residency with Enchanted Circle Theatre. She played a judge, weighing charges of theft and murder against Cortez and codefendants Columbus, Pizarro, and the like. She presided confidently over the testimony of witnesses who ranged from Taínos and Aztecs to Queen Isabella and Bartolomé de Las Casas, listening to their widely differing perspectives. I was deeply moved to watch my formerly shy first grader, whose questions were ignored and dismissed by her third-grade teacher, banging a gavel on the stage in front of the whole school, focusing us all to listen to the Taínos's testimony. It hadn't been for nothing. Those lessons had all been for this: that a little girl understood that history is as fascinating as it is complex, and that no single voice speaks an absolute historical truth.

Some people ask me why I teach first graders this way. If I had sixth graders, I would teach them the truth in sixth grade, but the fact of the matter is I have first and second graders. Although I hope that their future teachers will teach them the truth about Columbus (not to mention other aspects of U.S. history), this is my only chance to do it. I really do not think they are "too young to handle the truth." What I have observed from my limited teaching experience is that first and second graders are hungry for interesting stories. Spend a single recess period on the playground with young children and you can see how they are fascinated by conflict, passionate about clashing perspectives, eager for truth and fairness. My students, like Diana, who claimed her Taíno heritage, tend to take history quite personally. They take it to heart. They empathize with historical characters whose names might not be known. They want to hear multiple perspectives on the same incident. They aren't traumatized or depressed by it. They are charged by it. They become aggressive learners, demanding evidence in search of the multiple truths that make history.

CHAPTER 9

seeing ourselves and our families through students' eyes

All roads are good.

—Native American proverb

During my first year of teaching I was doing a unit on family diversity. All the students were bringing in family photos to share. I brought in an old black-and-white photo from the 1960s that showed me with my siblings. It had been taken in the summertime, at my uncle's house. My students were very curious to see the photo, impatiently taking turns to study it and reluctantly passing it along. Suddenly Carmen shouted excitedly, "Hold up! I didn't know you was Puerto Rican when you was little!"

Her classmates crowded around to study the photo and nodded in approving amazement. Curious about what they were seeing in the photo that so convincingly supported this hypothesis, I looked over Carmen's shoulder. I was about six years old and wore a white dress. I was skinny, with long dark hair, big dark eyes, and tan skin. Three of my siblings were blond. The two with brown hair were fair and freckled. I supposed I did look Puerto Rican. In fact, I looked like Carmen.

That same year I had a beautiful girl named Sopha in my class. She was Puerto Rican and Cambodian. She looked Cambodian, but spoke Spanish. She lived with her Puerto Rican mother and a loving circle of tias (aunts). She had very little contact with her father. During the spring of my first year of teaching, I took a course in antiracism for educators. One of our assignments was to look critically at the photos and posters on our classroom walls, and the books on our shelves, to see what diversity they reflected. I realized that the diversity on my walls and shelves was weighted heavily toward African Americans and Latinos, so I added some books and large calendar photos of Asians and Europeans. Each day, it seemed Sopha discovered a new one. She'd exclaim again and again, "That looks like my Papa San."

• • •

It struck me then how much children wanted to see themselves and their families in the classroom and in me. I make a point of addressing this visually, through the photos and posters in the room, starting with displaying a family photo of every student taken on the home visits. I address it through literature, through the picture books we read and the poetry we learn. Perhaps the most important way I do it is by sharing with the children about who I am, sharing my story, my family.

hyacinths: food for the soul

I often tell children stories from my childhood. One day in late winter, I brought in a hyacinth plant and introduced it at our morning meeting. One student asked, "Why did you get it?" So I told the class that

when I was about twelve years old, it was sometimes hard to get my mother's attention, because I had a brother and four sisters and two cousins also living with us. I figured that I could get more positive attention if I made myself useful.

One way I learned to do that was by getting very quick at mental math (this being in the days before pocket calculators). I would offer to go grocery shopping with my mother and keep a running tally in my head. Being an almost-teenager, I was easily embarrassed. In those days, the cashier rang up all of your groceries on the cash register and announced the total. If you were short on cash and said, "Oops, I only have $50" when the total was $52, the cashier would yell out, "OVER-RING ON REGISTER EIGHT!!" A manager would amble over slowly, loudly asking, "IS THIS WHERE THE *OVER-RING* IS?" while clanking a hundred keys. All the customers would stare and mutter impatiently while you scrambled to take $2 worth of stuff out of your groceries. They jangled keys and pounded the register and slammed the cash drawer open and shut about a dozen times before you were finished. I always wanted to put a paper bag over my head and crawl out of the store. I sought to spare my family this humiliation and tried, mathematically, to avoid over-rings at all costs.

One day in late winter I was shopping with my mother and saw her put a hyacinth in the cart. I asked her the price, and then, in an inappropriate and bossy way, I said, "Put it back! We can't afford that."

My mother looked back at me in her unperturbed manner (she had lots of practice) and said, "No."

"But Mommy," I protested, "we don't have that much money and we should just be getting food we can eat, not *flowers!*"

My mother breathed slowly, calmly, and then said, "They are not just flowers, they are hyacinths. We are going to get them, even if we have to put some food back, because hyacinths are food for the soul." We got the hyacinths. I still remember how their overpowering perfume brightened our cold, bleak kitchen and gave us hope that spring would come.

Later that morning, during writing workshop, Ellen approached me and asked, "Could I try to write your story about the hyacinths?"

I remembered how I spent my whole childhood, biting my tongue in school, struggling to silence those stories. I am saddened that many children still live with the burden of poverty, but I feel some sense of satisfaction that I have created a classroom community where a story like this one about my mother's steady wisdom in the face of hardship and adolescent arrogance can be told and can resonate for children of all economic backgrounds.

Figure 9.1 Ella's hyacinth story

> *Why Marry gets Hiasis evey year*
> *For all the kids in the world*
>
> Once upon a time there was a girl named Mary. She was 13 and she was a litte poor.
>
> Once she went to the store she was checking out the store ceeper shoted "you don't have anaf mony"!!! So she had to take out one of the things.
>
> So she leaned metel math and every Friday Mary would get piked to go to the stor because she would add up things they got so when Mary got to the stoor Mary would ask her Mother how much mony she had then when her mom got something Mary would ask how much mony that was and Mary would add up all the things. When Mary got to the check out place they would have anofe mony so that they could bey all the things thay wanted.
>
> So one day Mary was at the stor Doing her job when her mom just piked up a hiasent and put it in the cart. Mary was mad her mother had just piked up a very ickspsiv thing and thay couldend afford it.
>
> Mary yealed at her mother her mother just said in a sove vose we can afford it yo'll see and it will do good.
>
> When Mary got home her mother put the hiaset on the window sill and all over the hous Mary could smll it. it was doing good when Mary's dad came home it made him happy, and it also made her brothers and sisters fell happy and that why Mary gets hiasens every year!!

wearing bright colors

I find that teaching requires a good bit of humility as I seek to be a learner in my own classroom and forge a student-teacher partnership in this project of education. I must let go of pretense.

One morning I had to meet with my son's teachers at the middle school before class. My student teacher had greeted the children and supervised silent reading. I arrived just in time for morning meeting. The children were already seated on the rug as I sat down in my rocker. Before I could even start a greeting, Samuel looked at me with his huge eyes and said, "How come you not wearing bright colors like us?" Now, I am not a fancy dresser. I shop at the Salvation Army thrift shop. I usually just wear dark slacks or a skirt, with a brightly colored shirt and sweater. On this particular day, I had been a little anxious about the meeting and had made an effort to look "grown-up." I had worn black

slacks and sweater, with an ironed white blouse. I added a pin and matching earrings handed down from my grandmother. I imagined I looked very sophisticated, if not like myself. I looked at my students and noticed a look of worried concern. Two were wearing sunny yellow shirts, and one had on lemon-yellow pants. I remembered that the day before, I had worn a bright yellow shirt.

"Well," I explained, "I had to go meet with the principal at my son's school this morning. I didn't know her and felt a little nervous. I thought I should look grown-up, you know, like a parent, so I wore this outfit to make me look more grown-up. Do you think it worked?"

Samuel shook his head. "Your clothes look sad."

Krish agreed with Samuel. "You look like a funeral."

I touched my black sweater. "Too much black?" I asked.

Som Jet laughed. "No, the white! White is for a funeral."

"White?" I asked. "Not black?"

Krish said, "In India, we wear white for a funeral."

Som Jet waved a hand and said, "Thailand, the same."

"What are happy colors?" I asked.

"Your yellow shirt," Samuel answered. Gabriella, in her bright yellow pants, nodded.

"Your red sweater." Students offered more colors: orange, green, purple, blue, pink.

I said that there are sort of fashion rules and that I didn't know them very well, but they included rules like people shouldn't wear white pants after Labor Day, and people wear lighter colors in spring and summer and darker colors in fall and winter.

"Break those rules!" Krish said defiantly, raising his fist for emphasis.

I told them about how Einstein was my fashion hero, because he had a bunch of black suits, ties, and white shirts that all looked the same. Every day, he wore a clean outfit that looked exactly like the one he'd worn the day before. I said I wanted my clothes to be that simple, that I could get dressed every day without thinking, and ideally, without ironing. I said I wasn't as smart as Einstein, but I wanted to free up as much of my brain for thinking as possible.

"That's okay for Einstein," Ben said, not unkindly, "but you should keep wearing colors."

• • •

Bit by bit, children provide me with these reality checks as they help me see myself through their eyes. I must be honest and humble, and keep my sense of humor. Sometimes students comment on aspects of my physical appearance. Sometimes they notice that, like or unlike their mothers, I do not shave my legs or underarms. These observations generate comments such as, "Wow! I like the fur on your legs!" or questions such as, "How did you get those strings under your arms?"

Frank discussions about funny little observations like these lead to interesting learning. I point out that women naturally and normally have hair growing on their legs and under their arms, just like men do. This is sometimes a point of amazement. I explain that during the 1940s, when my mother was a teenager, it became the style for American women to shave their legs and underarms. In fact, in other cultures, this is not the expectation at all. Nothing bad happens if women don't shave; it is just an expectation in American society. Women can decide whether they want to follow that style or not. Pete Seeger recorded a funny song called "Putting on the Style," which pokes fun at pretentious people trying to show off the latest style. (You can find the lyrics in *Rise Up Singing*.)

There's a beautiful picture book by Jean Merrill called *The Girl Who Loved Caterpillars,* which is set in Japan hundreds of years ago. The main character is a nobleman's daughter who shocks and frustrates her family and neighbors by defying societal expectations (she studies caterpillars instead of writing poetry about butterflies) and not conforming to beauty standards, like blackening her teeth or plucking her eyebrows. This story can be a good point of departure for a discussion of gender stereotyping and body image.

These ideas can also be used to launch a discussion of critical media literacy. All those shaven models and actresses make us think that "normal" women are hairless, just like all those super-skinny models make us think that "normal" women are super-skinny and everyone else is just fat.

●　●　●

Each teacher has a unique story. Bits of that story can be woven into the day and become part of the fabric of the classroom community. I sometimes use food stamps in making up story problems. In discussions of economics or social studies, I use examples of when I worked minimum-wage or piece-rate jobs, like farmwork. I talk about going to college on a scholarship and graduating when I was thirty-six. These stories acknowledge economic diversity in respectful ways and affirm the possibility of change, that one does not have to remain in a minimum-wage

job forever, or that failure to get a college degree by the age of twenty-two does not seal the door to higher education shut for life.

I offer as much support and encouragement as I can for parents who take that scary step into college. In fact, at the end of my first year of teaching, Marilyn Rivera, the instructional aide in my classroom who had taught me so much, came to me and said, "I have some good news and some bad news. The good news is, after hearing you talk about going to college, my son Charlie and I have both enrolled at Holyoke Community College. The bad news is I'm quitting my job here." I was thrilled and devastated at once and wished her well on that brave path.

"do they have a box for travelers on that race form?"

Whenever my curriculum asks the children to share their stories about family or ancestry, I share as well. I try to do this in a way that honors all families and is sensitive especially to separated, foster, adoptive, and multiracial families.

I share with them my son's concept of "adopted ancestors," which he came up with the first time we read Patricia Polacco's picture book *Pink and Say* together. The story is about two young Union soldiers: Pink is a runaway slave from the South who saves the life of Say, a White boy from Michigan wounded in battle. Both are eventually captured by the Confederates and brought to the notorious Andersonville Prison, where they are separated. Say survives and his friend Pink does not. At the end of the story, which has been passed down from one generation to the next in Patricia Polacco's family, she asks the reader to say the name of Pinkus Ailey aloud, to remember him because he had no descendants. When we read that, my son, who is African American and Irish, said, "I will adopt him as my ancestor." I share that idea of "adopted ancestors" with my students because some of our ancestors may have been from groups so marginalized, dispersed, or oppressed that their family history is not well recorded.

This year, as part of our study of the continents in geography, I asked families to record on a map what continents their biological or adoptive ancestors came from. It was a way to celebrate our wonderful diversity. Esperanza, whose father is Columbian and mother is Mexican, Navajo, and Chinese, had ancestors from five continents. In my ancestor story, I said that my paternal grandmother's ancestors had been called "Irish gypsies," but that now they would be called Travelers or Romas. My students were curious about this. I explained that Travelers historically lived in wagons, or caravans, and traveled from place to place, trading horses or providing services such as mending metal household items as they passed through towns. They were often discriminated against and were stereotyped as dirty and untrustworthy. I explained that I don't use the word *gyp* for "cheat" anymore, because I learned it comes from the word *gypsy* and is used as a put-down.

I found an old, large photo from the 1970s titled "Irish Gypsy Camp." It shows two girls in a trash-strewn lot beside two broken-down old wagons. Although the photo was taken at some distance, one girl has her hand on her hip, and they both look defiantly toward the camera. We discussed the photo, which generated a great deal of interest. Many students thought the photographer hadn't asked permission to take the photo and the Traveler girls were mad that he "stole" it. They thought the girls were angry because the photographer might have planned to use the photo to put Travelers down, saying, "Yuck! Look how dirty it is where they live!" Some thought the photographer took the shot at such a distance because he was scared of them. I left the photo displayed and often noticed children going up to study it more closely. I read the picture book *Jethro Byrd, Fairy Child* by Bob Graham, about a little girl who meets a charming family of Traveler fairies. I also found a wonderful foreign film called *Eldra,* about a Roma girl in Wales who has little interest in assimilating.

My students' curiosity made me more curious, so I researched a little more, learning that Travelers still experience consistent discrimination throughout the United Kingdom. According to Save the Children's *Children's Rights: Equal Rights?* (Muscroft) the death rate for Traveler children is ten times higher than for non-Traveler children. Although Traveler children attend primary schools, their participation drops sharply in secondary schools and is described as "nonexistent" in higher education. My students wondered how one group of Europeans could discriminate against another, because they were more familiar with racial than ethnic discrimination.

When I visited the Holocaust Memorial Museum in Washington, D.C., in 2005, I paid particular attention to the exhibit about the Roma or "Gypsy" people, who were an early Nazi target for elimination. There was a Roma caravan, with a fiddle and bow on the seat. As I studied the photos of Romas who had been killed, I stopped short. There was a woman in a high-collared dress, with dark hair and shadowy eyes, who looked a lot like me.

I always teach Langston Hughes's poem "My People," which leads to a discussion of who our people are. My students' interest in Travelers provoked my own research and reflection. I wrote this poem:

My People
Why is it that I feel proud to say
I am from Irish linen, fairies, lace curtains and
black tea so strong the spoon stands up in it?
Why is it I am proud to say
I am from the hands of Scottish fiddlers who built
captain's quarters and chapels across Prince Edward Island
when ships and chapels were still made of wood?
All lovely and beautiful, but hardly like the me
that is me.

Out of all that, I only drink tea.

I remember when I was small:
coal black eyes, long brown hair and tan skin
a dark spot among my fair sisters and cousins.
Strangers would ask my mother, "Is that one yours?
Where did she come from?"

No, the me that is alive,
the resilient survivor,
the persistent part of me,
comes from my father's mother's
Irish Gypsy roots.
As a child, I thought tinker *was clever*
and gypsy *was romantic,*
until later I learned
those words were something like nigger,
a name like spit.
Now my people claim the name Travelers,
but over tea
a British school teacher confides in me,
"That one, Ryan, won't amount to much.
He's a Traveler, you know.
At least they won't stay long."

How stubbornly my family never told their stories
of endless roving in raggedy caravans,
of people fearing they would snatch their babies,
of being mistrusted,
of being pushed to the limits of town,
of proudly not giving a damn about
what other people thought of them.

But in spite of the not telling
our lives have become their stories:
For more than a dozen adult years
I had no home,
and it seemed fine.
Some of us still live
out of overflowing cars,
moving, moving, place to place,
Travelers,
not tourists.
And this,
our strange inheritance:
that we can fix our broken cars
on the side of the road,
that we can appear with a clop, roll, and jingle,
that we can disappear like smoke,
that we can always make something of nothing,
that we can live on the margins,
that we can move on
when others would stop,
that we can persuade,
that we are some kind of smart
in spite of our odd ways,
that we can tell stories,
that we can survive.

Near the end of the school year, the district sent home forms for each child's family to sign and identify his or her race(s). I am pretty terrible about paperwork like collecting forms. Every few days I would try to wring a few more of these forms out of reluctant backpacks. Finally I made another pitch for returning these "race forms" at our morning meeting, explaining that when I was a kid, some administrator just looked at you and checked off whatever single box they felt like. I said that even though this paperwork was a hassle, at least it was an opportunity for families to discuss race, itself an artificial construction, and ancestry, and check as many boxes as applied. Madeline said, "That's good, because you know how you have Traveler ancestors and I have Native American ancestors, but nobody would probably know that if they just looked at us? This way we can be proud of ourselves and write it down. Do they have a box for Travelers on that race form?"

finding ways in

All of these little stories, these sharings, are invitations to children to help them feel affirmed and connected, like they belong in this classroom community. Too often our reflex upon realizing our difference is to clam up, to hide our difference, to become invisible. This requires a huge investment of emotional energy on the part of the child, managing all the anxiety that accompanies the fear of being "outed." All that anxiety keeps the child's affective filter too high to learn well. Part of growing up is learning to feel comfortable in our own skin, to learn to like ourselves, to feel safe enough to take the risks necessary to learn. Some children need more affirmation and more love than others.

Sometimes in the course of telling a story, or making a text-to-self connection during a read-aloud, I mention when I was a single parent, or something about having divorced parents, or being in a biracial family that is "not all matching." Doing this in an ongoing, casual manner affirms and normalizes family diversity of all kinds.

During a spelling lesson toward the end of the 2005 school year, we were generating rhyming words for the spelling word *say*. Students were raising their hands, offering *day, play, clay, pay,* and so forth. Joe raised his hand and offered *gay*. I noticed, thankfully, that absolutely no one giggled. I added *gay* to the list on the board. Joe raised his hand again and asked, "Uh, Ms. Cowhey, why didn't you make that a capital *G?*"

I considered this. "Do you mean like 'Gay Pride March'?" He nodded. I explained that if it was the official name of a march, or on a poster about gay rights, you might write it with an uppercase *G*. If you were writing a sentence about "equal rights for gay people," you would just use lowercase. Joe nodded in understanding.

Madeline raised her hand. "Is there another meaning for *gay?*"
I explained, "It can also mean happy or joyful, like 'They danced gaily.'"
"Oh!" said several children in surprise.

"who made that stupid rule?"

In 2004, my second graders gathered on the rug, discussing the impending fiftieth anniversary of the historic *Brown v. Board of Education* decision. I asked how their lives would have been different without *Brown*.

"I wouldn't have all these friends . . . 'cause I wouldn't know them," said Sadie.

Michelle raised her hand and said, "I wouldn't exist." Michelle is a biracial girl, with an African American mother and White, Jewish father. Her mother, Barbara, had stayed for morning meeting that day, and she elaborated:

"Because of *Brown,* I was able to get a good education and went to a college that was integrated. That's where I met Michelle's dad. We fell in love and decided to get married."

Samuel, who is Panamanian and Pakistani, said, "My mom is brown and my stepdad is White, and they got married." He turned to ask Barbara, "In those days could a brown person and a White person get married?" Barbara said they had been married in Massachusetts in 1985, and it hadn't been a problem.

Angela, an African American girl, had quietly been following the discussion and finally raised her hand. "Because of that [the Brown decision], things are more fair, like I can go to this school and have all different friends. Still, not everything is fair, and that makes me sad."

Sadie asked Angela what still wasn't fair. "Well, your parents could get married, because you have a mom and a dad, but I have two moms and they can't get married. That's not fair."

Sadie considered this for an instant before asking, "Who made that stupid rule?"

With the honesty and incisive thinking I cherish in second graders, Angela and Sadie had cut to the chase. When it comes to discussing gay marriage in second grade, these are the questions that matter most:

Is it fair to exclude some families from the right to marry? Who made that rule (and how is it changing)?

Although the numbers vary from year to year, I have always had at least one child in my class with lesbian parents. In 2005, nearly one-third of my students had lesbian parents. I probably have more lesbian-parented families than most teachers (because of my city's demographics), but the reality is that teachers may not know by looking if they have a child with gay or lesbian parents, aunts, uncles, grandparents, or family friends.

Our school has a Family Center, which holds a weekly parents' hour with coffee and conversation, as well as a family portrait project, in which a professional photographer takes free family portraits at open house. These photos are displayed in the front hallway, heralding for all visitors the breadth of the school's diversity. Over the years, many parents have told me that even before speaking to anyone in the school, just looking at those family photos in the front lobby made them feel welcome, like they could fit in.

an eye-opener

At one of the first homes I visited just before beginning my first year of teaching, a parent greeted me wearing a button that said, "We're here. We're gay. And we're in the PTA." Beth and Karen Bellavance-Grace began talking about being foster parents for the state Department of Social Services and being adoptive parents. As we talked about family diversity issues, I asked if they would be willing to advise me on good books and teaching ideas. My education in teaching family diversity and learning from my families began on the first day of my teaching career, before I even set foot in my classroom.

When I speak to teachers and future teachers about gay and lesbian issues in elementary schools, they often ask how I can "get away with that." This is particularly ironic in Massachusetts, which was one of the first states to recognize the rights and needs of gay and lesbian youth in schools. In 1993, during the administration of Republican Governor William Weld, the Massachusetts Governor's Commission on Gay and Lesbian Youth recommended that

- high schools establish policies protecting gay and lesbian youth from harassment, violence, and discrimination;
- teachers and counselors receive professional development to respond to the needs of these students;
- schools establish support groups (gay-straight alliances);
- schools "develop curriculum that incorporates gay and lesbian themes and subject matters into all disciplines, in an age-appropriate manner."

Despite that progressive policy, established under a Republican governor, teacher self-censorship, often based on the fear of raising potentially controversial topics, remains the status quo in many schools.

Another problem, as progressive as the Weld commission's report was, is that it focused solutions primarily at the secondary level, with gay-straight alliances and so forth. Most people still get queasy talking about gay and lesbian issues at middle or—heaven forbid—elementary levels.

In my classroom, issues of family diversity often arise spontaneously. Once a group of my first-grade readers decided to act out *The Carrot Seed* by Ruth Krauss, a simple story about a boy who plants a carrot seed and cares for it diligently, despite the discouragement of his brother, mother, and father. After the skit, all the other students wanted a chance to act it out too. I said we could do it once more before lunch. I began pulling sticks with student names at random from a cup, to assign the four roles. After I pulled the first three sticks, a boy had already claimed the part of the brother. One girl had taken the role of the mother, and another girl had taken the role of the kid who plants the seed. The last stick I pulled was Nancy's, and the remaining role was for the father. A boy quickly said I should pull another stick. Nancy sprang to her feet without hesitation. "That's okay!" she said. "I'll be the *other* mom!"

In May 2004, same-sex marriage became legal in Massachusetts. Heidi and Gina Nortonsmith, parents of one of my students, had been plaintiffs in the *Goodridge v. Massachusetts Department of Public Health* landmark lawsuit that resulted in the legalization of same-sex marriage in our state. They were given the first place in line at Northampton's crowded city hall on the morning of May 17 to get their marriage license.

After the court's decision, my students got "marriage fever." During "sharing time" Madeline reported that she was the flower girl and her sister was the "ring barrier" at their friends' wedding. Avery Nortonsmith proudly showed the silver ID bracelet that he, his brother, and his moms all got on the day they were legally married, inscribed with the historic date. Astrid talked excitedly about preparations for her moms' wedding, how she and her sister and six of their girlfriends would be flower girls. I went to the wedding with my daughter and saw about half the families from my class. It was one of the most joyous and supportive celebrations I have ever witnessed.

My five-year-old daughter caught the "marriage fever" too and conducted wedding after wedding in her imaginary play. Each night she'd say, "Come on, Mom and Dad, you're getting married tonight."

"We got married eight years ago," my husband would remind her.

Undeterred, my daughter would say, "No, that was your *commitment ceremony*, but *this* is gonna be your *wedding*."

Even snacktime conversations raise the issue of gay marriage. Beth Bellavance-Grace, who now works as an aide at our school, told me about a kindergarten conversation she heard. A girl announced to her table, "I know who I'm gonna marry when I grow up. I'm gonna marry Eleanor."

"You can't marry a *girl*," a boy at her table replied.

"That was just in the olden days," she replied. "But now I can."

When we discuss family diversity, I define family as "the circle of people who love you." After I showed *That's a Family* one year, Marisol responded, "Yuck, that is so weird to have two dads!"

Jimmy turned to her and spoke with an air of sophistication. "What's the big deal about two dads?" he asked. "I got two dads. I got one in my house and one in the jail. Lots of kids gots two dads."

Marisol considered this a moment, then said, "Oh, I didn't think of that. I have two moms. I have my mom at home and a stepmom at my dad's house."

"See?" Jimmy said with a shrug. "I told you it's not so weird."

I had one student who was co-parented by three women. One morning we were having a math exhibition and the students had invited their parents. Thomas's three moms came in one at a time, each from their different jobs. Jimmy knew that his parents wouldn't be attending, but he kept looking to the door whenever another parent entered. He finally went over to Thomas and asked, "It be okay if I borrow one of your moms?"

In 2005 President Bush's secretary of education, Margaret Spellings, criticized PBS for producing *Postcards from Buster,* a children's show that included a family with lesbian parents. I wish Margaret Spellings could spend some time in my classroom. And I wish many Americans would approach the issue of same-sex marriage with the same openness as my second graders. As we celebrated the first anniversary of legalized same-sex marriage in Massachusetts, the national battle over marriage rights continued to heat up.

The refusal to extend equal rights to families with gay and lesbian parents hurts children like my students, giving them the message that their families are not equal, are somehow inferior. And, as my second graders will tell you, that's not fair.

responding
when tragedy
enters the
classroom

Los perros están ayudando a buscar
personas.

Rescue dogs are helping to look
for people.

*The love of our
neighbor in all
its fullness
simply means
being able to
say, "What
are you going
through?"*

—Simone
Weil

The first day of school is always full of emotion, as small children walk the fine brave line toward independence and their parents tentatively learn to let go. In addition to community-building activities, the first day of school is also filled with teaching lots of mundane procedures: where to put milk tickets, backpacks, and homework, when we go to art and the library, how we signal for quiet and needing to go to the bathroom.

In 2004, during my routine first-day lesson about how to do a fire drill, I had just finished explaining the importance of staying with the group when a girl in front asked if I would go back in the burning building to find a missing student. I reassuringly said that we would send in a firefighter to make sure everyone got out safely. She interrupted my breezy attempt to move along, persisting, "Then how come all those children got burned up in that school in Russia?" I hadn't seen that coming.

Things like that never come up at a good time. It had actually crossed my mind a couple of hours earlier when the hallways and classrooms were filled with happy and anxious families bringing their children for the first day of school, and I thought how September 1 probably started like this in Beslan. But I hadn't, between the milk orders, lunch count, attendance list, and clogged soap dispenser at snacktime hand washing actually thought what I might say if it came up. Other children began to talk about bombs, guns, soldiers, and bad guys. I signaled for quiet and briefly explained what had happened at the school in Beslan, Russia. Most of the children knew the story; only a few did not. They spoke next.

Yulia, who had been adopted about nine months ago from Ukraine, stood up, smoothing her pretty first-day-of-school dress with cherries on it. "I am from Russia," she began, looking at her classmates. "And I think I know that school." She turned to me, her huge brown eyes filling with tears. "And I think I know those children." She hung her head and sobbed. I knelt and hugged her, said I was so sorry, explained that it was Russia, not Ukraine, but that it feels like we all know those children.

Another boy, Joe, opened his eyes and mouth wide for a few seconds before he worked through his stutter to say, "It was so wrong that they hurt children. Why did those grown-ups do that?"

Then I could not help crying. This seven-year-old instinctively knows what the rest of the world knows—that all children should be kept safe from harm, even during conflicts. The United Nations Convention on the Rights of the Child states this clearly, yet grown-ups all over the world, from heads of state to the most desperate and disenfranchised suicide bomber, violate this principle as a matter of course. They all have their reasons, but there is no excuse for hurting and killing children. There's a Cambodian saying, "When elephants fight, ants perish."

black ants and buddhists

A couple of days later, we had our first real fire drill. A flicker of panic spread across my students' faces. I thought of Beslan too. In my calmest teacher voice I said, "Children, this is a fire drill. Come with me," and I walked them out to safety.

• • •

I never know when tragedy will walk through my classroom door, but I've learned it has no qualms about dropping in on the first day of school. How we respond to tragedy, as teachers, as parents, as humans, not only provides comfort and security, but also can provide hope and power for children in a world that is often unfair, and sometimes unspeakably violent.

Freire wrote, "Authentic education is not carried on by A for B, or by A about B, but rather A with B, mediated by the world—a world which impresses and challenges both parties, giving rise to views or opinions about it. These views, impregnated with anxiety, doubts, hopes or hopelessness, imply significant themes on the basis of which the program content of education can be built" (1970, p. 74).

The world does impress and challenge us, as well as sadden and startle us. Like it or not, the world comes into our classrooms, so all of our teaching and learning, one way or another, is mediated by the world. As much as I often hope my young students will have been sheltered from the news media in times of tragedy, they come in with views, spoken or unspoken, often laden with anxiety. If I attempt to ignore that, in favor of my predetermined agenda or curriculum, the outcome may be little or no learning at all.

On that first day of school, when a girl brought up the tragic school fire in Beslan, my agenda was to teach our classroom routines, to help the children get to know each other, to build a classroom community. Terrorism is not part of our second-grade curriculum, first day or otherwise.

I asked Yulia if she thought it would help if we wrote a letter to the children and families of the school in Beslan. She said she wanted to do that. Then all my second graders were gathered on the rug as I stood poised at the easel with my marker ready, asking how we should begin. They agreed on the date. Someone suggested, "Dear Russian Friends," and an argument broke out. "They already know they're Russian; they don't need us to tell them." "They are not our friends; we've never even met them." We hashed that out, and then got to the hard part. What do you say to people who just lost their son, their daughter, their mother, their best friend, their teacher?

We feel so sorry because so many people got killed and hurt and sad and scared. We know you must feel so sad today, but we hope you can feel happy and safe again someday very soon. We hope you are okay and your school is okay. You are so brave.

We are drawing these pictures for you and your school to help you feel better. Maybe you can hang them in your school so that children, teachers, and families can see them and know that children in the United States of America are caring about you.

We think that it was so wrong for people to ever hurt children or anyone, especially at school. We want all schools to be safe. We hope the people at hospitals get better fast. We hope your whole community can heal.

Love, The Peace Class, Second Graders at Jackson Street School.

That afternoon, at dismissal time I looked for Yulia's mother, to tell her about the discussion, how Yulia cried, how I explained the news. She thanked me and offered to take the letter to have it translated by a Russian friend of hers. The children decided to make drawings for Beslan, peaceful pictures that could remind them of happier times.

The next day we followed up on Joe's indignation that grown ups had done something that hurt children. I began to teach them about the United Nations. I used *For Every Child* by Caroline Castle to teach about the U.N. Convention on the Rights of the Child. They made captioned drawings about children's rights: the right to be called by their own names; to have food, clean water, housing, health care, education; to be kept safe from conflict. A couple of months passed. Sometimes my students would make a connection when something sad and scary happened, like in Beslan, or when they wrote a letter to comfort someone, or heard a news item that prompted them to think about the rights of children.

In early November, we received a thank-you letter from the House of Child's Creation in Beslan, Russia. I realized I hadn't been expecting a reply. I had addressed our envelope to "Beslan School, Beslan, North Osetia, Russia" and sent it off into the universe. The letterhead was in Russian, but the reply was in English: "Thank you for your words of sympathy. It is important for us to know that all the world is with Beslan, that you are sharing our grief. We feel the kind of your hearts." They enclosed a photo of our letter and drawings, displayed on a wall with other drawings. I showed it to Holly, a fellow teacher who had mentioned to me that she had Ukrainian visitors at her home. She said their delegation would be coming to visit our school the next day. I asked her to bring them by my classroom.

The next morning, I read the letter at our morning meeting. One of the children asked how close Beslan was to Ukraine. We tried to find it on the globe, but Beslan was not marked. Just then I noticed Holly bringing the Ukrainian delegation into the art room across the hall. I asked a student to invite them to visit us next. I asked Yulia if she would introduce us to them. When they entered, she introduced us, in perfect English. I whispered that she could speak to them in Russian, and she introduced us again. They were delighted. The women in the group cried and hugged and kissed her. My students were very impressed. We asked them to show us where Beslan was on the globe, in relation to Ukraine.

After some debate in Russian, a man in the group took the globe. He ran his finger across the Caucasus Mountains, toward the Black Sea, then back partway and said, "Beslan is here." The visitors stayed a little while. We learned they were Ukrainian educators, medical professionals, and mental health experts from an organization called Children of Chernobyl that helps children with severe special needs participate and succeed in school. These men and women were doing hopeful, healing work in the wake of the Chernobyl nuclear disaster, which occurred before my students were even born. They gave my students little metal badges that said Children of Chernobyl in Russian, and they pinned them on proudly.

At the end of that first day of school, my student teacher, Jackie, said, "When they brought up that school fire in Russia, I don't know what I would have done if I was the teacher." She was right. This never came up in any teacher preparation courses I took. No professor ever said, "Here's a rule of thumb in case a school shooting massacre hits the news," or "Usually the best way to talk about the collapse of the Twin Towers with youngsters is . . ." or "When our government begins a pre-emptive war with a military campaign titled 'shock and awe,' young children may feel . . ."

• • •

On the morning of September 11, 2001, I met my new student teacher and plunged into the day with my new class of first graders. I thought it was strange later when I saw my principal talking tearfully on her cell phone. A note went around to staff, saying that we could ask for coverage if we needed a break, or needed to make phone calls to family. At lunch, I asked at the office what that was for. A secretary told me there had been a plane crash. There was a fire at the World Trade Center.

One of my cousins is a New York City firefighter who responded to the first explosion at the World Trade Center. I figured he was there again, but why would I call him? Several of my cousins work in and near the World Trade Center, but I don't carry their home numbers, let alone their work numbers, with me at school. It wasn't until the end of the day, when my principal convened an emergency faculty meeting, that I understood what had happened. Like millions of other people, I phoned and e-mailed family members, to see how they were, to say I loved them.

Coming into school the next morning, I grappled with how to respond. I answered the children's questions, clarified their misinformation and confusion, and reassured them we were safe in school. Students described what they had done the night before with their families, saying prayers, lighting candles, and listening to their parents calling relatives.

One girl said she wanted to write a letter to her grandmother, to tell her what had happened and to let her know she was safe. Another student interrupted, "That's dumb. You said your grandmother lives on the next block from you. She's gonna know you're safe. Of course she knows what happened. Everyone in the world knows what happened."

The girl held her ground. "I just want to write to her about it, and to tell her I love her."

Another boy had a favorite uncle living in a remote part of Ecuador. He said he wanted to write to him. Spontaneously, other children thought of relatives they wanted to write to. Many wanted to write to their own parents. These six-year-olds, in their first week of first grade, with little writing experience, put pencil to paper with a simple but passionate message: "I am still alive. I love you. I'm glad you're alive." There was some comfort, some affirmation for the children in this, just as there was for me as an adult. Although many of the families had friends or relatives in New York, and some of those people had harrowing experiences, they were alive and accounted for. They were shaken and craving reassurance.

Then they wrote to their new pen pals, Zulu children in South Africa, children who lived in mud huts with corrugated tin roofs held down by old car tires, children with names they couldn't yet pronounce, children with whom they might become friends.

Figure 10.1 Student captioned drawing of firefighters

The firefighters helped to put the fires out.

They wrote a letter to my cousin's firehouse in Brooklyn, because they knew the firefighters were very tired and very sad.

I told my students about my sister Ellen, who lived in a basement studio in Fort Greene, Brooklyn. She had just returned home from an out-of-state trip. When she heard the news on the radio on the morning of September 11, she went through her nearly bare cupboards and found jelly beans and graham crackers. She filled some plastic jugs with water. She filled up her shopping cart and tied a folding table to it. She left the safety and solitude of her home and pulled the cart over to the Manhattan Bridge. She set up her table with a plate of crackers, a bowl of jelly beans, and cups of water. She taped up a little sign that said "Free." As thousands of frightened New Yorkers poured across the Manhattan Bridge, crying, coughing, and covered in dust, she offered them what she had: jelly beans, crackers, and water.

Throughout the day, people kept giving her more water and cookies and cups, like the loaves and fishes. I told my students that there was a lot we could learn from 9/11 about hoping, healing, and helping. For example, you should not prejudge the value of your gift or act of kindness, no matter how humble it seems. No one told Ellen, "We just witnessed devastating destruction and death and you think *jelly beans* will help?!?" Quite the contrary. People paused a long time to choose a certain color, made eye contact, and said, "Thank you." Many people took only one, in consideration of those behind them. My students wrote and drew about my sister and the jelly beans, about lighting candles and saying prayers, about going on peace marches, about firefighters and rescue workers, and about blood donors.

In early October 2001, Yolanda one of my first graders read a very simple story she'd written. It said, "It was on TV. Bad men knocked the buildings down." Quickly the other students began to concur that "bad guys" had done it. Yes, said others, "bad guys with beards." "And towels," some added. Then more agreed, adding that all bad guys had beards. Others joined, saying that all men with beards are bad guys. I interrupted and asked about specific bearded fathers in the class and asked if they were bad guys. I asked why the police didn't arrest all men with beards. A student answered, "'Cause all the bad guys would cut them off to look like good guys, and then we'd all be mixed up."

Clearly these children had been exposed to many images of Osama bin Laden attached to the term *Islamic terrorist*. Not surprisingly, they were working on the stereotype that all bearded Muslim men with turbans were terrorists. I began to teach about stereotyping. We discussed what they actually knew about Muslims, which was limited to beards, towels, and bad guys. I invited Marria, a devout Muslim friend of mine, to come visit my class to teach us more about Islam. She is a White woman who grew up in a nearby town. We had been in the same teacher preparation course. She could have been a parent at our school or a teacher in the room next door.

Marria taught us about the five pillars of Islam. She taught us how to say the greeting "*A salaam alaikum*" (may peace be upon you) and how to write it in Arabic. She told us about how she studied Islam, learned Arabic, and eventually converted to Islam. Many of the students made connections with what she told us, telling her how they learned Hebrew, how they used the Torah or Bible as a holy book like the Koran. They noticed similarities in Muslim traditions of *zakah* (charity) and their own, comparing the fasting of Good Friday and Yom Kippur with Ramadan, while acknowledging that Ramadan is *much* longer. I reinforced Marria's lesson with the picture book *Ramadan* by Suhaib Hamid Ghazi.

For the remainder of the year, they continued to make connections with Marria's visit, at first because I modeled it, and later because they continued to see the relevance of it. I planned our study of the lunar cycle to synchronize with the lunar month of Ramadan. As students shared their moon journal entries each afternoon, one little girl would say in amazement, "And they're *still* fasting!"

Some tragedies are worsened and distorted by an upsurge in prejudice. Deconstructing a stereotype and developing human relationships can reverse the almost reflexive responses of fear and distrust in the face of tragedy. As teachers and parents, we can model ways to learn about less familiar cultures and traditions and foster a sense of connection in children and ourselves.

• • •

Jackie, the student teacher who in September said she wouldn't know what to do if the children brought up the tragedy in Beslan, was planning to substitute for me for the first two weeks of January 2005, while I was on a short leave. On December 26, 2004, a tsunami struck Southeast Asia and killed more than 220,000 people. I had received an e-mail from my principal a couple of days after the tsunami saying that Julie Hooks-Davis, a parent of one of my former students, was planning to travel to Aceh, a province in Indonesia, on January 10. Julie is the director of the Institute for Training and Development in Amherst. She was planning to take funds to assist a nonprofit organization of *pesantren* (directors of Muslim boarding schools) and community leaders she'd worked with at her institute. She was willing to take cards and drawings from our students.

Jackie and I spoke early on the morning of January 3 as she prepared to begin the first day of her two-week solo stretch. We talked about how it was likely that the children had heard about the tsunami, and that many of them probably would have seen television pictures of the wave hitting and the devastation left behind. I told her to follow the children's lead, but to be prepared to respond if a child brought it up. Children might be anxious or curious, frightened or sad. We reviewed my "rules of thumb" for talking with children about tragedy:

Remind parents to eliminate (or at least severely limit and supervise) exposure to mass media, especially television. Adults will need to process and talk about the tragedy themselves, but they should do so out of children's hearing.

Check with families to see how/if they may have been personally affected by the tragedy. If so, seek their input on how best to proceed. Shortly after the tsunami hit, I called the mother of one of my students who was recently adopted from India, to see if her orphanage was all right. I called the families of former students who recently came from India and Thailand to make sure their relatives were okay.

Listen to the children, especially at less structured times.

Help them identify their feelings, concerns, and questions.

Allow for spontaneous connections, apparently out of context. Children are trying to make sense of the tragedy.

Be truthful, but brief. Do not offer gory details.

Clarify misinformation and discredit/discourage rumors.

Focus on those who survived: how they cooperated, solved problems, were resourceful or persistent. I learned this powerful rule from a child. One student was feeling sad on the first anniversary of 9/11, overwhelmed about the nearly 3,000 who died. Another child, Calvin, comforted him by saying, "It's sad those people died, but remember all those people who knew how to do a fire drill and helped each other and they got out *alive.* More people lived."

Brainstorm with the children some action they can take to help survivors. Engaging in deliberate acts of kindness can empower the children when the human or natural world seems cruel and arbitrary. This could be as generic as donating funds to UNICEF or sponsoring a flock of chicks through Heifer International, or as specific as helping a particular school or project with which you have a contact in the affected area.

Focus on those who help and stories of hope.

Help the children think of ways to *reach out in sympathy and friendship to comfort others,* by making a card, picture, or note. They can draw their own pictures of the scary thing if they need to, but the pictures they choose to send should be comforting ones.

Assure the children of their own safety, that family and teachers work to keep them safe.

In cases of natural disasters, like the tsunami, offer realistic assurances. For example, I say to my own children, "We live far from the ocean. We do not live in an area with earthquakes. The worst thing we have here is blizzards and ice storms. Those are not scary to us because we can just stay home, where we have a woodstove and can cook with gas. Aunt Amy hated snow and ice storms, so she moved to Florida. She learned how to board up her windows and fill jugs with drinking water during hurricane season and knows when to evacuate. Grown-ups learn what the dangerous things are in each area, and then they decide where they want to live. They learn how to keep their families as safe as possible from whatever dangers there might be. No place is perfectly safe, but most places are pretty safe."

• • •

Figure 10.2 Student drawing for tsunami victims

In a way, the tsunami was a test for Jackie, as a brand new teacher. It was also a test for me, as a mentor. She had assisted me with community service-learning projects and had organized one herself, with lots of family involvement. We'd talked about these rules of thumb, in relation to Beslan. Jackie was ready to try.

The children walked in the door on January 3, talking to each other about the tsunami. By the end of the morning meeting, they had made a plan to organize a bake sale for the tsunami survivors in Indonesia. They drew pictures and made cards.

I had received a donation of international flag posters, so each child received one as a gift for the new year. They looked up the flags of the countries affected by the tsunami. The children used maps and globes to locate Indonesia, India, Thailand, Sri Lanka, and other affected countries. Alex used his father's computer atlas and printed out colored maps that showed that Banda Aceh is 9,045 miles from our city. He mounted these on construction paper and hung them around the school.

Our second graders made posters to advertise their bake sale, welcoming donations of baked goods. Many planned to bake with their parents. A café donated coffee and cups. Fourth and fifth graders who saw the signs asked their teachers if they could help. Jackie coordinated with a fourth-grade teacher, Sue Ebitz, and a fifth-grade teacher, Susan Fink, who recruited their students to bake. The second graders and their parents would run the bake sale before and after school in the lobby. The fourth and fifth graders would run it through all three lunch periods in the cafeteria.

Jackie read our students excerpts of books about daily life for children and families in Indonesia, India, Thailand, and other south Asian countries. She also read from an Oxfam book about the importance of sanitation and water purification systems. (After Halloween they kept raising money for UNICEF until the class had $150, enough to purchase pipes and a pump for a village well.) They read a news clipping about a tsunami survivor who clung to a floating tree and drank rainwater for eight days while drifting in the Indian Ocean before being picked up by a South African cargo ship.

School was closed that Thursday because of an ice storm. Ms. Fink hadn't yet gotten a notice out with her students about baking, so she called her entire class to ask them to bake. Then she got her friend to bake, and baked some cookies herself.

On Friday morning, the lobby of the school was buzzing. Three eight-foot tables were laden with baked goods, and another was set up with coffee and hot cocoa. More baked goods kept coming in, and filled a shopping cart. Ms. Ebitz had brought a cash box and some change to start us out. My students were making sandwich signs about the bake sale. They remembered that this had been effective during our voter registration drive, so they connected the posters with yarn for kids and parents to wear out in front of the school. They made them for the adults who direct traffic in the parking lot. The second graders had decided that everything should be 50 cents, except for whole, big things, like pies or loaves of bread, which would be $4. They worked busily at their math, those who are mathematically gifted and those who struggle, shoulder to shoulder at the cash box. I heard adult customers patiently saying, "Okay, let's think what fifty and fifty would be . . ." Meena, who came from India two years ago, kept clapping her hands each time she added money to the cash box, saying, "We are helping! We are helping!"

One check came in with a sticky note that said, "Maxine is donating her Christmas gift money to help people in need in south Asia." During the day, an anonymous donation of $100 came in with a note to the students: "I was sorry to miss your bake sale, and want to contribute to help the people in South East Asia. Thank you for being such responsible citizens of the world." At the end of the day, Ms. Ebitz and some fourth and second graders began sorting and counting the money. The children were amazed to see hundred-dollar bills. They counted and rolled coins, and bundled stacks of bills. In the end, they counted $1,511.75, *and* decided to run another bake sale the following week.

· · ·

Freire wrote, "Students, as they are increasingly posed with problems relating to themselves in the world and with the world, will feel increasingly challenged and obliged to respond to that challenge" (1970, p. 62). While, on the one hand, we as teachers and parents do our best to shelter young children from exposure to mass media, the reality is that tragedy will enter our classrooms. It may be on the other side of the planet or in the life of a student or teacher. It may be the result of man's inhumanity to man. It may be a natural disaster, such as a tsunami, hurricane, or earthquake, an event no human could stop. Tragedy is part of the human condition.

The sudden, unpredictable nature of tragedy is part of what makes it so disturbing to us. For that very reason, we cannot rely on being able to find wonderful resources to help us teach our children through these times. Of course, we can scurry to the card catalog or hop online to look for books on these topics, but our immediate results will often be limited. There were no books about 9/11 in 2001, few books about tsunamis in 2005.

At those moments, I needed stories, words, and pictures, because they help us make sense of the world, help us comfort others, help us get things done. With a focus on helping and healing, my students and I used the stories of our own experiences and those of our families, and some from the radio and newspaper. We made pictures to express our feelings, and pictures to comfort others. We wrote letters, poems, posters, and stories. We used our words, got the help of translators, and even used symbols to communicate with people who speak other languages. Sometimes we find a gem like this:

May we exist like a lotus
At home in the muddy water.
Thus we bow to how life is.
　　—Zen reflection

Oftentimes, the tragedy will have more of an emotional effect on adults than on our children. We must remain open and present so that we can listen and respond, reassure and guide action. This is not an easy challenge, and we will be called to rise to it when we feel most vulnerable ourselves. All of this is true, and yet these may be some of the most important lessons we will ever teach our children.

building trust with families and weathering controversy

Life is inherently messy . . . but out of messiness comes great things.

—Margaret Wheatly

my house

ms. cowhey's bicycle

ms. cowhey's

me & my mom

In my first year of teaching, I was overwhelmed and completely uncertain about how to work with a very bright boy who called out constantly, was forever out of his seat, and was very aggressive with other children. When his mother said she thought he needed to sit in a desk in a row and do worksheets, I said we weren't doing that. She said my class wasn't a good fit and tried to change him to another class.

I felt like a failure, but I also felt a sense of relief, thinking that perhaps some more experienced teacher would know much better how to work with this very challenging student. The next day I got word back from the principal that she had told the mother that the boy had to stay in my class. I was stumped and a little desperate.

Despite our positive home visit, I was beginning to think this parent didn't like me. My philosophy of teaching and hers seemed completely at odds. For better or worse, we were stuck with each other, joined by her challenging son. What else could I do? I asked her to volunteer in the classroom.

I thought that maybe if she spent some time in class with us, she could see some merit in my nontraditional teaching approach. Of course, as a first-year teacher, I had no track record to support my odd ideas. I also thought that if she could see her son in action, she might be able to give me some pointers on how to work more successfully with him. She agreed to come in one morning each week. She could see how challenging he was. She knew sign language and taught me some signs to use with him for staying seated and focusing on me. We developed incentives for not calling out. She was able to reinforce at home what we were working on in class, using the same language.

When we were studying quilt patterns in our two-dimensional geometry investigation, she helped the children sew quilt squares in our sewing center. She brought in materials to share with the children about her volunteer work with the Names Project AIDS Memorial Quilt. She helped organize mystery math guests and bilingual family math nights. As the year ended, she made another request to the principal: that I loop up and teach second grade so her son could be in my class again. That request was granted.

● ● ●

Critically teaching young children about the world requires the teacher to be a learner. I always tell my students that we have to feel safe enough to take risks if we are to learn well. That goes for me as a learner as well. Sometimes those risks can cause controversy. Sometimes I make mistakes. Many teachers engage in a kind of self-censorship that limits the risk and the controversy, but that limits a lot of potential learning. I am not encouraging recklessness by any means. Rather I am feeling the tremendous weight of responsibility for the trust that families place in me when I commit myself to teach their children.

It begins with building trust. In late August, when I get my class list, I can wait about ten days for the office to generate a computer printout of addresses and phone numbers, or I can look them up myself right away. It takes me a half hour to do the latter. Then I send home a letter to all the families of my new students. In that letter, when I say it is a privilege to teach their children, I mean it.

I make home visits to meet my students and their families. I do that even if my new students are younger siblings of former students, even if the family is already familiar. As a teacher, I can't imagine when in the coming school year I will be able to spend thirty to sixty minutes with a child individually. Seems highly unlikely, doesn't it? I figure why not spend that time up front? I think of it as a worthwhile investment. The visits give the children a chance to check me out and tell me about themselves while on their home turf. They also show me some things about themselves, not necessarily consciously, maybe how long they sit still, how they relate to their parents or guardians, siblings, and pets.

One year I went to visit a beautiful boy named Ahmed. At least, that was the name on the class list and the name that everyone at school called him. I drove down to Holyoke, a nearby city, where his family lived. His parents worked in the food service at Smith College and brought him to our school through the school choice program. He answered the door with great enthusiasm and brought me into the kitchen, where he introduced his grandmother, mother, and baby sister. He asked if he could show me his "best thing." His mother nodded. I followed him down the hall. He hopped up on his high bed and showed me a beautiful boy doll with dark brown skin, huge brown eyes, and black hair like his. "He's beautiful," I said.

"He looks just like me," he said proudly. "And his name, his name sounds like mine."

"What is his name?"

"Daniel."

I thought about this. "How does Daniel sound like Ahmed?" I asked.

He leaned forward and whispered, "I have another name."

I leaned forward and whispered, "What is your other name?"

"Samuel."

"Ah! You are right, Samuel does sound like Daniel. But how come everyone at school calls you Ahmed?"

He shrugged. "They just do."

His mother called from the kitchen then to say that the coffee was ready. "Samuel, did you show Daniel to Ms. Cowhey?" his grandmother asked. He nodded. His aunt came in, saying, "Hey, Samuel, is this your new teacher?" He said yes, and introduced me. Later his baby sister crawled down the hall and his mother said, "Samuel, get your sister."

Samuel's mother, Ligia, told me that she had trained as a schoolteacher in Panama before coming to Massachusetts, but that she worked as a cook here, at the college during the school year and at camps in the summer, because her English was not too good and so that she and her husband (Samuel's stepfather) could work together. I learned that her husband's mother and sister were also both elementary school teachers, one retired and the other looking for a job. I learned that Samuel's father was a Muslim from Pakistan and had recently moved to Texas. I learned that Samuel was being raised Catholic and would make his first Holy Communion that year.

I learned that his family called him Samuel. Near the end of our visit, I asked Ligia why everyone at school called him Ahmed if his name was Samuel. She shrugged. "He has two names." On the computer forms at school, someone must have dropped his middle name, Samuel, keeping only his first name and his two last names. Ligia explained, "That's what his first teacher called him. So that's what everyone called him. I didn't want to argue."

So it was that Samuel, simply and eloquently, taught me my first lesson about him, using his precious doll and loving family as our text.

• • •

When I visit, I don't have a huge agenda. I use simple conversation starters. I ask the child, "What would you like me to know about you?" I ask the parents, "What would you like me to know about your child? About your family?"

In the living room of the first student home I visited, I noticed a prominently displayed photo of my new student sitting in a courtroom beside a standing judge, striking a gavel. It was his adoption day photo. His moms told me that they had been foster parents for years and that they'd adopted him just the year before. As a brand new teacher, I had a warm, fuzzy image of myself teaching a little unit about families. Suddenly it occurred to me that I wasn't really sure how to talk or teach about foster and adoptive families or families with lesbian and gay parents. I asked if they knew of any good resources or had any advice for me. One of the moms said that she'd helped the district develop a family diversity curriculum the year before and would help me with it. She offered to share books from home and talk with the class about foster care and adoption. She invited me to a workshop about issues of adoptive children in schools, which was very helpful.

Being a foster or adopted child is a huge part of a child's identity, especially for one who has recently been adopted. If the teacher feels awkward about the topic, she may decide not to bring it up. The concept is unfamiliar to children who are not from foster or adoptive families, and they may ask innocent but painful questions such as, "Why did your mom give you away?"

Although I never pry, I find that adoptive children, especially older adoptees, have a strong desire to talk about it. Inevitably, it will come up, especially if the child looks different from his foster or adoptive family or is old enough to remember or refer to memories of former schools, homes/orphanages, or birth parents. I found it was better to be proactive, honest, and humble enough to admit I wasn't confident about how to handle it than to bank on a strategy of avoidance.

Meena was adopted at the age of six from an orphanage in India. Toward the end of her second-grade year, she asked her mother if she could bring in a videotape from India to show her classmates her orphanage and friends. Her mother tried to discourage Meena from this plan, but she persisted. In the meantime, Meena told me about the videotape; I was unable to really understand what she wanted.

I called her mother, who shared her concerns. She said the videotape had been made by the orphanage to show a prospective adoptive parent her cognitive abilities, so it was an unnatural performance, an awkward show of a puzzled little girl reciting numbers and letters by rote, trying to please a social worker with a video camera. Her mother was afraid children might tease her because of it. She said there was another, more natural, videotape from her first orphanage that showed her class practicing yoga. She asked me to view them both and then talk with her daughter about it. Meena, her mother, and I reached an agreement to show a brief clip of the first videotape, to show how the orphanage looked (skipping the painful recitation parts), and a bit more of the yoga practice videotape.

Previously Meena had shared a baby picture of herself and told the class matter-of-factly that her birth mother had brought her to the first orphanage because she could not take care of her. She had also written a story for our class newspaper, "When I Came to America." Meena, who had been adopted and come to America so recently, made it clear that this was an important topic for her writing and sharing.

Meena was leaping with excitement when it was time to show the videotape. I prefaced it carefully, thanking Meena for her willingness to share her experience, reminding members of the class that we would be respectful and appreciative, that we could ask polite questions that Meena could choose to answer or not. Meena stood beside the television, proudly telling us the names of her friends and the women who cared for them (specifying who was mean and who was nice) and showing us the crib she had shared with another child. One child asked where the toys and books were. Meena laughed as she answered, "There *were* no toys and books!" My students were very impressed with Meena's skill in yoga, even as a five-year-old, and some connected it with her current prowess in gymnastics. Meena was very pleased with her sharing; her mother felt satisfied that Meena was honored through the process.

Of course, no single approach fits all situations. Such a sharing could bring up painful memories for another adoptee in the class, or be very affirming. Sometimes children share spontaneously, forcing me to think on my feet. In all cases, if I feel comfortable talking with the parents, I feel more confident handling it.

Home visits are a good way to learn about and understand the diversity of my students' families, but they also give families an opportunity to talk with me about other issues in their family's life. These may include issues such as the serious illness of the child or a family member, recent or impending death, birth/adoption, marriage, separation, divorce, custody dispute, incarceration, addiction, rehabilitation, unemployment, disability, or other family issues. It is important to know how these things might affect a child's moods, schedule, and energy level. It is often a relief for a parent or guardian to explain the context of family issues before they manifest themselves as anxiety or inappropriate behavior in the classroom. It allows me to have a little lead time to learn from the family and to try to connect the family to resources in the community if they have not yet found any.

The visits are also a way to learn about the interests and passions of the parents and other family members. At Angela's home, I noticed a beautiful Zulu basket and a woven kente cloth. It turned out that Angela's parents had visited South Africa about ten years earlier. I explained that our first math unit was about patterns and invited them to bring in the cloth and baskets. Angela, a shy African American girl, was beaming with pride as she helped one of her moms open the kente cloth. Sadie, another first grader, stuck her head in a large basket and inhaled deeply. From inside the basket, we heard her voice saying, "Hey, guys, you should come in here and smell this. It is sweet like cut grass. I'll bet this is what South Africa smells like!" In moments, half a dozen children were wearing huge Zulu baskets over their heads, inhaling deeply and dreaming of South Africa.

In that week before school starts, I find these home visits are the best way to use my time. Every other classroom has lovelier bulletin board displays. In fact, my bulletin boards are bare on the first day of school, awaiting the children's work. Just outside the door of the room, however, on the cinder block wall is a large poster that says, "These are our families, partners in education." It has photos of all the students and their families, taken when I visited. It is beautiful, and everyone looks at it. No one complains that the bulletin boards inside are bare. The family photos are a way to understand and affirm the diversity of our families as we begin the year. We are who we are, and we all belong here. Students are proud to point out their families on the poster. For many students it is reassuring to have a place they can go to look at a picture of their families.

During the home visits, I also invite any parents who are interested to volunteer in the classroom, on either a regularly scheduled basis or on an occasional basis, for projects or field trips. I tell them to watch for my weekly family letter every Monday.

These weekly letters provide context for the families to understand homework assignments, field trips, and discussions. As most parents know, when you ask a first grader what happened at school, they will tell you about recess. When you ask what they've learned, their first response is often, "Nothing." Many parents tell me they use the letters as conversational prompts at dinner every night, so they can ask specific questions like, "How was the ice cream you made with the chemist today?" or "Can you show me how to make some of those Japanese characters tonight?" or "What book did you discuss in philosophy today?"

The letters also give parents more insight into the play of their children. I always enjoy hearing from parents what they observe their children acting out in their dramatic play. For example, after our Native American arts and history residency, a parent observed her daughter and a classmate playing in the garden. They were discussing the need for shelter, and decided to use a large hole for that purpose. They then discussed the need to gather food for the long winter ahead, and began busily digging out the tubers of Jerusalem artichokes, brushing the dirt

Figure 11.1 Sample weekly letter to families

Dear Families,

　　We made great progress on the hand washing front this last week. We worked out a few logistical kinks and now manage to get all hands washed thoroughly before snack and lunch. Students will be finishing their "Keeping Healthy" booklets this week. We also talked about getting plenty of rest, exercise, and eathing healthy foods. This led to a discussion of healthy snacks. You might want to talk with your child about his or her favorite healthy snacks or new ones they might like to try.

　　On Friday we had a great tea party, hosted by Elliot, Addy, and Aidan. Last week they read a nonfiction book about tea. After they wrote reports about what they'd learned and found China, India, and Sri Lanka on the world map, Addy said, "Wouldn't it be fun to have a tea party?" They put their math skills to work, taking a survey to find out, "At a tea party, would you prefer hot cocoa or tea?" They decided to serve tea *and* cocoa at the tea party. They wrote letters to Ms. Agna to invite her to be a special guest at the party. She agreed to all their requests, everything from wearing her "I'm a Little Teapot" pin and kimono, to showing her Japanese slides and performing the Japanese tea ceremony. They wrote letters of confirmation and more letters of invitation. We took another survey about favorite types of muffins. Galit's mom, Deena, helped us with baking some lemon poppy and blueberry muffins. They figured out a schedule for the tea party program. On our final day of planning the tea party, Elliot giggled and whispered, "This is supposed to be a *reading* group, but we're not even reading!" Ms. Agna lent us her collection of tea related books and all the students spent some time on Friday browsing through pictures of tea pots and other tea details. Aidan, Elliot, and Addy recited a poem by the seventh-century Chinese poet, Lu T'ung:

　　　　When I drink tea,
　　　　I am conscious of peace.
　　　　The cool breath of heaven
　　　　rises in my sleeves
　　　　and blows my cares away.

　　The students were very quiet and respectful during Ms. Agna's tea ceremony, and most students even tasted the green tea. Needless to say, there was plenty of cordial chatting during the muffin and cocoa portion of the program. Thanks to all the families who helped out with making this idea a reality.

　　Our spelling program is going well, with lots of student enthusiasm. This week we will be moving on to a new set of words (in, is, you, that, it). On Wednesday, students will bring home the cut apart letters from their spelling words. For homework, I would like them to play a word scramble game, first making their spelling words, then trying to make as many words as possible (hit, hat, out, tin, etc.) by rearranging the letters.

　　On our South Africa project, I am planning to have a book sorting session on Thursday, January 24 from 3–5 P.M., in Barbara Black's room (101), to organize books for shipping. If you can volunteer, please let me know. I will also be doing a slide show/talk about the world conference against racism and my trip to South Africa at Williston on Monday, January 21 at 9:30 A.M. If you missed the slide show at Jackson Street and would like to come, please see me for details. Have a good week.

　　Peace, Mary Cowhey

off them, talking about how they could make birch-bark baskets to store them in their shelter.

Volunteering in the class on a regular basis can give a parent valuable insights, not only into how her or his own child learns, but also into the cultivation of a learning community. Some teachers have told me they don't like the idea of having parent volunteers because they don't want anyone in the classroom "watching" them teach. I don't think of it as watching. I think of it as helping. It takes humility to ask for help. By asking for help I am being clear: "I can't do this job perfectly on my own, but because your kid is in my class, I want to do the best job possible. Can you help me do better?" No one comes in my class expecting perfection. Frankly, they probably expect chaos. When they help out and see those beams of brilliance emerge from the noisy swirling dust, they share that sense of satisfaction in teaching. Just like the poster outside my classroom door says, parents are our partners in education. Parent volunteers make that sentiment a reality.

When we go on field trips, I send home not just a permission slip, but a letter to the family, explaining why we are going on the trip, what we'll do there, what we'll learn, and how that connects with what we are doing. I always find parents willing to go on trips, and I find those trips strengthen their connection to the class and our collective experience.

I try to visit the Barrett Street Marsh with students every season. On our spring 2005 trip, Miles's father, Jason, joined us again. His pack was stuffed with field guides, binoculars, and dip nets. When we got out to the beaver dam, he was surrounded by children eager to examine the creatures he dipped up from the muck: mayfly larvae, dragonfly nymphs, snails, red worms, leeches, and backswimmers: exciting treasures in our study of insect life cycles. The following Friday, he came to our room in the afternoon, holding a paper cup. He works for the state Department of Wildlife and Fisheries and had found a huge predatory aquatic bug in one of the tanks that day. It was shiny black, with a long swordlike mouthpart. We were in the middle of math when he came in. I brought the insect around from table to table as the children worked on their story problems, giving them all a chance to examine it.

Because of full-time work schedules and commuting time, many parents will not be available to volunteer at convenient times. I try to be flexible and find a way to respond positively to the offers family members make, right up to the last day of school. During our last week of school in 2005, Jason came back to teach a lesson about the life cycle of the trout, in relation to our chick hatching and study of insect life cycles. Adam's dad, Bob, is a doctor and a singer/guitarist. He also came in that last week to teach a blues song, "Ain't No More Cane on the Rising," because his son came home and sang "Go Down, Ol' Hannah," which he had learned in class.

Parents want to know what the curriculum is. It shouldn't be shrouded in mystery. Often district personnel may say it is available to the public on their Web site, but that is not easy or convenient for everyone to access. Sometimes what we're asked to teach is not developmentally appropriate for our students, or we lack the resources needed to do it well, or training has not been provided for teachers. Because of standardized testing pressure, and shifting mandates and standards, our district and state curriculum frameworks keep changing. Grade-level assignments change too. I like to let families know what I am teaching, and what additional materials, information, contacts, and resources I am looking for each year so that I can teach it as thoroughly as possible. I am always looking for people who can help me teach it better.

Of course, I hope the families will read most of the weekly letters I send home. Like most teachers, I make a point of responding promptly to their notes, phone calls, and e-mails. I also try to be proactive about contacting families about positive developments as well as concerns. I call parents to let them know when I observe a strong improvement in behavior or academic work, hear a great comment, or have a funny story.

I call to mention if their child had a concern or a good suggestion. For example, most of my students were excited when the PTO organized a field trip to a science museum to see an exhibit of giant insect models. One of my students, Barry, was upset because he loves art, and the trip was during our weekly art class. He and I brainstormed solutions and came up with the idea that we could make some illustrations with pastels and watercolors to illustrate the poems we would write about the insects. I am not artistically talented, so I talked to the art teacher about my promise. I told her I was thinking of something along the lines of Eric Carle's insect illustrations and asked if she had some tissue paper we could use. On a previous parent-led art project, we had mixed media—oil pastels and watercolors—so we did that too. Barry was quite pleased with the results.

I look for ways to get every parent involved in the course of the year. I try to schedule field trips and special activities at different times and on different days of the week, with plenty of advance notice so that family members can try to make arrangements to attend. Especially if there is a single working parent, I try to get to know significant other adults in the child's life, so that I can invite an important aunt, uncle, grandmother, or cousin. One of my students has a single working mother and a severely disabled brother. His mother had to use all of her sick days and most of her vacation days taking his disabled brother to medical appointments, so she was unable to participate in field trips. Her son understood this, but he still really wanted someone from his family to come. He asked if his uncle could come. I asked his mother, who said it would be more effective if I called to invite the uncle. I did, and he became a regular field trip volunteer.

I had one first grader who started the year as a selective mute. I was trying hard to make her feel comfortable and welcome. Her mother and little brother often came on field trips. Her father was assigned to a local air force base and worked long hours preparing marines for deployment to Iraq. A former navy SEAL, he often trained marines in orienteering and survival skills. My student told me that after our first field trip to the swamp, her mother showed her father where it was and the whole family went for a walk there. I invited her father to come in to teach a lesson about using compasses and topographical maps during our study of maps. He came first thing in the morning, in full military dress, and did the lesson before heading down to the air force base. His daughter was quite pleased and proud.

I had wondered if her family found the nonviolent orientation of our class at all problematic, with the name Peace Class, our study of Gandhi, and so forth. They didn't. I always communicated clearly in the letters about what we were doing and discussing on these and all other topics. As I got to know my student and her family over the course of two years (first and second grade), I learned that they trusted me. They were welcomed, respected, included, and relied upon. Their daughter grew to love school and was very happy and comfortable. She loved the hikes in the marsh and hatching the chicks. She became an avid reader and prolific writer. She became an active and articulate participant. Years later, her family continues to stay in touch.

weathering controversy

In my third year of teaching, I began working with my students on a unit about the history of racism. During a discussion about the Montgomery bus boycott and Jim Crow laws, a student asked, "Where did Whites get this idea that they were better than Blacks in the first place? What were they trying to prove?" Our investigation brought us all the way back to Columbus, the first recorded trans-Atlantic slave trader, who exported Taínos from the Caribbean to Europe as slaves.

I had recently discovered *Rethinking Columbus* edited by Bigelow and Peterson and started using those materials in my class, with gusto. One day I was rushed and hadn't fully prepared my history lesson. I planned to read a passage from *Rethinking Columbus* but had not had the time to fully read it through. I proceeded with the lesson anyway, but as I read the passage aloud, I realized it was pretty gory. It described how Spanish overseers would chop off the hands of Taíno slaves with a machete if they got caught in the sugarcane press. I wrapped that passage up, and we moved on to making captioned drawings about Taíno life after European contact. Eileen drew a picture of a Spanish overseer with a bloody machete standing beside a sugarcane press and a Taíno slave with tears on his cheeks and blood spurting from his severed wrist. I remember thinking I should never make that mistake again of rushing to teach a lesson without adequately previewing the materials.

That night, I saw Eileen's mother, Maureen, at a Family Center potluck. I had Maureen's other twin daughter, Kaitlyn, in my class as well. We began talking and she said, "You know my girls tell me everything that goes on in your class." I felt a tiny "uh oh" in the back of my mind. "They tell me the stories you tell about the horse that kicked your stubborn great-grandfather in the head. They tell me what problems you did in math. They tell me how you scratch your nose." I had a bad feeling about where this conversation was going.

"You know," Maureen said, "Teresa said she wants to talk to you." I felt a bigger "UH OH" then. Teresa, Maureen's partner, was a very reflective but quiet Puerto Rican woman, whereas Maureen was very outgoing and actively involved in the classroom. In the year and a half I'd known her, Teresa had never initiated a conversation with me. I was sure the girls must have told Maureen and Teresa the machete story. Maybe Teresa wanted to yell at me about traumatizing Eileen and Kaitlyn.

"Teresa wants to talk to me?" I asked. Maureen saw how anxious I was and seemed to take a funny pleasure in watching me squirm for a moment. I was trying to formulate my apology, having made an overzealous-new-teacher mistake of using inappropriate materials.

"Yeah," Maureen said slowly, nodding. She smiled. "She wants to thank you for teaching the truth about her people."

Often, when I speak at colleges and universities, students ask, "Don't you get in trouble with parents for teaching like this?" So I tell them this story, about the closest I ever came to getting in trouble with parents.

• • •

Even with all of my efforts to build trust with my families, controversy still arises. It might be related to something I teach. More likely it might be related to some academic or behavioral issue. Whatever it is related to, I'll handle it better if I've established good trust and communication with my families.

During my first year of teaching, my district adopted a new constructivist math curriculum called "Investigations." I had taught it as a student teacher and had gotten a week of training in it the summer before I started teaching, so I was feeling relatively confident about math. As I began sending home math games for the children to practice with their families, I was surprised by the negative feedback I got, particularly from many of the Puerto Rican families. I had gone to great lengths to get every game and homework assignment translated into Spanish (the Spanish edition of the curriculum wasn't available yet). One mother asked, "Do you think my son is stupid? Why do you send games for him to play? Where are the worksheets? Do you think he can't do real math?" I felt hurt. I had high expectations for all of my students. I wasn't trying to put anyone down.

I asked Marilyn Rivera, my instructional assistant, for her advice. She said that many of these parents had gone to elementary school in Puerto Rico; they learned math by memorizing facts from flash cards and doing worksheets of equations. The "Investigations" curriculum didn't look like real math to them. They felt like their kids were getting cheated. I thought about that. The good news was that they had high expectations for their kids and felt confident enough to advocate for them.

I decided to organize a series of bilingual Family Math Nights for first grade. I personally invited all of the families in my class, and they all came. We played the games. I asked the children to explain their strategies and their mathematical thinking. The parents were very impressed. Once they saw that their children were learning math this way, and learning it well, they were sold on the math program and were willing to do the homework games.

I had one student, Paulo, who was a selective mute. Before we did the Family Math Nights, he never did his homework. I tried sending the games home in English, then in Spanish, then in English and Spanish, but he never did them. At the first Family Math Night, in October, I realized that his mother, Alma, couldn't read. When the games were explained and demonstrated, she played with great enthusiasm.

I told Alma that if she ever wanted me to show her how to play a game, she could always stop by the classroom in the morning for a

demonstration. She was a rather burly and brusque woman. Soon after that, she stormed into the classroom one morning waving a homework paper, saying, "I don't know how to play this damn game." I asked her if she had a few minutes, and played a round of it with her and Paulo. "All right! I got it! Paulo, we play tonight!" she yelled, and she herded the rest of her children out of the room. It became a routine I looked forward to.

Positive and frequent interaction between teacher and parent can not only improve a child's achievement, but also change a parent's perception of her or his child. When I first met Alma, she told me, "Paulo won't say nothing or do nothing in school. He's not gonna learn nothing. I think maybe he'll be a landscaper like his father." At the end of the year she told me, "You know, I think Paulo's gonna be a teacher."

During my first year of teaching, the state Department of Education monitored our school on the basis that we were becoming a segregated school. Our elementary school had nearly 50 percent children of color, whereas the other elementary schools had closer to 12 percent. There were stories in the newspaper about the need to desegregate our school. Meetings were held, mostly attended by White people. Some of them said, "They must not care. Why don't *they* show up?" In fact, parents in my class did care. They liked the school the way it was and felt angry that the state or someone was trying to "kick them out." There was clearly a lot of confusion and anxiety about the desegregation issue.

Another first-grade teacher, Lisa, had the English language learner cluster in her class, and I had the bilingual student cluster in mine. Our colleagues sometimes complained that we shouldn't "let those parents come in the classroom and hang around in the morning, talking Spanish and all." Although their complaint was nasty, it contained an accurate observation. Many of the parents of color walked their children into our classrooms, kissed them, and told them to act right. The parents sometimes lingered to chat with each other; recently the topic had been desegregation.

Lisa and I decided to team up and organize a "desegregation breakfast," *una charla* (a chat). We invited all the parents from both of our rooms, our principal, bilingual teachers and staff, and the civil rights and early childhood coordinators for the district. We got coffee, bagels, juice, and cream cheese. Lisa took all the students from both classes and organized activities for them. We ran the breakfast in my room.

Several clear themes emerged from the meeting. Parents were adamant that they did not want to be forced to send their children to another school just to balance someone's statistics. They didn't mind more White kids coming to our school, and didn't mind a choice about where to send their kids, as long as they didn't lose the right to come to "our school," in no small part because of its feeling of community. Many said that between work and family obligations, they couldn't commit to joining committees or going to lots of meetings. One of the parents and I decided to join the district task force on desegregation. We worked for more than a year on a subcommittee investigating in-district school choice. The statistical "crisis" subsided later that year. Our proposal for a school choice program was put on the back burner but was implemented a few years later.

My point is that what may appear on the surface to be parent apathy, dissent, disgust, or disapproval may well be the key to solving a problem at a student, class, school, or district level. Some of the discouragement teachers experience comes from misinterpretation, which is especially likely if trust and context are lacking.

Here are some of my rules of thumb:

1. I try to embrace the contradiction, rather than duck it. Ignored problems usually don't go away. They tend to get bigger and uglier.
2. If I am the one to bring a problem up, it will be easier for me to articulate my concerns thoughtfully than to react defensively.
3. I try to be humble. I ask for help and advice when I don't know how to handle something or don't understand what is going on. I ask parents/guardians, aides, cafeteria workers, janitors, and my principal, whose cultural understanding and sense of school and community history may be far more sophisticated than my own.
4. If I make a mistake, I apologize right away. I explain what I've done or will do to set things right. I try to take responsibility, the same way I expect my students to accept responsibility.
5. Especially if there are linguistic and cultural differences between parents and me, I seek the guidance of an insider who can help me interpret what is going on before I make any assumptions.

I would be limiting my students and myself if I didn't consider trying anything new that could possibly result in a mistake. I'd be kidding myself if I didn't admit I have made mistakes and will continue to do so. Teachers inevitably have to deal with parents about difficult situations that arise, be they social, emotional, behavioral, or academic. Strong parent involvement and consistent, honest communication with families is my best insurance when (not if) I make mistakes or have to handle challenging situations.

CHAPTER 12

going against
the grain

March 8

Dear Annoncer,
I heard you say Moms and
Dads on the speaker I just wanted
to let you know that some people
in this school have 2 Moms or
2 Dads so you could say Gardian
s.

Love, Astrid

People are unreasonable, illogical, and self-centered; forgive them anyway.
If you are kind, people may accuse you of selfish, ulterior motives; be kind anyway.
If you are successful, you will win some false friends, and some true enemies; be successful anyway.
What you spend years building, someone could destroy overnight; build anyway.
If you find serenity and happiness, others may be jealous; be happy anyway.
The good you do today, people will often forget tomorrow; do good anyway.
Give the world the best you have, and it may never be enough; give the world your best anyway.
In the final analysis, it is between you and God. It was never between you and them anyway.

—Mother Teresa

During my first year of teaching, there was a school shooting tragedy in Kentucky, in which some students who felt like they didn't fit in brought weapons from home and shot a bunch of students and a couple of teachers. It was tragic, to be sure. A group of teachers clamored at our staff meeting that we had to "tighten up security" at our school. When asked for suggestions, their first idea was that parents not be allowed to walk children to their classrooms, because that allowed an unregulated flow of "strangers" in our building. I pointed out that if they were parents who came to the classroom, the teachers would know their names and faces and they would no longer be strangers; they would be family members. No, they argued, someone with a violent agenda could slip in. I said that by getting to know the families, I will know if there are issues of alcoholism, mental illness, domestic violence, child abuse, custody disputes, or other issues about which I need to be especially vigilant.

I pointed out that in the recent tragedy, the shooters were not violent strangers or even disturbed family members who "slipped in" but troubled students who were required to be there. No matter, they thought we should have a system in place so that parents and guardians couldn't go past the front lobby. I said that the school would be more secure if we had parents in the hallways, because they love their children. If they saw anyone acting suspiciously or causing trouble, they'd be all over them in a minute.

In the end, it was decided to set up a system where all nonstaff had to sign in and get a visitor badge before going down the hallways, and that a person without a visitor badge could be stopped. A counter was put across the front lobby to control the traffic flow. This created a need for volunteers to handle the visitor badge distribution and collection, and caused bottlenecks, which caused children to be tardy.

A week or two after this new system had been implemented, I was walking from my apartment to the Dumpster in my neighborhood when I saw Magda, a parent who continued to walk her sons to my classroom every morning. She smiled broadly and said hello. I noticed that on her coat she was still wearing the school visitor badge. I realized she wore it all the time. I was glad to see her creative resistance to the new rule. Later the fire department said the counter in the lobby was a hazard and could block quick evacuation in case of a fire, so it had to go.

· · ·

We live in a competitive society. For many people, competition is more natural than cooperation. Some people feel defensive when others do things differently. They may feel compelled to criticize or humiliate the one who is different. They may want the one who is different to go away or to be removed. If you teach critically, and if teaching critically is different from the dominant culture in your school, you may feel like you are going against the grain, swimming against the tide. I often felt this way. I feel it less often now.

When I started teaching, I had a one-year contract. I knew that my district laid off the new teachers every spring for the first three years. Many were not hired back after that first layoff. I wanted a chance to teach. I wanted this school and this principal. I was willing to take a year. I taught like I had a year to live. I don't mean that in a "Damn the torpedoes!" way, but rather that I was gung ho to try out all the ideas I had read about in my own classroom.

I set up my classroom using tables instead of desks, so that we could work in cooperative groups. I made home visits. I did not have cute classroom decorations. I hung up Romare Bearden's colorful collages and large beautiful photos of children, torn from old UNICEF calendars. I set up a woodworking center. Skeptical colleagues stood in my doorway and shook their heads, saying things like, "You'll get sued for that." (No child ever injured herself, and even my most aggressive students never whacked anyone with a hammer; I use it now only during my simple machines unit, because the hammering is so noisy.)

I felt self-conscious on the first day of school when all the other first-grade classrooms had monarch butterfly caterpillars and thought, "Are we supposed to do that?" I had shown a veteran teacher my lesson plans for the first week and asked her advice. She laughed at me and said, "You're planning to *teach* on the first day of school?" Of course, I felt rather stupid and asked what she was planning to do. She just laughed some more.

I did a lot of things differently from the other first-grade teachers and most other teachers at my school. Some of those things were ideas and practices from research. Many others were the children's ideas. Some were just based on my own hunches and opinions. I initially shunned some practices, like the teaching of handwriting, on the basis that it was conformist and uncreative. No one required me to teach handwriting, so I didn't.

A couple of years later, I had a first grader whose handwriting (I realized in retrospect) actually had gotten worse in the course of the school year. Because I did not teach it and had not established clear expectations in relation to it, I just thought she was rushing because she was so excited to get her story out. That summer, a brain tumor was diagnosed in her, and she later lost a good deal of her vision. I felt terribly guilty for not having pursued that casual observation about her handwriting.

In the meantime, my district decided to implement a new handwriting program. I was quick to sign up for the training and appreciated the thoughtful (if not exciting) approach to teaching this useful and necessary skill. Of course, handwriting gets a little more exciting when used for authentic purposes, such as making signs and banners that need to be standard, bold, and legible. I pay much closer attention and intervene more quickly now when one of my students doesn't meet the clear expectation. If my intensive interventions with family support don't work well enough (usually they do), I can consult with our occupational therapist to determine whether it is a difference I need to be concerned about, or just a difference.

That handwriting thing was a mistake none of my colleagues noticed or criticized. I criticized myself for it a lot, and took constructive action to improve my practice. There were plenty of things, however, especially my first year, that my colleagues *did* notice and criticize. I cried many times that year because I wasn't sure what to do. I just wanted to teach and teach well.

crimes of nonconformity

One day that first spring, some of my colleagues asked to meet with the principal regarding their complaints about me, which were all in the realm of nonconformity. In fact, they'd made a list of my crimes of nonconformity. It included the following:

- Doesn't eat lunch in the faculty room
- Allows parents into the classroom
- Has family events in the evenings
- Students do not walk in a straight line in the hallway
- Students are loud when they walk in the hallway

Of course, I was guilty on all counts. In an effort to fit in, I *had* gone to the faculty room to eat at the start of the year, but the conversations were extremely unpleasant. There was one loud teacher in particular who liked to "hold court" in the faculty room. I was uncomfortable with his frequent racist and classist comments about families who came from the subsidized apartments "across the street" and "welfare mothers" and stereotypical imitations of African American and Puerto Rican students. Students and often whole families were given unflattering labels.

I felt very uncomfortable and wasn't sure what I should do or say. I was new in the school and didn't want to alienate new colleagues. I didn't want to appear uptight or self-righteous. I didn't laugh, heartily or nervously, just watched. A few times I asked friendly teachers what they thought about that commentary and they would shake their heads or roll their eyes, saying, "Just ignore him," or "He always acts like that."

That first winter, I took a course that another first-grade teacher, Lisa, recommended about antiracism for educators. I read Beverly Daniel Tatum's *"Why Are All the Black Kids Sitting Together in the Cafeteria?"* I knew it wasn't enough to just not laugh. I had to say something to interrupt the cycle of racism. The next time he made a comment about the neighborhood across the street, I calmly said, "You know, I live across the street. Do you think that about me and my family?" Another day he made a joke about welfare mothers. I said, "You might not realize this, but I was a welfare mother for a couple of years, and I don't think that's funny." When he did another one of his stereotypical impressions of an African American student I said, "I find that offensive."

Things would get real quiet. Conversation would stop when I entered the faculty room, and I'd receive a couple of icy stares. The racist diatribes subsided, at least in my presence, but I didn't feel welcome. That was when I started to eat lunch in my classroom with Lisa. We could talk about readings from the antiracism course, or questions about teaching without static. The complaint almost struck me funny, like they minded my absence.

My principal was aware of the faculty room scene, and she began to make changes over time. She had the very large square table removed and replaced it with four or five smaller round tables so there could be different and even semiprivate conversations there instead of a single dominated and loudly moderated one. Lisa and I went back to eating in the faculty room and had our conversations there. A staff social committee cleaned and painted the faculty room, and installed a carpet, couch, and comfy chairs in one area, in addition to the tables. Over time, the loud teacher was transferred to another school and then stopped working for the district.

I remember Sonia Nieto once said she advised new teachers not to go to the faculty room, because conversation there was often so jaded and discouraging. She said her thinking on that issue changed over time, and now she urges new teachers to go eat in the faculty room. I don't go every day, but I go on a fairly regular basis and enjoy the company of other staff members in what has become a less-biased, more collegial place.

I never quite understood why some teachers so resented parents of first graders dropping their children off at the classrooms. I don't know what they suspected Puerto Rican parents of whispering to their children in Spanish—"Go poke the teacher with scissors," perhaps? I listened and quickly learned that all of those whispered Spanish conversations ended with "Give me a kiss," "Bless you," or "Behave yourself" (literally "carry yourself well"). Who could ask for more than blessed, kissed, hugged, well-behaved children? I was not in a hurry to make those parents go away.

It was also true that I had organized family events in the evening, like bilingual Family Math Nights. I started organizing them because parents unfamiliar with the new district-mandated "Investigations" math curriculum were angered by what they perceived to be a dumbing down of the curriculum. Some of those parents weren't playing the assigned math games with their children at home, not recognizing the value of that homework. Many of these parents expected a traditional rote approach and did not understand the constructivist philosophy behind the new curriculum.

I had gotten training from the local educational collaborative in running Family Math and Science Nights and had organized a series at the school the year before, when I was a student teacher, as part of my research on most effective family involvement practices to support student learning. I invited the other first-grade teachers to participate in organizing the Family Math Nights for our grade level and offered them the option of just sending home the leaflets inviting their students and families.

Lisa was enthusiastic about organizing it with me. Several parents, as well as Kim, the bilingual teacher who worked with my class, and Kathy, the ESL teacher who worked with Lisa's class, volunteered to help with outreach, translation, and running the activities. Two other first-grade teachers were discouraging, saying that no one would come, that it was a waste of time, and besides, it would set a negative precedent. One explained that if teachers did things like this on an unpaid basis, they would be considered "past practice" in future negotiations, and teachers who didn't want to would be required to do them. Because I was new in the teachers' union, I hadn't been aware of that. Teachers still aren't paid enough, and without teachers' unions, we'd be paid even less. It was a valid point. I located some grant money to pay all of the teachers involved, but no more teachers chose to help or to invite their students.

The Family Math Nights were a tremendous success. Hispanic parents who had been skeptical of the new math curriculum were impressed and better understood how to support their children. They also felt more empowered to ask questions and discuss math with teachers. The parents who attended were enthusiastic and spoke to their friends and neighbors. Eventually the nonparticipating teachers got notes from parents in their classes asking if they could have a Family Math Night too. Those teachers who had not distributed the leaflets to invite their families complained to our principal that Family Math Nights should be stopped.

Our principal, who was new in her position, had been supportive of the bilingual Family Math Nights and had helped me locate the grant money. We had already completed the planned series of three events in the fall, so it was not a problem to "stop" that year. My principal chose not to tangle with the complaining teachers on this point. The following year, two parents who had been involved the first year went to the Parent-Teacher Organization and volunteered to organize the Family Math Nights for all of the second grades. The parents of all second graders were automatically invited through the school newsletter. Because it was entirely organized by parents, there was little anyone could complain about.

The year after that, the Family Center, an organization within the school to promote family involvement, had a chunk of grant money and was interested in running Family Math Nights. The director came to ask my advice about it. I explained that research showed that the most effective way to involve parents least likely to participate with children who were most likely to benefit (lower income, less educated, non-native English speakers, folks with math anxiety) was to hold a series of smaller events, instead of one schoolwide event. I said that I could train volunteers the Family Center recruited, which would give the school a base of Family Math leaders for years to come. She said, "Considering school politics, I think it would be best if you weren't involved." Later, I learned that the Family Center planned to hire a trainer who lived across the state.

I was very upset. I had organized a successful series of events at the school while a student teacher and again as a first-year teacher, and had worked as a trainer. The Family Math programs were very popular with parents and, if properly implemented, could have a major effect on reducing the achievement gap in math. I had been prevented from providing Family Math for my class and grade level because it upset some teachers. Now I heard that some stranger who had no rapport with our families and no clue about our school culture would be a better choice than me for training the parent volunteers to run it.

I felt sick over the whole thing. I knew my ego was getting wrapped up in it. In addition to teaching, I was in graduate school and had a new baby. I didn't need more work or more battles. I cared deeply about Family Math, the principle and the actual program, but I realized I had to let it go and just focus on teaching. I wished them luck and said no more. The trainer from across the state backed out because it was too far for her to travel. They never implemented the program.

I can't fight every battle and still have the energy, sanity, and focus to keep teaching positively, keep loving my family, keep having a life. Even with allies among colleagues, families, and administrators, I can't win every battle. Sometimes, however sadly, I have to let go.

learning to walk with silent dignity

It was also terribly true that my class did not walk in straight lines (there was clearly some clumping going on) and that we were not completely silent. In fact, if we ever were silent, it was more by accident than design. I had observed that my class was not the only nonstraight, non-silent class in the school, but this was not the time to mention that. It was not my students' fault; I had never taught them, never expected or demanded this behavior from them. I had not fostered this straight and silent behavior because I thought it was authoritarian and conformist.

I had to think about it again. Our classroom was near the end of a hallway, so not much traffic passed our door, which was sometimes closed if we were engaged in a noisy activity of our own. This meant that we passed lots of other classrooms whenever we went anywhere in the school. I could understand that a classroom closer to the center of the school might feel annoyed or distracted if they had to put up with noisy hallway traffic interrupting their lessons. I discussed this criticism with my class. They agreed it was true and hadn't considered that it might be annoying and distracting to students and adults who were trying to concentrate on their work. Getting consensus about the silence wasn't too hard.

We had to think more strenuously about reasons to walk in a straight line. We finally came up with these:

- If your hands are not at your sides, you could feel tempted to run your hands along the walls and this could mess up, knock down, or tear the artwork of other students displayed in the hall. That would be disrespectful.

- If you are walking next to your friends, you might forget that you shouldn't talk and just start talking with them when you should be quiet.
- If you walk in bunches, it might be hard for another class to pass in the opposite direction.
- If you want to walk and talk in clumps or bunches with your friends, you could do that outside at recess time.

All of this criticism had gotten me thinking about my friend Ruth, and a conversation I had heard her have with her son, Frankie, a couple of years earlier when we were both single mothers in college. She had picked him up from the private school he attended, and we were riding in the car. A biracial first grader, he was complaining that his teachers were punishing him for things that White kids did too, but they went unpunished.

I was surprised at what seemed to be the harshness of Ruth's tone as she spoke to him. She said, "Look, Frankie. I'm not saying it's right, and I know it isn't fair. You're young to have to hear this, but you are just going to have to learn to be better and work harder than the others, because people are going to be looking at you. There will always be somebody who thinks you don't belong at their school because you're not White or because we don't have as much money as they do. Don't let anyone provoke you. They're wanting to make a bad example of you because they think you don't belong here, so you're just going to have to get used to having to act better than everybody else." Those words were hard to hear, but she loved her son fiercely. As a woman of color, she spoke from the wisdom of her own experience, and I knew she was right. It wasn't right or fair, but it was true.

I looked at my own students, their eyes shining with excitement and adventure. We were a loud and energetic bunch. I didn't want to handcuff and blanket them to stifle their lively nature. I asked if they remembered the part of the video about Martin Luther King Jr. we had watched earlier that year, about the march to Selma. They recalled it vividly. I said, "Martin Luther King taught those activists to walk with silent dignity. People threw rocks and bottles and garbage at them, called them names, and sprayed fire hoses on them, and still they walked with silent dignity, like no insult could hurt them. Do you think we could walk with silent dignity?" We tried it, a very slow, tall, dignified, silent walk, like we were marching to Selma, all the way to the cafeteria and back. We had found a way.

After that, instead of dreading the hallway walks and nasty rebukes, we anticipated them. We thought of other historical examples, such as Gandhi's salt march to the sea and Harriet Tubman conducting a group on the Underground Railroad (*extra* quietly). The leader got to announce, "We're going to walk to the gymnasium now. We're going to walk with silent dignity, like we're marching to Selma," and we'd step off. Finally, my class looked straight and silent, but more important, they looked sharp and proud. There wasn't another complaint about our hallway behavior all year.

> *Let no man drag you down so low as to make you hate him.*
> —George Washington Carver

When I first started teaching at my school, bullying was a problem—among the teachers. It had been that way for a long time, so it had become part of the faculty culture at the school. It was especially strong the first year. Intimidation was not subtle. A teacher came up to me in the faculty room and said, "You know why my nickname is The Terminator?" I didn't know. "Because the teachers I don't like, I get fired." Her friends laughed and a couple of other teachers smiled uncomfortably. I wondered how and if a teacher could have the power to get another teacher fired, but I didn't ask. I just said, "Thanks, I'll remember that."

One day a teacher came in my room and announced that my first graders would be taking a standardized test the next day. I was surprised, asked the purpose of the testing, and began to give my objections to standardized testing. She raised her hand to silence me, and then waved it dismissively, saying, "I've heard all that before. The other teachers who had those arguments, they're gone now."

I walked into a teacher meeting my first week and set my notebook on a table, about to take my seat. A teacher sitting nearby said, "You don't want to sit there. I'm pretty nasty." I smiled, said, "Thanks for the tip," and sat elsewhere.

I found that wonderful George Washington Carver quote that year and made it into a sign that I hung in my classroom. I taught the quote to my students and reminded myself of it daily. It was a hard year.

There's something to be said for staying, for quietly doing what you do, however strange it may seem to skeptical colleagues. Like Ruth said, you just have to act better and work harder. I was nervous when one of my students was assigned to The Terminator's class for the next grade. I was worried she would somehow find fault with his education. I got even more worried when I heard her in the office saying that she had scheduled a meeting with his parents and the principal the first week of school. It turned out that he was reading and doing math on such an advanced level that he didn't "fit" in her groups, so she wanted to send him to the next grade.

I do more assessment than our principal and district require. Many of my students are below grade level when they arrive in the fall. We are required to use the Developmental Reading Assessment in the early fall and again in late spring. I also use it in December and March and aggressively look for interventions (whole class or individual) or additional help to bring every student to or above grade level by the end of the year. My main motivation is to teach my students well, but I would not be truthful if I failed to say that I am also conscious of the critics out there who would be quick to pounce if my students were not making strong progress.

My principal has always made a point of honoring diversity, including a diversity of teaching styles. She believes that different children thrive in different environments and that it is important to offer a variety. Our classrooms range from the traditional to the progressive. In the nine years I've been in the district, expectations and frameworks have been clarified and some things have been implemented on a districtwide or schoolwide basis.

On any given morning at our school, you can walk in one classroom and see teacher, children, and parent volunteer gathered on the rug for a morning meeting and in another class see students standing to recite the Pledge of Allegiance. In the next room, they may be starting the day with silent reading at their tables. In the next one, they may be doing punctuation worksheets at their individual desks. Within a shared set of constraints, we all have a certain amount of freedom to develop our own teaching styles, to collaborate with colleagues, to engage in research, to work on our own projects.

I appreciate that freedom and don't try to impose my style of teaching on others. Increasingly, teachers check in to borrow books and other materials for lessons or units they have heard about and would like to try. The faculty bullying that characterized my school eight years ago has receded significantly. In its place is more collaboration and respect . . . not perfect, but much better.

I take all criticism seriously, whatever the source. Even if the motivation is less than well intentioned, I try to find what is valid in what is being said. Even if there is no direct complaint to my principal, I will often ask to discuss the criticism with her to get another perspective on it and get her advice. Even if the critic did not demand action, I try to take the criticism constructively and make some plan of action that would improve my teaching.

to pledge or not to pledge

One September about five years ago, a third-grade teacher came up to me and said, "I have to tell you a funny story." She said that John, who was in my class for first and second grade, failed to recite the Pledge of Allegiance when she directed the class to do so. She asked him why he didn't recite it. He said, "We never did that in Ms. Cowhey's class." She asked why not. He shrugged and said, "Because she's a protester, I guess."

The story got me thinking. It was true: I had not taught my students that traditional morning routine of saying the Pledge of Allegiance. Why not? On a gut level, I would have felt fraudulent. It seemed like one more conformist thing that I wasn't going to do if I wasn't told to. I thought back to my first-grade experience in Catholic school in the 1960s. Every morning I stood up and faithfully recited,

> *I pledge a legion to the flag of the Union States of America*
> *And to the public, four witches stand,*
> *One nation, invisible under God,*
> *With liberty and justice for all.*

I didn't know what *pledge, allegiance, united, republic, nation, indivisible, liberty* or *justice* meant. I'd heard of the American *Legion* Hall, where old men went. I knew there was a *public* school, where my Jewish neighbors went. I knew my dad was in the *union,* and that it had something to do with work. I knew what *invisible* meant, and I knew that you couldn't see God, so that line sort of made sense. The nuns were very enthusiastic about this, so I figured it was a kind of prayer. We always followed it up with this:

> *Hail Mary, full of grapes,*
> *The Lord is swishy*
> *Blessed ot thou among swimming*
> *And blessed is the fruit of thy room JESUS [head bow]*
> *Holy Mother, Mother of God,*
> *Pray for us sinners*
> *Now at the hour of our death. Amen.*

That one was equally mysterious. I understood the "full of grapes" part because my mother had explained to me that the wine used for Communion was made of grapes. The nuns in their long habits were swishy when they walked, so I supposed the Lord could be swishy too. I wasn't sure about that swimming part, but I let that go, because I knew there were fishermen in the story. The fruit in her room went with the grapes okay. I knew Mary (for whom I was named) was the Mother of God, and we were obviously the sinners in this prayer. I never understood "now at the hour of our death" because we never died when we said it. I tried hard to make sense of all this, but in the end, I recited it without question because everyone else did. And I didn't want to get whacked with a ruler.

The more I thought about it, the more I realized I did not make the children recite the Pledge of Allegiance because I think it is developmentally inappropriate. As a native English-speaking first grader with a strong vocabulary, I hadn't understood many of the words in it. What about my students with more limited vocabularies, and those learning English, and those who are not citizens? I think it sets a negative precedent to teach children to repeat and promise to do things they don't understand or believe. It makes a promise worthless. It trains people to be nonthinkers.

No parents or students had ever complained about my lack of pledge recitation. I checked the latest revision of the state curriculum frameworks and saw that I was now supposed to teach "national symbols, holidays, heroes and songs." All right, then, I would *teach* the Pledge of Allegiance.

I wrote out the Pledge of Allegiance on a chart. One of my students recognized it and shouted enthusiastically, "I know how to do that! I learned that in kindergarten." I asked if he would like to demonstrate for the class. He and several of his kindergarten classmates rose and recited it, in a rendition that sounded like mine in first grade. I thanked them and asked if they or other students could help me define some of the very tricky words in it. The first graders who had learned to recite it in kindergarten showed little advantage over those who had not when it came to defining words such as *pledge, allegiance, united, states,* and so on.

After we developed definitions for the new vocabulary, I distributed sheets with the pledge, typed double-spaced. Because we now understood that a pledge was a promise and had discussed that you should never promise to do something you don't understand or believe, I asked them to go through and make whatever changes necessary so

black ants and buddhists

that they could understand every word of the pledge. Here are Michael's changes:

I promise you can count on me to the flag of the together governed
    places of America,
And to the Republic, for which it stands,
One country, can't break up, under God,
With freedom and fairness for all.

Next, I distributed lined paper and asked them to rewrite the pledge in their own words. Here is Michael's rewrite:

I promise you can count on me to respect the flag of the United States of
    America and the government it stands for,
One country that God is watching. Indivisible,
With freedom and fairness.

Since then, I've taught the Pledge of Allegiance every year. I explain that we don't say it every day because I think that's a mighty big promise for first or second graders to make. I also explain that I don't think noncitizens should be pressured to recite it, because I would feel uncomfortable pledging allegiance to a country of which I was not a citizen. I tell them that as they grow up, they'll decide whether they want to just stand respectfully during the pledge or actually recite it, but they'll do so knowing what it means.

Over the years as I've taught this lesson, we had many discussions about the last line, "With liberty and justice *for all*." "What about Iraq?" my students wanted to know. "Does that mean *all* in the world or just *all* in the United States?" Other students pointed out discrimination against Blacks and gays and said, "It's not even fair to *all* in the United States."

All this to say that even if I shut my classroom door when I teach critically, eventually, word will leak out. My students will go forth to other classrooms, ask questions, and think differently. So will their parents. Sooner or later, people will know.

For example, we always do a lot of learning about family diversity and honoring all families. Last year our school hired a new secretary. One hectic afternoon, heavy snow developed, causing after-school-program cancellations. The new secretary come over the public address system and concluded her cancellation announcement by saying, "So if you need to call your mom and dad to let them know, you can come to the office to use the phone." Several students looked up from their math problems, eyebrows raised. Astrid raised her hand and said, "The announcer lady just made a mistake. She said, 'call your mom and dad,' but a lot of kids at this school don't have a mom and dad. They have one mom or two moms or an aunt or a grandmother or other guardian. Saying that could make them feel left out. They should say 'parents and guardians' instead."

I said, "She's new, and maybe she doesn't know that yet or hasn't thought about it. Would you please write her a kind note about that?" So Astrid did. I was pleased that Astrid had listened critically to something as mundane as a cancellation announcement and that she recognized exclusive language. She did not respond in anger or act like a wounded victim. She took prompt action, using oral and written language, to correct a mistake, to make our school a better place.

thinking critically about teaching differently

When I first started teaching, I felt pretty alone, like an odd duck. Some of my early teaching decisions were based on little more than a sense of social justice and my well-worn tendency to reject conformity. I cried a lot that first year and doubted myself often. My husband, Bill, a former engineer who had just become a first-year teacher himself, listened; we consoled and encouraged each other. I was able to talk with my teaching friend, Lisa, to process what was happening at school, with my students, their families, the faculty and administration. I could talk with my principal about major concerns. Although she couldn't solve all the problems with the wave of a wand, I felt she was an ally who shared my concerns and was working to address them (maybe not as fast as I wished) from the administrative end.

It took me months to develop a sense of who my allies were on the faculty and to gain the confidence to risk interrupting the status quo. The reality is that the forces that maintain the status quo have allies, often loud and numerous. When you go against the grain, you enter a world of complex dynamics that can't all be studied out beforehand. Some folks show their true colors right away.

When my husband went for a second interview for his first teaching job, he asked the principal, "What kind of diversity do you have here?" There was a long pause, and then the principal answered, "We've got a few of them, but they don't give us much trouble." When the principal called to offer my husband the job the next day, Bill turned him down. There's no sense in starting to work for an educational leader with whom you have major disagreements from the start.

I've learned to observe carefully what happens when I make changes, noticing who my allies and opponents are. I may find allies in administration and opponents among colleagues, or vice versa, but more likely, I'll find some of both. The reasons they oppose and the methods they use are complex. I tread more carefully now; I am less likely to charge around like a bull in a china shop. My principal has demonstrated that one can often make deeper, more lasting institutional changes through a series of sometimes subtle, thoughtful, deliberate moves over years than by hasty, bold actions and decrees that generate backlash and resentment.

It is not easy to go against the grain, to challenge the status quo in an institution as established as a school. I sometimes rock the boat by doing something different, doing something new, or not doing something that was always done before. When I choose to do something different, I think first about what my reasons are, and am prepared to talk with students, parents, colleagues, and administrators about those reasons. As a bottom line, I consider whether my idea is developmentally appropriate and safe (physically and emotionally). Can I articulate the educational benefit? Is the topic or skill the children will gain through it relevant to the curriculum frameworks? How will this help the children? I think about what is expected and required and why. I rethink it each time I do it.

Sometimes, I go with my gut and the rationale evolves over time, as I observe the results. My ability to articulate that rationale also develops over time. I need to be able to talk through ideas with someone I really trust (partner, friendly colleague, principal, mentor) so I can reflect on these questions. If I can't talk through it, I probably am not ready to do it.

I try to be brave in the face of intimidation, but I always listen carefully to criticism. I'm no Mother Teresa, but I try not to provoke critics unnecessarily by dressing inappropriately, chatting on a cell phone, or doing personal e-mail in the presence of students, or otherwise acting unprofessional. This is not to be judgmental, but to be aware that plenty of other people may be. People may criticize, but let them criticize the educational changes I make, not that I showed my navel.

"take this hammer"

Get the attention of busy people by singing about voting and freedom.

Take this hammer (huh)
Carry it to the captain (huh) [repeat those two lines 3x]
Tell him I'm gone (huh) [2x]

If he asks you (huh)
Was I running (huh) [repeat those two lines 3x]
Tell him I was flying (huh) [2x]

If he asks you (huh)
Was I laughing (huh) [repeat those two lines 3x]
Tell him I was crying (huh) [2x]

—traditional African American work song

As the school year drew to a close, I was teaching a unit on simple machines. Although I'm not talented musically, I like folk songs. I thought about "If I Had a Hammer," then "John Henry." I don't play guitar or sing very well, so I invited another teacher to bring her guitar and join us. I also started digging through old tapes and Pete Seeger albums and found a couple more songs, including "Michael, Row Your Boat Ashore" and "Take This Hammer." Bit by bit, our unit on simple machines evolved to include a mini-unit on African American work songs.

Of all the songs, the one that most captured my students' interest was "Take This Hammer." I was singing it one morning as I was working in the classroom when Gabriella came in early. "You're singing that song!" she exclaimed. "It sticks in my brains! I'm singing it all the time now!"

When I introduced the song, I told my students what little I knew about it, that it originated as an African American work song in the South, and that Leadbelly (Huddie Ledbetter) had recorded it. I told my students that as a person who can't carry a tune very easily, this is the kind of song I like, because the most important thing is the beat, in this case, the rhythmic pounding of the hammer (huh) at the end of every line. I had written the words on a chart—each line repeats at least twice—and we sang it through once with a tape. Then we stopped and I asked them what they imagined was happening in this song, if there might be a story in those words.

Michelle said she thought African Americans developed a lot of songs about simple machines because "for a long time, they did most of the work in this country." Because we didn't know exactly when the song originated, we weren't sure if it referred to work under slavery, under a chain gang, or under the oppression of a hard, terribly-paying job with a cruel boss. I explained that a captain could be an overseer, a foreman, or some kind of medium-level boss.

As we discussed the first verse, the children thought the worker either was very honest and didn't want to steal the hammer, or didn't want to be *accused* of trying to steal the hammer, or didn't want to bother carrying a heavy hammer while running. Another idea was that he was telling another worker to pick up where he left off, or to carry on the work. Michelle's grandmother, a retired music teacher, said she thought the worker was saying, "Take this!" to the hammer in anger with each blow. My students thought the "I'm gone" might mean running away from slavery, escaping from a prison chain gang, or quitting a lousy job.

In the second verse, my students thought "I'm flying" meant that he was running so fast his feet left the ground, or that he wanted to get away from there so bad and so fast that running wasn't fast enough— he had to be flying. I reminded them how in some African American legends, slaves flew away.

In the last verse, some children said the boss might think he'd be laughing, like, "Ha! Ha! I'm getting away from you and this terrible job!" I asked why the worker then said, "Tell him I'm crying." One student thought it might be a trick, that he really was laughing, but wanted the boss to think he was so upset about leaving the terrible job, he was pretending to love what he really hated. Some thought the workers might have this "trick" in the song in case the captain overheard them singing it.

There were many different theories about why he'd be crying. Seamus thought that if he was running away from slavery, he might be leaving behind family members he loved, and felt bad that he didn't have a way to get them out too. Benjamin said that if he was escaping from a prison chain gang, he could be so scared about them hunting for him that he'd be crying. Gabriella thought that maybe he was crying because he had quit that lousy job but didn't have another job to go to, and was scared because he didn't know what he would do now.

On the last day of school, we sang this song for our music teacher and another class of second graders. I watched the expressions on my students' faces as they mimed the powerful hammer pounding and sang the lyrics, each child having embraced some combination of its many possible meanings. It seemed a fitting way to end the year: We had learned that you couldn't study tools and machines and forget about the workers who use them. We learned that a song we both sing can mean one thing to you and something else to me. Either way, it is important to take the time to imagine the perspectives of the ones who made that song and to talk to others about what they imagine.

Back in the classroom, I noticed some of the notes children had written on the bottom of our morning message. Many were of the "I'm going to miss you so much" variety, but Seamus's note caught my eye. Seamus, who had given me quite a run for my money over the last two years, had written, "You're the best teacher in the world. P.S. I want to go away but I still love you." It reminded me of a magnet I once saw on my sister's refrigerator: "It's been lovely, but I have to scream now." But then I thought, "That's the point of this work that I do. I nurture children so that they *can* go away."

I gathered the children on the rug, and we reflected on the last day of our two years together. I told them I felt proud of how they'd become such fluent, expressive, thinking readers and writers, problem solvers, philosophers, poets, and scientific observers. I asked if they could feel the power of those tools in their hands, and if they felt ready to "take this hammer."

As the question hung for a moment in an unfamiliar silence, I thought about all the things I hope for my students, whom I had watched grow from timid six-year-olds into strong eight-year-olds, from nonreaders and strugglers into independent readers who love reading. I hope for their academic success, of course, but I hope for their social success as well, that they will learn about and respect differences, that they will listen and speak well enough to negotiate ways to cooperate. I hope some of them become teachers. In Seamus's note to his third-grade teacher, he wrote, "When I grow up, I want to be a teacher too." I hope they never stop asking questions. If they choose to have children, I hope they will teach their children well, and remember what it was like to be a child. I hope that their empathy remains keen and that they never turn a blind eye to injustice. I hope they will be happy and loved in their lives and that they will work to make the world a better place.

Then Seamus interrupted my thoughts. He nodded thoughtfully and said, "I think so."

•   •   •

Now it is summer, and as I write this, I think about what I hope for my readers. I want to pass on a powerful hammer, this idea of critically teaching young children about the world. Whether you are a teacher, parent, student teacher, administrator, professor, potential teacher, or someone who just cares about the education of children, I hope this book gives you the willingness to try to wield this hammer to build a different way of teaching and learning, to make your bit of change for the better.

APPENDIX

sample progression for "exploration and contact" unit

H ere is an outline of the way I taught my "Exploration and Contact" unit most recently. This is not meant to be used verbatim but to illustrate how curriculum can progress and flow in response to student questions, interests, and current events. I never teach it the same exact way twice.

To lay a foundation for this work, I do a map and globe unit first. I try to make that more relevant by doing a study of our own ancestors (biological and adopted) and read children's literature related to ancestors and immigration. We also ask families to share their own travel stories and read children's literature related to travel. Then we are ready to use our expanded map and globe skills and understanding of travel and immigration to begin to think about the concept of exploration.

Some of the lessons described below extend beyond one period and continue the following day. I teach an integrated curriculum, so I work and rework these lessons, questions, and ideas throughout the day, during language arts, morning meeting, and philosophy, not just during "social studies."

Lesson 1: What Do Explorers Do?

We begin by learning about a few contemporary and recent (twentieth-century) explorers, like Ann Bancroft and Liv Arnesen. I read aloud

Ann and Liv Cross Antarctica by Ryan and Arnesen. We discuss and chart the logistical planning to meet the survival needs of the explorers (water, food, shelter, appropriate clothing), their means of transportation (skis, parasails, sleds), methods of navigation and communication (global positioning system, satellite phone), challenges/dangers encountered, and people they meet.

Extension: I sometimes tell the story of African American Arctic explorer Matthew Henson, who accompanied Admiral Peary to the North Pole, using the chapter about him in *Against All Opposition* by Haskins or *North American Explorers* by Oney. I also sometimes use excerpts from *Shipwreck at the Bottom of the World: The Extraordinary True Story of Shackleton and the Endurance* by Armstrong to tell the story of Ernest Shackleton's harrowing expedition to the Antarctic in 1914, which inspired Bancroft's dream to explore there. We compare and contrast these same categories of survival needs, transportation, navigation, communication, challenges, and encounters (noting that the Antarctic was uninhabited) in the Arctic/Antarctic regions in the early and late twentieth century.

Lesson 2: Following Explorers on the Map and Globe

I read aloud *Captain Bill Pinkney's Journey* by Pinkney. We discuss and chart the same categories discussed in the previous lessons; we compare and contrast. Children use large world maps (and a couple of globes) at their tables and work in groups to follow Captain Bill Pinkney's journey, using a checklist to guide their exploration of the map. They record each of his stops as they find them on their maps.

Lesson 3: Vocabulary Lesson

We define and chart relevant content-area words: *explore, visit, discover, steal, share,* and *trade,* referring to Bancroft/Arnesen, Henson/Peary, Shackleton, and Pinkney expeditions for examples. I tell a story about an aunt calling, then showing up at the door with a cake at dinnertime, asking children to use the vocabulary words to describe what she is doing. We continue the exercise with children making up other scenarios, using the vocabulary in context.

Lesson 4: Why Did Trading Matter?

I read aloud *Caravan* by McKay and discuss factors that motivate exploration, including trade. I ask if they think there are any places in the world today where people still make caravans like that to trade. We revisit our content vocabulary chart again. We discuss contemporary trading in our community, like walking to the farmers' market, riding the bus downtown, driving to the mall, how we go to get what products, and how we trade/pay for them. I teach additional vocabulary: *buy, sell, fair, trade, barter, exchange, price, cost, profit, supply, demand, rare, import, export.*

Extension: This is a good opportunity to learn more about economics by making a field trip (even walking to a grocery store or farmers' market) or bringing in a visitor such as a parent or community member who works in farming, retail sales, or wholesale businesses that use "fairly traded" products such as coffee or crafts. They can describe how they trade. We use the new vocabulary in context. Children can draw/write/dictate captioned drawings to show what they learned from the field trip or visitor.

Lesson 5: Questions: How Did Humans Get on the Earth? How Did People Get to the Americas?

I pose these questions as ones that humans (including storytellers, historians, anthropologists, and other scientists) have asked for thousands of years. We brainstorm what children know and wonder. Inevitably some children raise (and others question) the biblical story of Genesis. Others argue the theory of evolution. I use a time line and illustrations to explain the theory of human evolution, presenting scientific evidence that supports the theory that all humans evolved in Africa. I read aloud Native American and African creation stories. I do not try to bring this discussion to a single group conclusion. I use it as an opportunity to explore multiple perspectives on a universal question: all people have wondered where they come from.

Lesson 6: The "Likely, Unlikely, and Possible" Game

Using the table of theories of pre-Columbian exploration from *Lies My Teacher Told Me* by Loewen (see Figure 8.1), I introduce my "Likely, Unlikely, and Possible" game. I tell a brief summary of a theory, like Ice Age migration. I give the children a couple of minutes to discuss the theory with their tablemates to decide as a group whether they think that theory is likely, unlikely, or possible. On the chalkboard or easel, I make a table listing the theories down the side and likely, unlikely, and possible headings across the top. Each row has a horizontal dotted line across

it, to record "before and after" votes. Each table gives me a sign to indicate their vote. Thumbs-up means likely. Thumbs down means unlikely. A shaking hand means possible.

I make quick tally marks in the three columns to record the initial table votes. Then I use illustrations, photos, and legends from *Lies My Teacher Told Me, Who Came First? New Clues to Prehistoric Americans* by Patricia Lauber, *Against All Opposition, National Geographic, The Discovery of the Americas: From Prehistory Through the Age of Columbus* by Maestro and Maestro (stop before Columbus), and other resources to present further evidence. Next I give the groups the opportunity to discuss the evidence and vote on the likelihood of each theory again. I record the "after-evidence votes" in the bottom half of each box. I repeat this process for at least half a dozen theories, including Phoenicians in reed boats, lost Japanese fishermen, St. Brendan and his monks in a leather boat, Vikings, and African explorers from the Mali empire with 200 ships.

The tables are discussion and voting groups, not competitive teams. No score is kept. The tally marks are for the purpose of showing us how our opinions can reasonably change in the face of new evidence. We also consider that some evidence is more convincing to us than other evidence. An important part of our job as historians is to judge the quality of the evidence. Perhaps later some of us will discover additional supporting evidence.

I often continue this game for a second day. As a literacy extension to this lesson, the children draw and write or dictate captioned drawings about these theories of pre-Columbian exploration, indicating how likely the theory is, based on what evidence.

Lesson 7: Introduce Taíno Life and Culture

I have students locate Puerto Rico on a map and ask them if they know what the island's name was before it was called Puerto Rico. I read aloud *The Song of El Coquí and Other Tales of Puerto Rico* by Mohr and Martorell and teach the song "Coquí." Sometimes I read aloud *Atariba & Niguayona: A Story From the Taíno People of Puerto Rico* by Rohmer.

Lesson 8: Taíno Life and Culture

I show the *Taíno: Guanin's Story* video to continue our study of Taíno life/culture, stopping the video before European contact. I send home a few pictures from the *Taíno* activity book for students to use in talking with parents about Taíno life and culture before European contact.

Lesson 9: Taíno Cultural Landscape

I show the *Caribbean National Forest: El Yunque* video. We discuss the fact that this area of Puerto Rico has been protected from development, and these pictures give us an idea of how Boriken looked at the height of Taíno culture there, before European contact. I explain that the Taínos had an oral tradition. We focus on Taino petroglyphs and practice drawing them. The petroglyph worksheet can be done in class or for homework, to prompt additional family discussion.

Lesson 9: How Did the Taínos Get to Boriken?

I read excerpts about the migration of the Arawaks from Venezuela north through the Lesser and Greater Antilles, describing how archaeologists have been able to document their trail using shards of their distinctive pottery. We discuss Taínos as explorers in canoes that could hold 100 people, drawing on *The Tainos, The People Who Welcomed Columbus* by Jacobs. I refer to kindergarten teacher Maria Garcia's T-shirt that says, "TAINOS: Ancient Voyagers of the Caribbean." We discuss the structure of Taíno society, daily life, roles, food, shelter, and religion.

Lesson 10: Assessment Re: Taíno Life

We brainstorm, and then the children write and illustrate captioned drawings of what we learned about the Taínos. I mount and display their captioned drawings in the hallway.

Lesson 12: One Version of the Columbus Story

I read aloud *Follow the Dream: The Story of Christopher Columbus* by Sis or another heroic version of the Columbus story. We discuss and record descriptive characteristics of the Taínos and Columbus.

Lesson 13: Another Version of the Columbus Story

I read aloud *A Coyote Columbus Story* by Thomas King. We discuss and record descriptive characteristics of the Taínos and Columbus again.

Lesson 14: How Do You Get at the Truth in History?

In a follow-up discussion later the same day, I hold up both books and ask, "Which story is truer? How can we get at the truth in history?" I

record students' ideas on a chart. For me, this is one of the most important lessons in the unit, in terms of critical thinking. The ideas, questions, and arguments children raise in this discussion help shape the rest of the unit. I want this discussion to include the following ideas: multiple perspectives, primary-source documents, biased reporting, quality of evidence, and the idea that one can question and challenge the truth of what is printed in a book.

Lesson 15: Alien Invasion Simulation

I randomly divide the class into two groups and conduct the alien-invasion simulation. (See Chapter 8 for details.) We process and record how people in each group feel. We discuss text-to-self connections between our own feelings in the simulation and stories we've already read. Could we say that all the Spanish felt the same? All the Taínos?

Literacy extension: Students write and draw how they felt.

Activity extension: Reverse roles and repeat the simulation, discuss, write/draw.

Lesson 15: Singing "1492"

I teach the song "1492" by Nancy Shimmel. We discuss the use of different terms, such as *Caribs* rather than *Taínos,* as well as other nations named: Aztec, Cree, Onandaga, and Menomineee. We discuss the poster that says, "Indigenous people's rights are human rights."

Lesson 16: Explore Multiple Perspectives

We conduct the history experiment with one actor and three witnesses reporting separately. I explain that Columbus was not the only witness and his journal was not the only record. We use excerpts from *The Taínos* to tell the story of Fray Antonio and the Laws of Burgos. We discuss the following questions:

How do you think the Spanish colonists reacted?

What do you think happened when Fray Antonio returned to Spain? Was Fray Antonio a "tattletale"? Was it appropriate for him to "tell on" the colonists? What do you think the king did? Was Fray Antonio brave? If so, why? Do you think his courage will save the Taínos?

Lesson 16: Ending Taíno Slavery, Starting the African Slave Trade

I continue telling the story of Bartolomé de Las Casas, using *The Taínos* and *Lies* for excerpts and census figures. We discuss the fact that although de Las Casas and the monks may have been well meaning, in an effort to "save" the Taínos, they were still planning to force them to relocate to villages they had built for them and to convert them to Christianity.

Although the monks eventually succeeded in freeing the Taínos from slavery, the Spanish colonists argued that their mines and farms would not be profitable without free labor. The colonists threatened to abandon the colony. The "solution" the Spanish came up with (after most of the Taínos were dead) was to start importing slaves from Africa, which began centuries of African slavery in the Americas.

We discuss what might have happened if the Catholic Church and king of Spain had said, "Tough! No slavery allowed! Do your own work yourself. If you can't manage, pack up and come home." Would the European colonies have continued to grow if there had not been any slavery or exploitation? Why did the church and the king think enslaving Africans was okay if they just said enslaving Taínos was not?

Lesson 17: Exploring Multiple Perspectives Through Language Arts

We do a choral reading of "Honeybees," poem for two voices by Paul Fleishman (in *Joyful Noise: Poems for Two Voices;* also see *Rethinking Our Classrooms* edited by Bigelow, Christensen, Karp, Miner, and Peterson for the poem and teaching ideas).

Assign students to work with partners to write poems for two voices (could be two insects, or two characters from Haiti in 1512, such as two Taínos, a Spanish colonist and a Spanish Dominican priest, a Taíno slave and a Spanish colonist, and so on). Younger students grasp the concept more easily when writing about insects or animals. Older students are more capable of writing about historical characters.

Lesson 18: Thinking About Other Explorers

I introduce other explorers by continuing to read aloud *The Discovery of the Americas* from Marco Polo to the end. I include the fact that Balboa

 APPENDIX

235

had thirty Africans with him who cut the trail through to the Pacific, using excerpts from *Against All Opposition*. We trace Magellan's route on the map and globe.

Lesson 19: If They Sailed There, How Did They Sail Back?

I tell the children the story of my childhood skepticism and historical experiments as I struggled to figure out the answer to this question. (See Chapter 8 for details.) I read aloud Eric Carle's *10 Little Rubber Ducks*. We look at maps and globes to see which ones show wind and ocean currents and which ones do not. I review map and globe vocabulary in context and teach additional vocabulary: *navigate, sail, wind, ocean, current, speed, direction,* and more.

Lesson 20: Navigation 101

I invite a guest expert (sailor) to teach a lesson explaining the basics of navigation, wind, and ocean currents. Students use large-scale maps on each table with wind and ocean currents marked, moving small marker pieces to show routes of various explorers. Extensions include learning about the development of navigational instruments such as the compass, sextant, and others and how to navigate by stars.

Lesson 21: Effect of Contact

I read aloud *The Invisible Hunters: A Legend From the Miskito Indians of Nicaragua* by Rohmer. After the read-aloud, students act out this dramatic, bilingual story in a reader's theater.

Lesson 22: Columbus Didn't Discover Us

I show the video *Columbus Didn't Discover Us* by Leppzer. We discuss what indigenous people in the film want (land, peace, and so on). Should they have it? Why? Can they have it? I pose the questions, "What if a Native American knocked on your door and told your family that you were living on stolen land, that it was time to give it back, that you had twenty-four hours (or even a month or a year, although Native Americans were rarely given that much notice) to pack your stuff and go? If all the people without indigenous ancestors had to leave, where would/could they go?" We discuss that these are hard and complex questions, without easy answers.

Lesson 23: *The People Shall Continue*

I read aloud *The People Shall Continue* by Ortiz. I emphasize that in spite of slavery, war, disease, and poverty, Native Americans do continue, survive, and struggle for justice. I focus on what we can do, as citizen activists. We can connect with Native Americans in our own communities; learn about local, national, and international struggles of indigenous people; and support them by writing letters to Congress, going to demonstrations, and so on. I relate the comment by the woman in the film about caribou to current events and environmental issues.

Lesson 24: Contemporary Native American Life

I read aloud a number of photo-illustrated books about contemporary Native American life from a series called We Are Still Here: Native Americans Today. Three that I use most regularly are *Clambake: A Wampanoag Tradition* by Peters, *Ininatig's Gift of Sugar: Traditional Native Sugarmaking* by Wittstock, and *Four Seasons of Corn: A Winnebago Tradition* by Hunter.

These books by Native American authors counter negative stereotypes (without teaching them) by featuring contemporary Native American children engaging in familiar everyday activities (using computers, living in modern houses, playing football, going to school) as well as traditional tribal activities.

Lesson 25: Contemporary Native American Struggles

I invite a Native American community member to discuss contemporary struggles and student questions that come up in the course of our study, such as, "If Columbus hadn't come, would Taínos still exist?" Advice from Otoe Indian Norma Sandowski to our class included the following:

1. We cannot undo history, but we can try to learn and teach the truth.
2. We can be activists for the self-determination of Native people.
3. We can be activists for the responsible care of the Earth (thinking of the seventh generation).

4. We can press the U.S. government to honor its treaties.
5. We can recognize, think critically, talk with others, and write letters about Native American stereotyping in children's literature, advertising, team mascots, and other media.

Classroom Resources

Armstrong, J. 1998. *Shipwreck at the Bottom of the World: The Extraordinary True Story of Shackleton and the Endurance*. New York: Crown.

Bigelow, B., and B. Peterson, editors. 1998. *Rethinking Columbus: The Next 500 Years*. Milwaukee, WI: Rethinking Schools.

Bigelow, B., L. Christensen, S. Karp, B. Miner, and B. Peterson, editors. 1994. *Rethinking Our Classrooms: Teaching for Equity and Social Justice*. Milwaukee, WI: Rethinking Schools.

Carle, E. 2005. *10 Little Rubber Ducks*. New York: HarperCollins.

Ciment, J., with R. LaFrance. 1996. *Scholastic Encyclopedia of the American Indian*. New York: Scholastic.

Eastern National Park and Monument Association. 1996. *Caribbean National Forest: El Yunque*. Conshohocken, PA: Eastern National Park and Monument Association.

Fleishman, P. 1998. "Honeybees," in *Joyful Noise: Poems for Two Voices*. New York: HarperCollins.

Fontánez, E. 1996. *Taíno: Guanín's Story* (video recording), Washington, DC: Exit Studio.

———. 1996. *Taíno: The Activity Book*. Washington, DC: Exit Studio.

Haskins, J. 1992. *Against All Opposition: Black Explorers in America*. New York: Walker and Company.

Hunter, S. M. 1997. *Four Seasons of Corn: A Winnebago Tradition*. Minneapolis: Lerner Publications Company.

Jacobs, F. 1992. *The Tainos, the People Who Welcomed Columbus*. New York: G. P. Putnam's Sons.

King, T. 1992. *A Coyote Columbus Story*. Toronto: Douglas & McIntyre.

Lauber, P. 2003. *Who Came First? New Clues to Prehistoric Americans*. Washington, DC: National Geographic Society.

Leppzer, R. 1992. *Columbus Didn't Discover Us* (video recording). Wendell, MA: Turning Tide Production.

Loewen, J. W. 1995. *Lies My Teacher Told Me: Everything Your American History Textbook Got Wrong*. New York: The New Press.

Maestro, B., and G. Maestro. 1990. *The Discovery of the Americas*. New York: Lothrop, Lee & Shepard Books.

McKay, L. Jr. 1995. *Caravan*. New York: Lee & Low Books.

Mitchell, B. 1996. *Red Bird*. New York: Lothrop, Lee & Shepard Books.

Mohr, N., and A. Martorell. 1995. *The Song of El Coqui and Other Tales of Puerto Rico*. New York: Viking.

Oney, Y. 2004. *North American Explorers* (World Discovery History Reader). New York: Scholastic.

Ortiz, S. 1988. *The People Shall Continue*. Emeryville, CA: Children's Book Press.

Peters, R. M. 1998. *Clambake: A Wampanoag Tradition*. Minneapolis, MN: Lerner Publications Company.

Pinkney, B. 1996. *Captain Bill Pinkney's Journey*. Peru, IL: Open Court Publishing Company.

Rohmer, H. 1988. *Atariba & Niguayona: A Story from the Taíno People of Puerto Rico*. San Francisco: Children's Book Press.

———. 1987. *The Invisible Hunters: A Legend from the Miskito Indians of Nicaragua / Los Cazadores Invisibles: una leyenda de los indios miskitos de Nicaragaua*. San Francisco: Children's Book Press.

Russell, G. 1997. *American Indian Facts of Life, a Profile of Today's Tribes and Reservations*. Phoenix: Russell Publications.

Ryan, Z. Alderfer, and L. Arnesen. 2003. *Ann and Liv Cross Antarctica*. Cambridge, MA: Da Capo Press.

Seale, D., and B. Slapin. 1993, 1996. *Teaching Respect for Native Peoples* (poster). Berkeley: i*arte Oyate.

Senior, M. 2004. *Did Prince Madog Discover America?* Llanrwst, Wales: Gwasg Carreg Gwalch.

Severin, T. 1977. The Voyage of "Brendan." *National Geographic,* vol. 152, no. 6: 769–797.

Shimmel, N. "1492." Recording on the CD *I Will Be Your Friend*. The CD and songbook (one per school) are available free from Teaching Tolerance (www.teachingtolerance.org). (Lyrics can also be found in *Rethinking Columbus*.)

Sis, P. 1991. *Follow the Dream: The Story of Christopher Columbus*. New York: Knopf.

Wittstock, L. W. 1993. *Ininatig's Gift of Sugar: Traditional Native Sugarmaking*. Minneapolis, MN: Lerner Publications Company.

Yolen, J. 1992. *Encounter*. San Diego: Harcourt Brace Jovanovich.

Zinn, H. 1980. *A People's History of the United States*. New York: Harper Perennial.

The Peace Class News

Volume 1, Number 1 • Jackson Street School • Northampton, Massachusetts • November 8, 2004 • Free

Welcome to the Peace Class News

By Mary Cowhey

Thanks for joining us in yet another idea. While I do stay awake at night thinking of ideas, this one came from a Peace Class parent, Jo Glading-DiLorenzo, who offered to help our students write and publish a classroom newspaper. That was back in August, before we actually started doing things. By the time we started learning how to write news stories, we were doing so many things it was clear this would have to be an ongoing publication.

So here is our first issue, written with great enthusiasm, by the Peace Class. It's free. Maybe it will be monthly. So far, I am the editor-in-chief, and Jo is our publisher. We'll probably have about twenty-two different departments, with about as many department editors.

While we have an excellent staff of writers, we consider all submissions of photos, articles on science and nature, community, politics, international topics, book reviews, education, sports, and other subjects from readers. I would also like to welcome letters to the editor, because we'd like community feedback on our newspaper. Volunteers are also welcome, especially in the still-mysterious realm of digital photography. You can e-mail the editor at mcowhey@hotmail.com or write Peace Class News, Jackson Street School, 120 Jackson Street, Northampton, MA 01060.

Butterfly

We were glad because the butterfly hatched today in the Peace Class.

A Busy Class

By Sophie

A couple of days after the voter registration drive Ms. Zagrodnik came in with a butterfly in a cocoon. Right now the butterfly is hatching. We're also doing a food drive for the survival center. The Peace Class has been going a lot of field trips. On one of the trips somebody's dad picked up a snake. I'm afraid of snakes. When we got on the bridge there were these prickly things. My friend fell in the water on the way home from a field trip, but she got out.

A New Butterfly!

By Winnie

When the children in the Peace Class came to school they noticed a monarch butterfly chrysalis had fallen on the floor of the aquarium. Mrs. Cowhey, the teacher, tried to hang the chrysalis on the top of the cage but it fell once and then again. Then she put it on a piece of paper on the floor. A few minutes later one of the children noticed the butterfly was born. We went over and picked it up with a flower and put it in a cup so it could hang upside down. When the butterfly was born its abdomen was very big. It flapped its wings. Its abdomen shrunk and its wings grew. Its birthday was October 21, 2004. Its life before birth was hard.

The Day We Registered People to Vote

By Rebecca

We, the Peace Class, registered 36 people to vote. It was in the lobby at Jackson Street School. It happened on Oct. 7, 8, and 12. We went on a public bus to Northampton City Hall to deliver the voter registration cards to the registrar of voters so the people could vote in the election on November 2.

2nd Graders Register Voters

By Sophie

Second grade students at Jackson Street School marched all the way to City Hall (after they took the bus halfway). They sang songs of freedom on the way. They delivered 36 voter registration cards to the city Registrar of Voters. When they got to the Mayor's office they had a little snack and then went back to school.

Children Help Their Community

By Jonah

Mrs. Cowhey's 2nd Grade Class is Doing a Food Drive! The food drive happened Oct. 21 and 22, 2004. Not only was the food drive helping the community it was helping the children in Mrs. Cowhey's class learn about the Survival Center. The children did the drive to help their community.

Kids Go to City Hall

By Luke

We marched and we sang to Northampton City Hall and we also took a public bus. And we helped 36 people register in the Jackson Street School lobby for a week in October.

REFERENCES

Professional Resources

Bigelow, B., and B. Peterson, editors. 1998. *Rethinking Columbus: The Next 500 Years.* Milwaukee, WI: Rethinking Schools.

Bigelow, B., L. Christensen, S. Karp, B. Miner, and B. Peterson, editors. 1994. *Rethinking Our Classrooms: Teaching for Equity and Social Justice.* Milwaukee, WI: Rethinking Schools.

Boyer, R. 1955. *Labor's Untold Story.* Chicago: United Electrical Radio & Machine Workers of America.

Brown, R. 2003. *The Crafts of Florida's First People.* Sarasota, FL: Pineapple Press.

Denton, P., and R. Kriete. 2000. *The First Six Weeks of School.* Greenfield, MA: Northeast Foundation for Children.

Freire, P. 1998. *Teachers as Cultural Workers: Letters to Those Who Dare Teach.* Boulder, CO: Westview Press.

———. 1970. *Pedagogy of the Oppressed.* New York: Continuum International Publishing Group.

Hughes, L. 1994. *The Collected Poems of Langston Hughes.* New York: Vintage.

Hughes, L., M. Meltzer, and C. E. Lincoln. 1983. *A Pictorial History of Blackamericans.* New York: Crown. (Note: This is the fifth revised edition of *A Pictorial History of the Negro in America,* first published in 1956.)

Jacobs, F. 1992. *The Tainos: The People Who Welcomed Columbus.* New York: G. P. Putnam's Sons.

Keene, E., and S. Zimmerman. 1997. *Mosaic of Thought.* Portsmouth, NH: Heinemann.

Kriete, R., with contributions by L. Bechtel. 2002. *The Morning Meeting Book.* Greenfield, MA: Northeast Foundation for Children.

Lee, E., D. Menkart, and M. Okazawa-Rey. 1998. *Beyond Heroes and Holidays.* Washington, DC: NECA Press.

Loewen, J. W. 1995. *Lies My Teacher Told Me: Everything Your American History Textbook Got Wrong.* New York: The New Press.

Mandela, N. 1995. *Long Walk to Freedom: The Autobiography of Nelson Mandela.* New York: Back Bay Books.

Mullane, D., editor. 1993. *Crossing the Danger Water: Three Hundred Years of African-American Writing.* New York: Anchor Books.

Muscroft, S., editor. 2000. *Children's Rights: Equal Rights?* London: The International Save the Children Alliance.

Nieto, S. 2003. *Affirming Diversity.* Needham Heights, MA: Allyn & Bacon.

Reit, S. 2001. *Behind Rebel Lines: The Incredible Story of Emma Edmonds, Civil War Spy.* New York: Gulliver Books.

Russell, G. 1997. *American Indian Facts of Life, a Profile of Today's Tribes and Reservations.* Phoenix: George Russell Publications.

Senior, M. 2004. *Did Prince Madog Discover America?* Llanrwst, Wales: Gwasg Carreg Gwalch.

Stenmark, J. K., V. Thompson, and R. Cossey. 1986. *Family Math.* Berkeley: University of California.

Takaki, R. 1994. *A Different Mirror: A History of Multicultural America.* New York: Back Bay Books.

Tatum, B. D. 1997. *"Why Are All the Black Kids Sitting Together in the Cafeteria?"* New York: Basic Books.

Thich Nhat Hanh. 1993. *The Blooming of a Lotus.* New York: Beacon Press.

Zinn, H. 1980. *A People's History of the United States.* New York: Harper Perennial.

Web Sites

www.syrculturalworkers.com. Box 6367, Syracuse, NY 13217. Syracuse Cultural Workers: Tools for Change. Catalog for posters, music, children's books, calendars re: human rights, children's rights, the environment, diversity, peace, etc.

www.oyate.org. Oyate is a Native organization whose work includes evaluating and distributing resources by and about Native people. *Teaching Respect for Native Peoples* (poster), *A Coyote Columbus Story,* and other great picture books and teaching guides are available through Oyate. Oyate, 2702 Matthews St., Berkeley, CA 94702; phone (510) 848–6700.

www.yourexpedition.com. Site for Bancroft-Arnesen expeditions.

www.teachingtolerance.org. Site for Teaching Tolerance, published by the Southern Poverty Law Center, 400 Washington Avenue, Montgomery, AL 36104. They publish a free magazine and other excellent materials for teachers.

www.nativebooks.com. HONOR (Honor Our Neighbors' Origins and Rights), HONOR Resource Center, 6435 Wiesner Road, Omro, WI 54963. They list hundreds of resources written, reviewed, or endorsed by Native American teachers, writers, and leaders.

www.taino-tribe.org/jatiboni.html. Web site of the Jatibonicu Taíno Tribal Nation of Boriken.

www.mtholyoke.edu/omc/kidsphil. Site for Philosophy for Kids, for information and resources about teaching philosophy with children, including question sets and video.

Literature Resources

Atkins, J. 1988. *Get Set! Swim!* New York: Lee & Low Books.

———. 2003. *A Name on the Quilt.* New York: Simon and Schuster.

Ballard, E. 2003. *The Bracelet.* Layton, UT: Gibbs Smith.

Blood, P., and A. Patterson. 1991. *Rise Up Singing.* New York: Sing Out! Publications.

Bogart, J. E. 1999. *Jeremiah Learns to Read.* New York: Scholastic.

Bruchac, J. 2000. *Squanto's Journey.* New York: Harcourt.

Brumbeau, J. 2000. *The Quiltmaker's Gift.* Duluth, MN: Pfeifer-Hamilton Publishers.

Bunting, E. 2004. *Fly Away Home.* Boston: Houghton Mifflin.

Burningham, J. 1994. *Hey, Get Off Our Train.* New York: Crown Books.

Carle, E. 2005. *10 Little Rubber Ducks.* New York: HarperCollins.

Castle, C. 2001. *For Every Child: The United Nations Convention on the Rights of the Child in Words and Pictures.* New York: P. Fogelman Books, in association with UNICEF.

Cherry, L. 2002. *A River Ran Wild: An Environmental History.* New York: Harcourt Children's Books.

———. 1990. *The Great Kapok Tree: A Tale of the Amazon Rain Forest.* New York: Harcourt.

Coerr, E. 1989. *The Josefina Story Quilt.* New York: HarperCollins.

Cohn, D. 2002. *¡Si, Se Puede! Yes, We Can!* El Paso, TX: Cinco Puntos Press.

Cole, J. 1986. *The Magic School Bus at the Waterworks.* New York: Scholastic.

Cooney, B. 1982. *Miss Rumphius.* New York: Scholastic.

Cronin, D. 2000. *Click, Clack, Moo: Cows That Type.* New York: Simon and Schuster.

Demi. 2001. *Gandhi.* New York: Simon and Schuster.

Estes, L. 2004. *The Hundred Dresses.* New York: Harcourt Children's Books.

George, J. Craighead. 1988. *My Side of the Mountain.* New York: Penguin Putnam Books.

Ghazi, S. Hamid. 1996. *Ramadan.* New York: Holiday House.

Graham, B. 2002. *Jethro Byrd, Fairy Child.* Cambridge, MA: Candlewick Press.

Haskins, J. 2003. *Against All Opposition.* Vancouver, BC, Canada: Walker & Company.

Hazen, B. Shook. 1983. *Tight Times.* New York: Penguin Putnam Books.

Hoose, P., and H. Hoose. 1998. *Hey Little Ant!* Berkeley, CA: Ten Speed Press.

Hughes, L. 1994. *The Dream Keeper and Other Poems.* New York: Scholastic.

Hunter, S. 1997. *Four Seasons of Corn: A Winnebago Tradition.* Minneapolis, MN: Lerner Publications Company.

Jendresen, E., and J. Greene. 2004. *Hanuman.* Berkeley, CA: Ten Speed Press.

Karusa. 1995. *The Streets Are Free.* Willowdale, ON, Canada: Annick Press.

Keats, E. J. 2001. *Ezra Jack Keats' Pet Show!* New York: Penguin Putnam Books.

King, C., and L. B. Osborne. 1997. *Oh, Freedom! Kids Talk About the Civil Rights Movement with the People Who Made It Happen.* New York: Scholastic.

Klamath County YMCA Preschool Staff. 1993. *Land of Many Colors.* New York: Scholastic.

Krauss, R. 1972. *The Carrot Seed.* New York: HarperCollins.

Lasky, K. 1997. *She's Wearing a Dead Bird On Her Head!* New York: Hyperion.

Lawrence, J. 1997. *Harriet and the Promised Land.* New York: Aladdin Paperbacks.

Lester, J. 1985. *To Be a Slave.* New York: Scholastic.

———. 1998. *From Slave Ship to Freedom Road.* New York: Dial Books.

Levine, E. 1995. *I Hate English!* New York: Scholastic.

Lionni, L. 1995. *Matthew's Dream.* New York: Random House.

———. 1973. *Swimmy.* New York: Knopf Publishing Group.

Lobel, A. 1979. "Dragons and Giants" from *Frog and Toad Together.* New York: HarperCollins.

McGovern, Ann. 1997. *The Lady in the Box.* New York: Turtle Books.

Merrill, J. 1992. *The Girl Who Loved Caterpillars.* New York: Penguin Putnam Books.

Mitchell, B. 1996. *Red Bird.* New York: Lothrop, Lee & Shepard Books.

Mochizuki, K. 1995. *Baseball Saved Us.* New York: Lee and Low Books.

Morrison, T., and S. Morrison. 1999. *The Big Box.* New York: Hyperion.

Oney, Y. 2004. *North American Explorers.* New York: Scholastic.

Ortiz, S. 1999. *The People Shall Continue.* Emeryville, CA: Children's Book Press.

Parr, T. 2004. *The Peace Book.* New York: Little, Brown.

Peters, R. M. 1998. *Clambake: A Wampanoag Tradition.* Minneapolis, MN: Lerner Publications Company.

Pinkney, B. 1997. *Captain Bill Pinkney's Journey.* Peru, IL: Open Court Publishers.

Polacco, P. 1994. *Pink and Say.* New York: Penguin Putnam Books.

———. 1988. *The Keeping Quilt.* New York: Simon and Schuster.

Radunsky, V. 2004. *What Does Peace Feel Like?* New York: Simon and Schuster.

Rahaman, V. 1997. *Read for Me, Mama.* Honesdale, PA: Boyds Mills Press.

Riis, J. 1997. *How the Other Half Lives.* New York: Penguin Group.

Ryan, Z. Alderfer, and L. Arnesen. 2003. *Ann and Liv Cross Antarctica.* Cambridge, MA: Da Capo Press.

Scholes, K. 1990. *Peace Begins with You.* San Francisco: Sierra Club Books.

Seeger, P. 2003. *Turn! Turn! Turn!* New York: Simon and Schuster Children's Books.

Seidler, A., and J. Slepian. 1987. *The Cat Who Wore a Pot on Her Head.* New York: Scholastic.

Seuss, Dr. 1984. *The Butter Battle Book.* New York: Random House.

———. 1976. *The Sneetches.* New York: Random House.

Steig, W. 1984. *Rotten Island.* New York: David R. Godine Books.

———. 1976. *The Real Thief.* New York: Farrar, Straus and Giroux.

Surat, M. 1990. *Angel Child, Dragon Child.* New York: Scholastic.

Tashlin, F. 1996. *The Bear That Wasn't.* New York: Dover Publications.

UNICEF. 2002. *A Life Like Mine: How Children Live Around the World.* New York: Dorling Kindersley.

Van Allsburg, C. 1990. *Just a Dream.* Boston: Houghton Mifflin.

Van Laan, N., reteller. 1997. *Shingebiss: An Ojibwe Legend.* Boston: Houghton Mifflin.

Waddell, M. 1996. *Farmer Duck.* Cambridge, MA: Candlewick Press.

Wittstock, L. W. 1993. *Ininatig's Gift of Sugar: Traditional Native Sugarmaking.* Minneapolis, MN: Lerner Publications Company.

Yolen, J. 1992. *Encounter.* New York: Harcourt, Brace, Jovanovich.